Entropy Academy

Entropy Academy

How to
SUCCEED at HOMESCHOOLING
Even if You Don't Homeschool

Alison Bernhoft

PROPRIOMETRICS
PRESS

Printed in the United States of America.
First Printing, 2016 ISBN-13: 978-1-943370-01-6
Library of Congress Control Number: 2016931918
Propriometrics Press: propriometricspress.com
Cover & Interior Design: Agnes Koller, figdesign.ca
Cover Photo: Nabi Tang / Stocksy United
Photographs: Alison Bernhoft

Publisher's Cataloging-In-Publication Data
(Prepared by The Donohue Group, Inc.)

Names: Bernhoft, Alison.
Title: Entropy academy : how to succeed at homeschooling even if you don't homeschool / Alison Bernhoft.
Description: [Carlsborg, Washington] : Propriometrics Press, [2016]
Identifiers: LCCN 2016931918 | ISBN 978-1-943370-01-6 (print) |
    ISBN 978-1-943370-07-8 (ebook)
Subjects: LCSH: Home schooling. | Education–Parent participation. | Entropy.
Classification: LCC LC40.5.E68 B47 2016 (print) | LCC LC40.5.E68 (ebook) | DDC 371.042–dc23

To my children, co-constructors of Entropy Academy and simply the most amazing people I know.

Contents

Introduction

*M*y head always told me this would happen: that the day would come when I had no one to teach, no small feet thundering round the house, no eager voices clamoring for attention. My heart, however, knew that I would always be surrounded by family, that there would be an infinite supply of small children to love, educate, and care for.

The truth is out: my head was right. Our older children are all away at various colleges, while the youngest is the first of our children to begin high school at a genuine, certified institution. For the first September in living memory I have no courses to plan, no academic goals to plot, no social activities to coordinate. I tell myself that it's not an empty nest, it's a successful launching pad; that our goal in bringing children into this world was to send them out into it as well-balanced, independent young adults. But the house still seems awfully quiet.

Looking back on twenty-plus years of homeschooling, I wonder what I would have done differently if I had known then what I know now. If I could talk to myself twenty years ago, what would I say? What advice would I give? I would definitely tell myself to relax and enjoy the ride; I would reassure my worries and offer copious encouragement. I would tell the gremlin that sat on my shoulder, haranguing me about what a "real" homeschooling mother would or wouldn't do, to get lost. It might pretend to have my children's best interests at heart, but it's a beast of pure destruction. What's more, I would continue, the most important person in any homeschool is the mother. It doesn't matter how brilliant the curriculum is, how enriching the extracurricular activities; "If Momma ain't happy, ain't nobody happy."

My biggest enemy was always a crushing sense of inadequacy. Nobody congratulated me on a job well done, I received no kudos or accolades. My children were never heard to say, "Way to teach algebra, Mummy, good job!" I frequently felt like giving up. Often, I battled depression. In order to assuage the guilt I felt at making what I saw to be such a colossal mess of their education, I devised ways of making the house do the teaching. That way, they'd still be learning, whether their mother was in inspired pedagogical mode or (as was far more likely) not. The kitchen and bathroom were particularly amenable to becoming centers of "automatic learning." No one, whether family member or guest, could long endure in either location without having their grey matter tickled: *I wonder why that perpetual motion machine on the windowsill keeps spinning…I wonder which color hyacinth will bloom first, pink, yellow, or blue…What is the square root of twenty-five?*

I had dual concerns: not only should the children receive a proper education, but I also wanted them to be socially adept—to have friends, to be sociable, to feel that they belonged in the community. For myself, I craved evidence that I was doing the right thing by them; I was tired of withering before the accusatory looks of my mother's friends. "Homeschooling should be illegal," one of them berated me in the supermarket one morning, gazing reproachfully at six-year-old Iain pushing my cart. "That boy belongs in school."

Going out during school hours became an act of defiance. Part of me wanted to reassure onlookers that this really was the best thing for my children, and part of me wanted to tell them to mind their own business and stop giving me the evil eye. I remained silent because, in all honesty, I shared some of their doubts. Yet, as I saw the children developing stronger relationships with each other and becoming thoroughly engaged in the world around them, the specter of social misfitdom receded to the skeptical corners of strangers' minds. Gradually, I became convinced that homeschooling worked.

HOW WE STARTED

When Robin and I were trying to decide whether or not to homeschool our firstborn, Iain, I was struck by the passage in Isaiah, "God is the potter and we are the clay." The image that came to my mind was that God was in charge, but he wanted to use my hands to shape my son. I was only too happy to oblige. I also realized, with something of a start, that if I was a child of God and Iain was a child of God, this made me Iain's sister in God's eyes. It made my son my equal. This definitely went against the grain. After all, I was much bigger than Iain, and I knew far more things. Of course I was more important! But then I read St. Paul writing to Timothy in his letter to Philemon, informing him that the slave Onesimus was every bit as important as his master: it was the same message in a slightly different guise. It started to make sense to me.

A corollary of this is the saying, "God has no grandchildren." Young children are raised, as it were, under the umbrella of their parents' faith; but at some point, that faith has to become their own. The Catholic Church has arranged for various steps in the process of emancipation: First Confession is followed by First Holy Communion, then Confirmation a few years later. The goal: a young adult standing in right relationship with God at the outset of his or her independent life.

My decision to treat Iain as an equal was a set point change that affected how I treated each one of my children. *No matter how infuriating Andrew might be, he is still just as beloved by God as I am.* I found this a sobering thought. And now that Iain is much bigger than me and knows far more things, I'm glad he learned at an early age to value people (specifically me) for their personhood rather than their size, strength, or acquired knowledge.

OUR RELIGIOUS BACKGROUND

Religion has always played a vital role in my life, as well as in my husband's. Robin and I met in a meditation cult in Santa Barbara, at the feet of our guru. I stopped meditating three years later in London, largely because it's hard to find two twenty-minute periods of tranquility a day with a baby nursing on demand. On second thought, for "hard," read "impossible." Besides, I felt there was more to the spiritual life than the watered-down Hinduism we'd been fed. I was challenged to reexamine my beliefs by Barbara, an Australian mother living in the same dingy block of flats in West Ealing, who was a joyfully charismatic Christian. Robin and I reconverted to Christianity, and were attending a charismatic Episcopalian church in North Seattle when our second son, Andrew, was born with Down's syndrome. The prosperity gospel that "God wants us all to be healthy and happy" meant that I must have done something horribly wrong to deserve a baby who failed to measure up. Church members tickled Andrew under the chin and gushed about how "special" he was, but the theology was inescapable: God blesses those he loves, and visits affliction on those he doesn't.

Dismayed to find ourselves relegated to the latter category, we sought understanding; we found none at that church. Over the years we kept asking, but it was not until Robin was spearheading anti-euthanasia campaigns in Washington and California in the early nineties that he started to find answers to our questions in the most unexpected place: the Roman

Catholic Church. I was unimpressed and more than a little scandalized; my ancestor, Bishop Ridley, was burned at the stake by "Bloody Mary" in 1555, and is commemorated, along with Bishops Cranmer and Latimer, in the Martyrs' Memorial in the center of Oxford. How could I turn on my own family? A little historical research revealed that they had burned for political, rather than religious, reasons. But still, I had my doubts: *Don't Catholics worship Mary, not to mention the saints? Aren't they required to follow Church dogma like unquestioning sheep? Aren't they—well, frankly, a bit weird?* More than one of our Protestant acquaintances made derisive comments about Catholics being required to "check their brains at the door" when they went to church.

Robin was spending a great deal of time on the campaign trail with Father Robert Spitzer, a Jesuit priest who was a treasure trove of information on the Church's real teachings. Robin duly related these insights to me. My Protestant friends were aghast, and sent me lurid tracts exposing the Catholic Church as the Whore of Babylon. I ripped these open eagerly, hoping to be able to rebut Robin's next attempt to convert me. But the pamphlets all started by falsifying the Catholic position, and then used scripture to prove why this misrepresentation was wrong. The intellectual dishonesty was disappointing at best, scandalous at worst. I soon realized that I would get no help from them, and as I read what the Church actually teaches, I came to recognize it as true. On the third Sunday of Advent, 1994, Father Spitzer officiated as Evan was baptized, our marriage convalidated, and our whole family was received into the Church. We had come home.

The Catholic faith is big enough to include everything, and I believe that all subject matter is fair game for home-schooling, in due time—with the exception of pornography and gratuitous violence. God reveals himself through nature. We see him in the very large—the immensity of space and the movement of the stars; we see him in the very small—in DNA of breathtaking complexity, revealed by the most power-ful microscopes. We see him, if we look with open hearts and minds, in everything in between. The idea that God is some-how at odds with science has always seemed preposterous to both Robin and me, and our faith handily survived a detailed appraisal of Darwin's theory of evolution. We learned to debate both sides of a political argument, and to take an objective look at the strengths and weaknesses of the democratic sys-tem. Additionally, the children enjoyed all kinds of art, from Michelangelo to Marvel comics, Shakespeare to the Magic Tree House, *The Ten Commandments* to *Legally Blonde*.

Catholics believe that a child's sense of right and wrong is established by the time he is seven, the "age of reason." Building on this sense of right and wrong, the adult con-science is formed. As the children approached the teen years, we trusted them with increasing freedom, believing that if teenagers aren't encouraged to make their own decisions, re-bellion or its flaccid counterpart, passivity, are likely to ensue. We had only minimal rebellion with Iain, and when he was preparing to leave for college, I asked him if he felt we had done an adequate job of forming his conscience. He gave me a big smile. "You did a perfectly splendid job, Mum. I don't have any trouble with it at all." Fortunately, I was able to appreciate his humor.

I've heard that the Bank of England trains its tellers to recognize counterfeit money by making them familiar with the real thing. They get so used to the look and feel of the genuine article that they recognize a fake instantly. I wanted to give my children the same familiarity with Truth, to feed them a healthy cultural diet before gradually introducing the darker things of life. If they were raised in an atmosphere of excellence, I trusted that their young spirits would develop a natural abhorrence for depravity in all its many guises. It's easiest to spot a counterfeit when it's held up to the light.

COMPUTERS

There is no doubt about it: technological developments since 1980 have completely revolutionized the way we think about education. The generation now growing up, popularly dubbed "digital natives," is more familiar with the workings of an iPad at eighteen months than many, or even most, adults, and by the age of eight or ten can create a website in the time it takes their resident adult to peel and chop an onion. Warren Boxleitner, a reviewer of interactive children's media (quoted in Ray Kurzweil's *The Singularity Is Near*), calls the iPad "a rattle on steroids"; looking at a room full of preschoolers bent intently over their tablets, he comments, "All of a sudden a finger can move a bus or smash an insect or turn into a big wet gloopy paintbrush." It all sounds quite wonderful: can it be that the touch screen has taken smelly, uncomfortable, often inconvenient, hands-on education—including the archaic monster of field trips that involve getting into a real car and enlarging one's carbon footprint by burning actual gasoline in search of something interesting—and relegated it to the garbage icon of history?

Initial impressions are positive: judging by the rapt attentiveness with which these two- to four-year-olds are focused on their iPads, the problem of short attention spans is solved.

But is it?

Maria Montessori was fond of saying, "the hands are the instrument of man's intelligence"; she believed that children learn concepts best by working with materials, rather than by being taught about them. Children literally learn through their fingers. The jury is still out on whether virtual materials on a touch screen educate as effectively as the real thing: does an interactive app about the seashore have the same, perhaps even superior, educational value as tracking down a hermit crab in a chilly tide pool and getting a nipped finger as a reward? Or does the salt tang in the air, the challenge of clambering over barnacle-encrusted rocks without shredding feet or fingers, even the unpleasantness of a faceful of sand thrown by a recalcitrant gust of wind, offer a superior learning experience?

Is finger painting somehow better if the pediatric finger pads actually feel the contrasting textures of paint versus paper, and there are dirty digits to wash afterwards? Ray Kurzweil, author of the largely (to me) impenetrable *The Singularity Is Near*, foresees a future where computers will have acquired the very best of human intelligence, indeed, may even have overtaken us and be running the world. He asserts that children's brains will grasp a 3-D reality as easily on a screen as in the real world—if, that is, they are aware of any difference.

Reading Kurzweil makes me feel like a hopelessly reactionary Luddite. No matter how responsive a screen may be, or how interactive the app, I cannot concede that it will give the well-rounded experience a loving human can provide. Oh, it may teach the *facts*, and that right well; but can it impart confidence and excitement, crack a joke, or sing a silly song on the way home? Can it equal the good feeling when Granny stops what she's doing, listens intently, and chuckles with glee at the inventiveness of her beloved grandchild's story?

Obviously, my answer to this string of rhetorical questions is a resounding "no!" But I have to be realistic—I could be wrong. You could follow my advice, spend the next twenty years making pyramids out of sugar cubes, enriching your gardens with worm castings, playing your way through Bach's 48 Preludes and Fugues, writing poetry, staging historical reenactments…and at the end, discover Kurzweil was right. It *is* all about computers.

But I still think you'd have come out ahead.

GENTLE READER—WHO ARE YOU?

When I began writing this book, I intended it to be an instructional how-to manual for homeschoolers. I wanted to show how effortlessly education can be incorporated into everyday life, and how much fun a family can have doing just that. The more I thought about it, however, the more I realized that any family with young children can adopt a lifestyle of learning—whether they homeschool or not.

Most teachers will agree that students who excel at school tend to have active, involved parents and grandparents: the more children learn at home, the more they benefit from what school has to offer.

As my children grew and I began to look at homeschooling more objectively, I was struck by the number of people who homeschool out of fear—fear of a lunatic gunman opening fire in their child's classroom, fear that their child will be inculcated with heathenish, amoral teachings. I wanted to show an alternative motivation: I home educated because I absolutely enjoyed it, and because I loved what I saw it doing to my children. Homeschooling is sometimes belittled as the last resort of apathetic, aging hippies, and I wanted to inform critics that home education can happen in Prague or Pompeii as well as at the kitchen table: that the persistent image of runny-nosed, barefoot truants scratching the alphabet in the dirt with a stick and using their head lice to practice counting could not be farther from the truth.

In the end, I chose to tell the story of our family—what worked, what didn't work, what made our family life more meaningful, and what was a waste of time. I hope that by laying bare the scaffolding of the school I built for my children and their friends, and describing the joy we found in bringing it to life, that here and there along the way each reader may find something to take into their own home. I won't try to tell you how to educate your children; over the years I've read scores of how-to books and they've all left me feeling thoroughly daunted, which is exactly the opposite of my intention here. What I can tell you is how I did it, warts and all. The children have not only survived to tell the tale, but also are flourishing; I made plenty of mistakes, but children are incredibly resilient. It's the successes that leave their mark, the accidental strokes of genius that cannot be planned or anticipated. All the planning in the world is only premeditated guesswork. Exactly why Entropy Academy worked so well is quite literally beyond me. The answer lies in the six children you will come to know in the course of these pages.

THE BERNHOFT CHILDREN

Allow me to introduce my children to you the same way I first met them—as they emerged from the birth canal. All was going well in my Lamaze-coached first delivery, and I was getting quite adept at relaxing into the pain of each contraction. Then, with the first, tantalizing glimpse of pink scalp and wispy, indeterminate-colored hair that we would so soon be snuffling appreciatively, the finely honed birthing machine ground to a halt. "Push!" exhorted the doctor. I regarded him stupidly. What *was* he talking about? Why wouldn't he just leave me in peace to go to sleep? Now Robin was siding with him: it was two against one. It just wasn't fair! *What is this thing called "push" that they want me to do?*

The combined efforts of Robin, the doctor, and two nurses finally managed to convince me that the end point of the birthing process occurs when the baby is *outside* the mother; rather against my better judgment, I consented to use every iota of strength I could muster to push this baby out under my own steam.

Head raised, our firstborn gave this brave new world a good, hard stare as he entered it. Recognizing the life-changing significance of this first encounter, I looked down at nine pounds, eight ounces of pure beauty, and uttered perhaps the most profound words ever spoken by a new mother: "It's a baby!"

"Well, that was the general idea," muttered Robin. "What did you expect?"

After several days of vacillation, we named him Iain.

A precipitous, unmanageably painful delivery ushered in our second-born. He was in deep distress; what we could see of him through the meconium was dark bluish-grey, and did not move. Robin feared he was dead. He spent the first days of his life in the ICU. We were told he had Down's syndrome.

Floppy and unresponsive, he lacked the strength to nurse; I dutifully pumped, trying not to reflect too closely on the contrast between Iain's confident and exuberant draining of the milk supply, and this arduous, painfully slow and ineffectual attempt to do the same. Andrew was three days old before I saw the color of his eyes. They were a murky brown.

My primary recollection of Fiona's birth was how incredibly painful the afterbirth was, and how sharp her toothless gums felt as they latched on to nurse. Traumatized by Andrew's birth and the subsequent loss of our daughter, Cara, at seventeen weeks *in utero*, I found it hard at first to relate to this gorgeous, nine-pound, five-ounce specimen of normal, blessedly alive babyhood. Confident in her nursing abilities, she suckled determinedly on my elbow; she was not at all happy to be redirected to the more conventional source of nourishment. And this was before she'd heard Frank Sinatra sing *I'll do it my way*, which could well be her life's theme song.

Friends and onlookers alike expressed great surprise about pregnancy number four; the general consensus seemed to be that after a healthy baby, and a girl at that, we should stop while we were ahead. Lorna entered the world in the still hours of the night, and a great quietness was upon her. She looked up blearily, quizzically, as if she were already trying to make sense of this vale of tears, made a half-hearted attempt to nurse, and went back to sleep. She had been very placid *in utero*, and this seemed to be her temperament. *Never mind if she's a bit slow,* I thought, *at least she's healthy.*

Fast forward: she slept most of her first year, rousing periodically to kick her feet and squeal at Iain's dramatic renditions of the Battle of the Alamo, or highlights from the previous night's baseball game. She moved around by rolling, preferably into a corner, where she howled until someone came to her rescue. Later, she learned to crawl backwards into the same favored corner, with the same ear-splitting results. But when she finally started walking at almost sixteen months, it was as if her afterburners kicked in; she took off like a pediatric rocket, and shows no sign of slowing down almost two decades later. Neither before nor since have I seen such a transformation in a child's personality.

Iain was inordinately proud of having been stuck in the birth canal and causing me such difficulty, and unbeknownst to me, must have given baby number five some explicit coaching as the due date approached. This was, I was convinced beyond any shadow of a doubt, our third boy, to be born on All Fools' Day. But as the hours of April 1 ticked inexorably away, I recognized with a sinking heart that familiar feeling: all desire to push had flown out the window, and I was left with my considerably older and weaker abdominal muscles to push this baby out with no help from the primordial birthing force.

It was an April Fools' baby all right—a female, born on April 2. The joke was on me. I don't remember there being a peal of thunder to greet her, but there should have been; Sheila positively erupted into the world, looking about as disgruntled as it is possible for a baby to look. *This*, I said to myself, *does not seem like a child destined to accept the status quo.* Little did I know how prophetic this utterance was to prove.

We knew from the ultrasound that our sixth baby was a boy, and his arrival was blessedly free from difficult or noteworthy circumstances. With his dark, curly hair plastered to his head, he bore a striking, and rather disconcerting, resemblance to the Welsh singer Tom Jones, but this was soon forgiven and forgotten in the joyous business of introducing the other children to their newest, and what was to prove their last, sibling. Evan seemed even-tempered and content with his lot in life— which, as the center of a cotillion of adoring fans, he might well be.

Now you've made the acquaintance of each of our children. They are Entropy Academy—and they rock.

1

ENTROPY

*A*llow me to tell you a story.

A young (well, youngish) mother in London is going shopping with her one-year-old son. As she leaves their flat, she carefully locks the dead bolt with a key.

Now see! The mother and her baby are coming back. They are coming home!

Oh dear, something is wrong! The mother is worried. She sees the key, left in the lock. "Goodness gracious," she thinks, "someone could have broken in. *Anyone* could have broken in. Perhaps the flat has been ransacked!"

She opens the door. "Oh dear!" she exclaims. "The flat *has* been ransacked!"

But then she looks more closely. She thinks, "I meant to put away that pile of clothes this morning." She remembers,

"Those books have been on the floor since Tuesday…I was going to fold those towels last night…"

The flat hasn't been ransacked after all! Do you think the mother is happy?

The answer, as I can tell you from personal experience (I was, of course, the mother in question), is yes and no. Relieved, certainly, but also horrified at this evidence of her slovenliness. "Surely," I hear you say, "this must have marked a turning point in your life? The beginning of an Ascent unto Cleanliness and Tidiness?"

Well, not quite, though I do try. But here's where entropy comes in. Entropy, the second law of thermodynamics, states that, left to themselves, things tend to a state of greater and greater disorder. This phenomenon can be observed anywhere on the planet but is particularly concentrated in certain locations: my kitchen, for instance.

Entropy is definitely a good thing. Without it we would not be able to enjoy the glories of the compost heap; instead, we would be wading through a waist-deep mess of dead leaves, interspersed with everything else that had died in our garden over the past few thousand years. There would be no decay, there would be no food chain. The world as we know it would not exist.

So let us (I decided to) be thankful for entropy. Celebrate it, even. We marked an annual "Entropy Day" on our calendar: we wore our clothes backwards or upside down and ate dinner sitting under the table, starting with dessert. (Lorna hated all these ideas, by the way, having a very keen sense of propriety, though she didn't mind having dessert first. Even though I thought it was fun, I didn't make her wear her clothes crookedly.) And I frequently reminded myself that the house wasn't messy because I was evil; it was simply obeying a primordial law of nature.

Entropy may be a good thing, a necessary thing, but it certainly makes life difficult. In particular, it makes homeschooling difficult. The average office is replete with systems analysts to maintain order, while at school the taxpayer funds a small army of administrators to keep things running smoothly. At home, it's all up to the poor parent, who finds herself (or, increasingly, himself) trying to teach more than one grade level while simultaneously dealing with that agent of instant entropy, the toddler (and let us not forget the nursing infant, thrown in for good measure). Small wonder so many families burn out. I often felt like one of those circus acts where the performer gets a dozen plates spinning on long poles; by the time the twelfth plate is rotating securely, the first three are looping wildly, threatening to crash to the ground. Which to rescue first? Those two! But now these three are threatening self-destruction—and that one is surely going to fall. Some days my only consolation was that at some point the act would be over and we'd all be safe in our beds.

Our school always was Entropy Academy, but it took me a while to realize it. Here is an early example of what I later came to call "Living with Entropy": it has to do with pencils.

In 1984, we returned to the US from a year in England where Robin was working as Senior Registrar (equivalent to Chief Resident) at the Hammersmith Hospital in London. We were fortunate enough to find a depressed housing market in Everett, just north of Seattle, where Robin, at the tender age of thirty-seven, was about to begin his first real-world (or non-academic) job. Our entire apartment in San Francisco would have fit quite comfortably into the living room and balcony of the house we bought on a bluff overlooking the Puget Sound.

When Iain and I began homeschooling three years later, I still hadn't finished unpacking. Half-empty boxes were everywhere: entropy reigned supreme. Many a morning found me stymied in my educational endeavors by not being able to lay hands on a single pencil. Such a simple thing to thwart my high ideals! Hoping the solution lay in quantity, I utilized an office supply company that delivered pencils by the hundred, postage free. Surely this was an end to my problems? No such luck! The house developed an insatiable appetite for pencils: as fast as Reliable could deliver them, the house gobbled them up. Eventually, however, critical mass was reached. Given a generous number of pencils per cubic foot of house, I could always be certain of finding at least one.

I tried to designate a box for pencils, label it, and train Iain and myself to return pencils to the box when we were done with them. It was an ingenious idea, breathtaking in scope, elegant in its simplicity. But it reckoned without...Andrew.

From the time he acquired the ability to move at will,

Andrew demonstrated a passionate commitment to rearranging the contents of our house. If I carried him past any movable item, he dealt it a swift kick or swipe with his elbow that delivered it speedily to its designated resting place on the floor. If I put him down for a nap with a baby gate in the doorway, every movable article in the bedroom ended up in the hallway. By the time he could walk, his attention had honed in on writing instruments, particularly the humble pencil. He could squirrel them away by the gross. Realizing how greatly this frustrated me seemed to increase his resolve. I imagined that at some point, possibly when we moved, a treasure trove of pencils would come to light. I was wrong. We never did find out where he put them all.

I have to admit, I may have been responsible for the disappearance of a certain number myself, as may Iain: let us not give Andrew all the credit. But neither should we quibble over details. The take-home lesson—or perhaps, the stay-at-home lesson—remains: find the most economical way possible of dealing with entropy, and seize it with both hands. This lesson was to serve me well in the glory years of Entropy Academy.

HOW WE STARTED TO HOMESCHOOL

Neither Robin nor I had particularly stellar educational experiences—I was miserable in Bristol, England, while he was bored in Fargo, North Dakota. Life as a child seemed to me a complex game with ever-changing rules: teachers had one code, my classmates another. I never could discover how to keep either camp happy. Unable to fit in, I escaped by playing the piano or, when I didn't have a piano at hand, drawing horses. Robin took a rather less introverted approach to solving his problems, becoming a wildly popular class president. In the process, he acquired people management skills that were to prove useful in his later medical and political careers.

It was with some trepidation that we approached Iain's kindergarten year. We had heard of homeschooling, but thought it freakish and—frankly—more than a little weird. We visited the local elementary school and found a lovely, big, sunny room (yes! even in Washington State) with a lovely, medium-sized, sunny teacher. It still didn't feel right. I wanted Iain to be home with me. But what was best for him?

What decided us was the brochure the teacher sent home with us: "What your child will learn in kindergarten." With the exception of some pre-computer skills, Iain already knew everything on the list and more. He had learned his colors, shapes, and numbers by helping sort the laundry, playing games, and listening to the stories I read to him every day. He knew cups, pints, and quarts from playing with measuring cups in the bathtub and helping me bake cookies. Those same cookies had taught him relative size—"Andrew's cookie is bigger than mine!"—while fractions were the domain of pizza. School supply stores sell plastic pizzas cut up into quarters, sixths, and eighths. How much easier, not to mention more motivating, is a slice of real pizza at the end of a math lesson, than a chunk of plastic. Iain had learned concepts such as "fragile" while unloading the dishwasher. He knew his letters from stories, games, cereal boxes, and street signs. It seemed I had taught him everything he needed to know with no special effort, in the normal course of daily life. I was relieved. I thought, "I can homeschool him this year and even if he doesn't learn a thing, he won't be behind when he enters first grade. And I know he'll pick up computer literacy in a snap when the time comes."

Despite the evidence staring me in the face that my laid-back method of teaching was working extremely well, I felt compelled to engage in a formal phonics program. I was terrified that Iain was missing out somehow, that he would fall behind those orderly students with their hyper-efficient mothers whose pictures graced the homeschooling magazines that materialized in my mailbox each month, striking terror into my heart. I purchased a well-used school desk, put it in the basement "school room," found a pencil, and started teaching. Iain's ignorance of the phonemes presented a lack in his education that I, dutiful teacher that I was, must needs supply. Every day we "did school": it was fraught with tension, but it had to be done—or so I thought.

But I couldn't shake the idea that the way I'd taught Iain thus far, with learning happening spontaneously in the course of real life, was preferable. The Irish poet William Butler Yeats wrote that education is "not the filling of a bucket, but the lighting of a fire." Our phonics curriculum felt far too much like filling a bucket for my taste, and after three frustrating weeks, it was relegated to gathering dust on a shelf. Iain found reason to read in his newfound passion for baseball; mastery of the phonemes followed as he sounded out his favorite players' names in the local newspaper, with minimal assistance from me. "Learning at home" apparently did not have to revolve around one-on-one, sit-down "teaching at home."

OUR FAMILY GROWS

I found the lifestyle of having my children at home all day to be deeply satisfying. Frustrating, challenging, maddening at times—yes, it was all these, but I couldn't imagine it any other way. And when Iain received his first standardized test results, I was gratified to learn that he scored in the 99th percentile. Apparently homeschooling not only felt good, it worked.

Not that this time wasn't without its heartbreak. Andrew's birth had been very hard for me; I who had always been the outsider at school, the last one to be picked for a team, the introvert nobody wanted to play with, was now ostracized with my special-needs baby. Other mothers gushed, "He's so cute— he's so special!" But I read in their eyes the unspoken, "And I'm so glad he's not mine." Through it all I was racked with guilt at the thought that our decision to have a home birth might have caused him irreparable damage. *What about all those people who had warned us that having our baby at home was selfish and irresponsible—had they been right?*

We decided to try for another baby, and soon I was pregnant again. At eighteen weeks, I went for a checkup: the doctor could find no heartbeat. An ultrasound was scheduled for the next day, and Robin was able to take time off work to be with me. As I lay on the table, the radiologist glanced at the scan, announced to no one in particular, "This baby is dead," and marched out of the room. I might as well have been a cow, for all the human interaction that took place. Robin followed him to try to extract a few more details. I was left for what seemed an eternity with only the unmoving image on the screen for company.

That was a Thursday. It was decided that I should wait out the weekend and see if the baby miscarried spontaneously. It didn't. Those were perhaps the longest days of my life, walking around knowing that the baby I had carried within me for four months was dead. On Monday, we scheduled the operation for the following day. I couldn't bear the thought of them cutting our baby up, of never seeing him or her to say hello, and goodbye, so rather than the efficient dilation and evacuation, we chose to have the baby induced. The doctor told me it would take between twelve and thirty-six hours. It took thirty-four and a half. As I held her tiny body in my hand, I thought it was I who had died, that the body I held was my own. The grief was numbing; pain would come later. To this day we don't know why she died. We called her Cara, Italian for "dear one."

Three days after her death, I had a dentist appointment.

"I thought you were pregnant," he said breezily when I acquiesced to an X-ray. I briefly recounted the events of the previous week; he shifted uncomfortably. "Never mind," he said. "It's probably all for the best."

All for the best? I wanted to sock him right in his impeccably white, straight teeth. I like to think that if I hadn't been so emotionally drained, I would have. It was his trivialization of my loss that was so galling, reducing it to a platitude that might grace a cross-stitch pillow in a chintzy gift shop. Sometimes the legendary British reserve can be jolly annoying, not to say downright infuriating—perhaps exactly what the dentist needed was a lesson in how to talk about death, and I was too well brought up to give it to him.

So now I had three babies: one normal, one handicapped, one dead. The trend was unmistakably in the wrong direction. I fell into a deep pit of depression. Any type of movement was an effort; creativity was out of the question. Dimly, I worried about Iain's preschool education, which had shuddered to a demoralized halt. I knew that these years were of crucial importance to his development, but it was impossible for me to impart anything remotely resembling excitement about learning when an obstinate jam jar lid could reduce me to a helpless puddle of tears.

I thought a lot about what kind of family I wanted. Robin was one of four children, while I formed part of the traditional English family: two parents, a boy and a girl. I found the notion of four or more children slightly scandalous, while to Robin it was perfectly natural. We had agreed to take it one child at a time—though we would both have been thrilled with twins—but things were not turning out quite as planned. More than anything else, Cara's death made me realize how passionately I wanted a large family. I yearned to hold a live baby, to help it grow and develop, and I wanted Iain to know the joys and frustrations of having siblings who could keep up with him, challenge him, maybe even outsmart him.

When I became pregnant again, fear was my constant companion. Every night I would fall into bed exhausted and go to sleep instantly, only to dream an hour later that I was in a rapidly rising submarine. I knew that as soon as the submarine breached the ocean's surface, I would awaken and remain awake the rest of the night. Those dark, sleepless hours were a hotbed for fearful misgivings. *What if this baby dies too? What if I have another handicapped baby—how will I cope?* I didn't undergo amniocentesis to discover any birth defects, partly because of the procedure's risks to the baby, but mostly because the only "treatment" for most birth defects is abortion, a step we were not willing to take.

I felt desperately alone. No one called to say, "I'm so sorry this has happened to you. Let me take you out for a cup of tea—I'll find a babysitter." No one called at all. But when I came back from the hospital with my beautiful baby Fiona, the house was full of flowers, many from people I didn't even know. Doctors and their wives who had not known how to help

me before, were now on safe ground. Flowers they could do.
I learned that people may care a great deal but not know how
to express it. In my turn, I was too bewildered to know how to
respond. I have often regretted my failure to thank those kind
individuals who reached out to me.

The fear diminished with each pregnancy, the submarine
taking a little longer to come to the surface: I joked that at this
rate, by baby number ten I'd be sleeping through the night.
But Mother Nature had different ideas, and we had to be content with six. Every time we welcomed a new baby, I marveled
at the nature of love. I used to think of it as a pie to be divided
between the children, with the arrival of each newborn meaning a slightly smaller slice for everybody else. What I learned is
that love is exponential: the more children, the more pie there
is to go around. Even as they grow older and leave home, the
strength of those relationships endures. My children are each
other's best friends, and I am grateful beyond measure for each
one of them.

CHANGES COMING...

But by 1994, when our youngest, Evan, was a newborn, I
was growing tired of the constant struggle to find friends and
activities for each of the children, not to mention for myself.
Robin's pro-life work seemed to be fizzling out. He prayed for
guidance, made a multitude of phone calls, and decided that
our prospects would be distinctly rosier in Ireland. I took a fair

bit of persuading—moving an entire household six thousand miles makes no appearance whatsoever on my list of fun things to do—but eventually gave in. We packed up our house, put it on the market, and in the early dark of a bitter December morn peeled Iain off the carpet where he was lying in the active throes of stomach flu, found last-minute room in the hand luggage for Fiona's roller skates, and headed for the airport to begin our new life.

We would live to regret the "Eire" of our ways.

2

The Ephemeral Emerald Isle

I begin this chapter with another story, this one not about me. A man is traveling on a train, somewhere in England. He has a cup of tea and a packet of biscuits (as the English call cookies) on the table in front of him. A woman boards the train, buys herself some tea and biscuits, and sits down opposite him. They each take a sip of their tea, studiously avoiding eye contact (this is England, after all).

The woman takes a biscuit and nibbles at it reflectively. The man reaches out and takes one too. Somewhat peeved, she takes another one. He does the same. *What effrontery,* she thinks. *How rude! I'd willingly have given him one had he asked, but for him to help himself like that is really beyond endurance.* Glaring balefully at him, she devours another biscuit.

Boldly meeting her eye, so does the man. It's a standoff. *I cannot believe this man's rudeness—his sheer audacity!* Before she can decide her next move, the train pulls in at a station; the man drains his cup and stalks off, leaving what remains of her packet of biscuits. As he exits, he gives her what Paddington Bear would call "a hard stare." The train gathers speed and the woman sits, quietly fulminating; she unbuttons her coat, slips her hand into her pocket and there—oh, horror! oh, mortification!—is her packet of biscuits.

This is what is known as a paradigm shift: events and circumstances have not changed, but how we feel about them has. The woman's righteous indignation pops like a balloon as we realize along with her that it is she who has behaved boorishly. All the evil imprecations she heaped on the unfortunate man's head now fall on hers. Everything is different because her thinking has changed.

My own paradigm shift came in Ireland. We had weathered the transatlantic trip, moved into our rented eighteenth-century box of a house, purchased a large supply of peat to take the chill off a minuscule area immediately in front of the fireplace (thanks to the fifteen-foot ceilings, the heat that didn't go straight up the chimney hovered somewhere above even the tallest heads), and were learning to live in a house with no closets, no cupboards, and no drawers. Things were not working out the way I had expected, to put it mildly.

Our first (and, though we did not know it, our last) Irish

Christmas was a distressingly bare bones affair: having flown in only a couple of weeks previously, we had nothing but hastily concocted ornaments to put on the tree, and very little in the way of presents to put under it. My face all but cracked, so bravely did I try to maintain a façade of cheery goodwill—but the children weren't fooled for a minute. No, it wasn't fun pretending to be poor for a season. No, it was not cool to celebrate the holidays with just our family and no friends. No, they didn't think the *Ojo de Dios* ornaments we had hastily mass-produced from yarn and drinking straws made a refreshing change from our shiny glass treasures that were even now nosing their way across the Atlantic.

The *pièce de résistance*, however, was not revealed till dinnertime on Christmas Day. No matter how high I turned the oven, no matter how charred the turkey skin (and yes, children, I *know* we just had turkey at Thanksgiving), the flesh of the bird remained shiny, pink, and, well, *raw*. With miraculous promptness (by Celtic standards), the landlord came three days later to troubleshoot our reluctant cooker. He found that the previous tenants had removed the piece of metal that comprised the roof of the oven, leaving an open box trying valiantly to heat the entire kitchen. Small wonder the turkey had refused to cook!

Whatever would possess people to steal the lining of an oven, and what were they planning to do with it once it was in their possession? And what, more to the point, was I doing, trying to achieve some degree of normality in this country that increasingly reminded me of what Alice found in *Through the Looking Glass*? How had I reached this point?

My first mistake dated back almost a year: I had allowed Robin and Iain to serve as the advance guard, sizing up the country, the city, and the housing prospects, while I stayed home nursing the newborn Evan. I had suppressed a gnawing suspicion that I would regret entrusting a task so vital to the wellbeing of our family to the observational powers of my two biggest boys, but wilted at the prospect of transatlantic travel with a baby.

Robin focused on Kinsale, a picturesque town about twenty miles from Cork, in southern Ireland. There were, he assured me on his return, dozens of homeschooling families in the area, and he had found an elegant, eighteenth-century house to rent. Choking down my misgivings, I set about the not inconsiderable task of packing up all our belongings and saying goodbye to the place I had struggled so hard for the past twelve years to make into a home. As I did so, I was dismayed at how tenuous were the ties holding us down; it was as if I'd spent all those years hammering tent pegs into rocky ground, and the moment I stood up to straighten my back and survey my handiwork, a slight breeze lifted the tents and floated them gently away. *Maybe leaving here is for the best after all*; for the first time, I began to feel optimistic about the move. We had not been able to sell our house, but decided to go anyway and leave it on the market, hoping a buyer would soon materialize. All other lights were an encouraging green.

How eagerly I sought a reassuring green light as our plane
began its descent into Cork airport! I thought I found one
in the almost luminous green patchwork of fields that rose
up to meet us…but alas, I was mistaken. From the moment
we touched down, all lights were red. I discovered that most
of the homeschooling families were immigrants from the
Netherlands, come to find the freedom to grow marijuana in
their state-of-the-art greenhouses. The first homeschooling
get-together looked like a Woodstock reunion, populated by
children running around barefoot in the December dews, hair
matted with vegetable matter. Robin and I conversed easily with their parents, whose English was fluent, but it soon
became apparent that our world views were, to put it mildly,
somewhat at variance. I did, however, manage to strike up a
friendship with an artist whose two sons were about the right
age for Iain and Andrew; her educational philosophy seemed
unconventional but intriguing. I was at her house drinking coffee one day when I glanced at the bookcase and saw her VHS
collection. There, in plain view, was *In Bed with Madonna*. I
went home in a state of shock and asked Robin if the film was
as bad as it sounded. "It's worse," he said. "The dog didn't even
get into the credits." It was time to look elsewhere for friends
for the children—and myself.

One by one, my rosy Irish stereotypes crumbled. I was
dismayed to find that most Irish children spent the long, dark
winter evenings riveted to the television, and were especially

enthusiastic about American programs. I was sure I could come up with something more constructive. In my innocence, I assumed that finding Irish dance classes should be—well, if not necessarily easy, at least feasible. I went to the library, but the librarian didn't know anything and referred me to a mother who might. Over the course of the following week, I made dozens of phone calls, each leading to another, always elusive, contact. Eventually, I was sent full circle back to the librarian who exclaimed, "Oh! You want *Irish* dance classes? Oh, well! They'd be in the meeting hall at four o'clock on Tuesday." I choked back an acerbic, "You could have told me that a week ago, you know!" and instead thanked her copiously. I duly enrolled the girls, was relieved to find that the classes actually happened with some regularity, and unearthed further lessons in what Fiona later termed "really, really, really lame gymnastics."

Iain, meanwhile, was attempting to play Gaelic football at the local school. Problems arose when practices were cancelled, which happened at the drop of a hat. Since cancellations were announced at school, the only way for Iain to find out if that day's practice was on was to trudge through wind and rain and wait, shivering, in a muddy field to see if anyone else showed up. Rain was of no help whatsoever as a predictor: it rained for at least a part of every day we were there, sometimes from a cloudless sky. Unsurprisingly, Iain's enthusiasm soon dwindled, and with it went my attempts to find him a niche in the community.

Robin tracked down two terrific Catholic homeschooling families, but the Irish concept of distances got in the way of our building any close relationship—we were constantly assured that anywhere we wished to go was "about ten minutes (pronounced *temmins)* away," but the elusive *temmins* always proved at least half an hour, and could easily be three times that with traffic. So our daily existence was, by and large, extremely isolated. The children missed the US terribly; I didn't allow myself even to think of it, the contrast was so painful.

Teaching was an ordeal that took place in the dining room—an elongated, corridor-like room, considerably higher than it was wide. The standard tall, narrow windows of ancient, wavy glass let in any stray beams of light that might accidentally stumble by, reminding me very much of a fishbowl. Walls and floorboards were painted with the shiniest super-gloss paint imaginable, and thus the room acted as a most effective echo chamber. "Deafening" doesn't even begin to describe it. The noise was no doubt worse because I had removed the voluminous, floor-to-ceiling net curtains that formerly graced every window in the house. Presumably intended to prevent anyone outside from seeing in, they gave me the uncomfortable feeling of living in the dregs of a cold mug of milky coffee.

Hoping to render Fiona fluent in Gaelic, as well as find her some friends, we sent her to the local Gaelic-speaking school. Initially, Fiona was ecstatic to be going to school dressed in a grey jumper, yellow turtleneck, and red cardigan, but as the weeks went by, she began to look more and more enviously at the domestic activities we were enjoying at home—tea parties on the lawn, exploring the further reaches of the house, and discovering that even the weak Irish sun was enough to set dried grass on fire, with the aid of a magnifying glass. Every afternoon we asked her excitedly how many words of Gaelic she had learned at school that day, and every afternoon her answers were disturbingly evasive. Only as the school year came to a close did we find the reason: teachers and students alike had been kind enough to accommodate her by speaking only English. In the immortal words of Rabbie Burns, "The best laid schemes o' mice an' men/ Gang aft agley…"

We set about looking for a house to buy, and soon made an unpleasant observation: everybody we met seemed either to have cancer, to have a family member with cancer, or to have just lost someone to cancer. It was while we were looking at a picturesque, seventeenth-century Dutch house that we got our first clue as to why this was. The house was fronted by a sparkling, apparently idyllic stream. "You don't want to be after eating any fish from that stream," the helpful real estate agent instructed us, "they've all got tumors. There's a chemical factory opened just upstream, and the water hasn't been the same since. And if you fall in, be sure to be after rinsing yourself off quickly—and wash your clothes right away, right, right." Eager to attract new industry, the Irish government had apparently relaxed its environmental standards to a disastrous extent. The economy might have been flourishing, but the population definitely wasn't. And if fish couldn't live near that house, our children certainly weren't going to live in it. We looked farther afield.

We heard about an almost-completed house, designed by a highly respected architect, that sat on a hillside, commanding spectacular views. It sounded perfect but, as we drove three hours to see it, I tried to keep my expectations low. It was just as well I did. "Almost completed" it may have been at one point, but unfortunately, before the finishing touches could be detailed, the owner's wife had run off with the highly respected architect. The jilted husband had wreaked a terrible revenge on the house—doors and windows were rotting holes, left to welcome every passing thunderstorm, and his eight German shepherds had done what dogs do best—liberally, and on every available level surface. Where they couldn't reach—some of the more ornate moldings above waist level, for instance—the owner had apparently taken a trowel and smeared excrement, with impressive attention to detail. The stench was indescribable. Even Pollyanna would have been speechless. We drove home in silence.

Undaunted, we kept looking. "Elegant Georgian property, façade flanked on both sides by symmetrical, period greenhouses and well-tended orchards" sounded—well, a little imposing for us, perhaps, but worth a visit. What the agent had neglected to mention was that every single pane of glass in the "period greenhouses" was smashed (at least *that* was symmetrical), and that rampant suckers from the "well-tend-ed" fruit trees had encroached into the greenhouses, compromising the brickwork. I walked up the garden path and peered through the letterbox into the front hall. Rainwater dripped slowly onto the stairs from a hole in the roof. A sudden movement caught my eye—it was a dog, running unattended in the empty property. *Not again!* I shuddered, turned tail and fled.

That real estate agent's use of euphemism has since attained legendary stature in our family. In her thesaurus, *charming* and *elegant* were synonymous with "dilapidated," while *full of character* signified little more than a pile of rubble. To this day, when we drive past a broken-down barn with sagging roof and crumbling walls, someone is bound to call out, "There's a Virginia O'Malley—all it needs is a vision, and a little loving attention."

We began to think that building a house might be the answer, and set about designing one. It was while I was dreaming up my ideal kitchen that I realized I already had it—sitting unused and unsold in Everett, Washington. *Why build in Ireland what we already have in America? Is life here so much better?* I reviewed our current situation: it was not a pretty sight. Robin's job prospects, which had looked so rosy from the other side of "The Pond," were as bleak as a treeless winter landscape peopled exclusively by crows, and the social scene in Kinsale was not much better. The "difficulties" of life in Everett, which had so recently overwhelmed me, now looked positively idyllic. Indeed, their siren song was proving hard to resist.

Almost dizzy with excitement, hardly daring to think out-side the subjunctive case, I began to plan a return. *If we went back to Everett, could I somehow make it work?* This is where my paradigm shift came in: where before I had thought, *I don't like this, let's try somewhere else,* my new approach was, *I don't like this, what can I do to change it?*

I began with the lack of communal educational opportu-nities for the younger set. *We would need a teacher—could it be me?* I might not be the best teacher on the planet, but I had two advantages over the competition: 1) I was (or would be) in the right place, and 2) I was willing to give it a go.

Next on the agenda was a venue. When we lived in Everett, Iain had attended a homeschool history and culture class on Mercer Island, some thirty miles to the south. Many of his fellow students had younger siblings; surely somebody in the area would volunteer a room for our use. The question that really made my knees quake, however, was would anyone really entrust their child's education to me?

On the off-chance that they would, I set about planning content. Being at heart something of a frustrated poet, I de-termined to place poetry at the core of my classes. Prose was easily incorporated: a brief hunt through some of my favor-ite children's books revealed a wealth of avenues to explore. I sketched out a couple of classes and found myself eager for more—maybe this would work after all. Iain's culture class teacher said she didn't have room for another class in her home, but recommended someone who might; and two transatlantic phone calls later, all was arranged. Just like that, my children had classmates and I was their teacher.

Three months after our arrival in Kinsale, an enormous moving van had carried all of our worldly possessions up the driveway and disgorged them in front of our rented house. I had given up unpacking our kitchen stuff when I found that none of our baking dishes fit inside the tiny oven, and that there was not a single drawer in which to store our cutlery and utensils. Now the same boxes, mostly unopened, were put back on an identical truck, and trundled down the driveway to begin their lengthy voyage back to America.

When we went through customs in New York, I was ecstatic to see black faces again, realizing how much I'd missed America's multiculturalism in an Ireland that is almost unremittingly white. As our friends drove us home from the airport in Seattle, the smell of damp cedars was like perfume. We were home. And this time, I thought I knew how to make it work.

3

THE AUTOMATIC HOMESCHOOL

*A*ll too soon, the new school year rolled around and with it
my first, heart-in-mouth experience of teaching a "real" class.
There were eight students aged four to seven, plus Fiona, who
at the grand old age of nine was designated teacher's helper,
and Evan, three, whose job it was to make sure Fiona had
plenty to do. Theresa, age eight, was my other assistant.

To say I was nervous would be putting it mildly. Terrified of
forgetting what I wanted to say, I had written out every word in
longhand. My subject was ducks, our first book *Make Way for
Ducklings* by Robert McCloskey. Not being exactly computer
literate, I had laboriously handwritten my chosen five poems
and photocopied them for handouts. Each child selected one
of the poems to memorize for the following week. I discovered
that most poets inspired by the duck are moved to great things,

five stanzas at least: I had to expand the lesson to include vultures and the eagle before I could come up with five short poems.

It was easy to fill an hour with ducks. I led into a discussion of camouflage with a question: *If you were Mrs. Mallard sitting on a nest all day, would you rather have bright, beautiful feathers that say, "Look at me, Mr. Fox, I'm over here!" or soft, brown feathers that blend with the grass?* Evan was alone in preferring a short-lived, multicolored glory. For homework, the students colored in duck outlines: one resplendent male, one drab, inconspicuous female. The first class was a resounding success—not only did the children not boo me or throw rotten fruit, they even seemed to enjoy my efforts, and were excited about the following week.

They were so enthusiastic, indeed, that in our second class I did a reprise of the same book; I had the children retell the story while I showed them the pictures. Then we examined the miracle of a flight feather with a magnifying glass, and compared it with down and contour feathers. We learned that the flight feather, with its elaborate zipper system of interlocking barbules, is strong and flexible as well as light. In contrast, downy feathers entirely lack barbules and are soft and fluffy to provide warmth, while contour feathers are midway between. A quick joke—How do you get down off an elephant? You don't get down off an elephant, you get down off a duck—and with this first exposure to the wonders of equivocation, the second class was at an end.

As the weeks went by and I settled into a routine, lesson plans became far more lax. The week I talked about the Highlands of Scotland, my lesson notes consisted only of the names of three books. I wish I knew what I said; whatever it was inspired Theresa to a passionate love for all things Scottish, and she recently became the champion Highland dancer of the Seattle area. I am reminded of a poem I find inspirational:

> *Don't worry if your job is small*
> *And your rewards are few.*
> *Remember that the mighty oak*
> *Was once a nut like you.*

"Tall oaks from little acorns grow," indeed, and I feel privileged that my class set in motion Theresa's fascination with the country north of Hadrian's Wall.

My goal was to encourage the children to look more closely at their everyday world. We read Jan Brett's *The Mitten* and marveled at how the mitten stretched to accommodate all those animals. What kind of fabric stretches best, I asked, woven, or knitted? The children examined their clothing to find out. We looked at our shirts, and found that button-ups tended to be made of woven fabric, while shirts that must stretch to pull over the head were generally knitted. In a burst of inspired craftoid zeal I had them try finger knitting; we also "wove" scraps of fabric through yarn tied around polystyrene meat trays. We wondered which was invented first, knitted or woven fabric: since fabric does not last as long as stone, say, or even leather, how could we answer that question? I told them that scraps of woven fabric have been found in Turkey at sites dating back to 7,000 B.C. In what sort of conditions would textiles most likely be preserved—hot or cold, wet or dry? There is no one correct answer; things have been preserved in hot desert sands, as well as glaciers and chilly Irish peat bogs. My goal was not for the children to come up with a specific answer, but to get them wondering.

The better the book, the more the teaching possibilities. *Blueberries for Sal* by Robert McCloskey lends itself well to investigations of mistaken identity, hibernation, or food preservation. Charlotte Zolotow's classic *Over and Over* describes the passing of the seasons, any of which may be singled out; our favorite was autumn, when we investigated the myriad of ways that seeds are stored and dispersed. Chris Van Allsburg's *Two Bad Ants* helps us look at our kitchen from a different perspective, while Phoebe Gilman's *Something From Nothing* celebrates the glories of cumulative, repetitive language while also revisiting woven and knitted fabrics. Pretty soon, ideas for lessons were exploding in my head like popcorn.

Sometimes I would take a theme and organize books around it: "Kings and Queens," for instance. I mentioned that far more English authors have written books about royalty than Americans. Why should this be? It didn't take the children long to figure out that it was because Americans have never been ruled by a king or a queen. Why does that matter? It took them a bit more thinking to realize that people don't usually write about things they have not experienced. What about the things people only experience in their imaginations, like trolls and talking animals and fairies? Can we write about them? Yes, if you have a good imagination, but it is very difficult to create convincing fantasy. We talked about fact and fiction, and how important it is to keep them separate. If I write about an imaginary king, he can be good or bad, wise or foolish; but if I write about George III, I can't say, "He was a good king, greatly loved by his subjects," because history tells us he wasn't, and a good writer doesn't rewrite history.

I ran the class for a year and could have gone on indefinitely—there are so many inventive and inspiring children's books to choose from, with more published every year. I found it an easy way to introduce my children to a vast range of subjects, and to help other families at the same time by including their little ones. Peer pressure is often talked of in negative terms—it's what causes young people to smoke, do drugs, and engage in promiscuous activities, or so we are told. Positive peer pressure, on the other hand, can be a powerful force for the good. It makes students eager to come to class and gives them an incentive to do their homework well, particularly memorization for recitation in class. Young people learn good things from each other when an attitude of respectful cooperation is encouraged. The beneficial effect of peer pressure is the main reason I worked so hard to keep Entropy Academy afloat over the years.

IT'S A HOUSE! IT'S A SCHOOL! IT'S...*THE AUTOMATIC HOMESCHOOL!*

Now I was out of the house one morning a week—really, one whole day—and that was enough for me. I enjoyed being home too much to spend long hours driving the children to outside activities, and instead set about making the house an environment where they couldn't help but learn.

THE KITCHEN

I began with the kitchen, which was where we spent most of our time, and purchased two large maps: the world map went on the kitchen table, the US map on the wall. I was scandalized to see that the world map cut Asia in half so that America would be in the middle of the map. Fuming quietly (well all right, fuming noisily, as my children will tell you), I cut the map down the International Date Line and stuck Asia back together with Scotch tape. I put it on the table and covered the whole thing with clear contact paper. It wasn't heatproof, but it lasted a while—somewhere between two and ten years, depending on my tolerance for singed and melted bits on the kitchen table. Over the years we tried out different maps; our favorite was one that showed all the flags of the world at the bottom. Periodically we would turn the table around so everyone got to admire the flags; it amazed me how many the children knew. And that map didn't cut Asia in half!

The map was there, undeniably, and the children saw it every day. But there is a world (literally) of difference between seeing and noticing, and I was thrilled to find a game that had them examining the map most carefully: one person takes the first two letters of a country and the last two letters of a neighboring country, makes a four letter word, and challenges the family to name the countries. For instance, SWeden and NorwAY make SWAY, while BRAY is a "two-fer," Brazil and either Paraguay or Uruguay. To my knowledge, the word BURE exists solely to draw attention to Burkina Faso and Côte d'Ivoire, two small countries of West Africa that might otherwise be eclipsed by their larger neighbors, Mali and Niger.

The map of the States on the wall was primarily for reference, but Iain used it to learn his states by pinging rubber bands at them from across the room: "This one's for Tennessee…watch out, New Mexico, here I come!" As the children grew older, and particularly when they started driving, road maps jockeyed for position on the wall: Washington State, Everett, and the greater Seattle area were all readily available for trip planning or simply browsing. These maps helped us develop a strong sense of "north," which a reliance on today's GPS technology does little to cultivate.

On the wall calendar next to the telephone, I kept track of appointments and social engagements. I also used it to familiarize the children with various artists and places: one year it was medieval music manuscripts, another, the surrealist artist René Magritte and his iconic bowler hat self-portraits. The hills of Tuscany tempted us to travel— one day!—while the intricacies of M.C. Escher made us question our powers of perception. One year, the Seattle Art Museum held a marvelous exhibition of the works of Leonardo da Vinci, while another year it featured Vincent van Gogh (pronounced by the Dutch guide with an impressive amount of throat-clearing): both spawned a wall calendar. I always felt slightly guilty about not using the calendars as the basis of an in-depth study of the artists (as the "real homeschooling mother" on my shoulder would surely have done), but just seeing the pictures was enough to acquaint the children with some great artists, and took no effort on my part. Now, that's what I call homeschooling!

One readily accessible drawer was devoted to *Highlights* magazine, the most enduring of all the periodicals we sub-scribed to over the years. I kept back issues in a milk crate, and took them out two months at a time; thus the content was always appropriate to the season, plus there was the ex-citement of rediscovering a favorite story or poem from years gone by. A choice smattering of science articles, interspersed with jokes, ideas for artwork, regular features, and stories from around the world, made it easy for me to accomplish many of my educational goals for the early childhood years without ever mentioning the word "school." In particular, open-ended thinking problems stretched our imaginations and had us thinking "outside the box."

Another objective that was easy to meet in the course of everyday life was stretching comprehension and its hand-in-glove partner, building vocabulary. That you can't do one without the other was amply borne out for me by recalling my early exposure to baseball as a young bride. I spent the first game Robin took me to (between the LA Dodgers and the SF Giants, our two rival "home" teams) wondering two things: i) how to tell which team was which, and ii) when it would be over. Reading about the game in the paper the next morning did absolutely nothing to enlighten me.

This is why reading comprehension is so difficult to teach in a vacuum. "Strike three," "ball," and "stolen base" all mean radically different things in baseball than in normal life: but how can you understand the rules of baseball unless you know what these terms mean? It's an educational catch-22, if you will, and the best solution lies in an ongoing Q&A between the child/ignorant one (that'd be me) and a parent/knowledge-able adult (in my case, Robin.)

As I learned at the game, words are tools. Without the correct vocabulary, I could neither understand what was hap-pening on the field nor discuss it on the way home. For some young children, lacking the right words is so frustrating that they simply give up trying to communicate. And the bane of teenagers everywhere, replacing precise speech with, like,

y'know, like, "like," is rather like (word used correctly) a build-
er trying to construct a wall using nothing but a trowel and cement. A wall can't stand without bricks; neither can a sentence
be articulated without the right words. And these words can be
modeled repeatedly by a parent while reading stories, eating
lunch, or playing outside.

THE ISLAND

We were lucky enough to have some counter space on top of
the kitchen island, and here could always be found something
live and something growing. An early "something live" was
Fiona's frog, sprung from a *Grow-A-Frog* kit she received for
her birthday. Having dubbed it "Froggy," Fiona proceeded to
ignore it completely; she lived in a state of blissful unaware-
ness as its tail dwindled to a stump and its legs grew long and
strong. Then came the dreadful morning when she tripped
merrily into the kitchen with her medical kit and ailing me-
nagerie of soft toys and dolls, ready to play "doll hospital" with
her sisters. She stopped in her tracks. Something was wrong.
Her frog floated face down, unmoving, in suspiciously cloudy
water. He was dead.

O *misery!* O *despair!* Fiona's enormous blue eyes welled up
with tears, which hesitated only a moment before cascading
down her cheeks. The medical kit fell to the floor, powerless
to help in this real-life tragedy. She was inconsolable. Her frog
was gone! We buried him under the palm tree while Robin

played a suitably tragic dirge on my grandfather's bagpipe chanter and Fiona wailed out her grief. Thereafter, any time she was thwarted, sad, or just plain overtired, her eyes would fill with tears and she'd whisper tragically, "I miss my Froggy."

The incident has gone down in family legend. Years later, when Iain went off to college and Evan was inconsolable, I told Iain he could consider himself as Evan's Froggy. "Thanks," he said. "You've no idea how much that means to me."

For several years, the kitchen island boasted a colony of stick insects. These tiny creatures taught us a bitter life lesson one morning, when we found every single one of them dead on the bottom of the cage. Robin's bagpipe chanter got another workout as they joined Froggy under the palm tree, and more bitter salt tears were shed. *Ochone!* I was on the verge of rinsing out the tank and going to the pet store for some hermit crabs when the observant Evan noticed movement—a tiny creature was struggling to emerge from a pinhead egg. Phew! Saved by lethargy! The bug, and twenty or so of his brothers and sisters, never knew how close they came to an intimate encounter with the garbage disposal. The second year we knew what to expect, so their sudden demise had a less traumatic effect. Ignoring my suggestion that we spray the diminutive corpses with gold paint ready to hang on the Christmas tree, Lorna and Sheila wrapped them in toilet paper painstakingly inscribed with their names, and buried them in the flowerbed. No bagpipe chanter. The third year they were dumped, unmourned and entirely without ceremony, on the compost heap. The fourth year something happened to the eggs, and the stick bug era was over.

But for those three years, everyone who ventured into our kitchen learned something about stick insects, from camouflage to cannibalism. (I'm sorry, I should have broken the news more gently.) We also learned an important lesson about the ratio of Emotional Return to Energy Expended in Pets: stick insects don't need to be walked twice a day or groomed or cleaned up after but—how shall I put this? They're not much fun. You can put one on your hand and watch it do push-ups, you can put one on a tree and close your eyes for five seconds…poof! It's gone! But that's about it. It won't come when you call, roll over and play dead, or fetch a ball. Its capacity for heroism in dangerous circumstances is strictly limited: try substituting a stick insect in the Lassie movies and you'll see what I mean.

As for the "something growing" on our kitchen island, we always had, at the very least, an aloe vera plant to slice up and put on burns and rashes—the best treatment, my husband swears. Come the autumn, I would plant hyacinth and daffodil bulbs in bowls of potting soil, keep them in a dark cupboard till the roots were well developed, then bring them out so we could watch the flowers grow and unfold. One hyacinth bulb was grown in a special glass so we could watch the roots grow down into the water. This bulb grown without soil had its nutrients exhausted after one season, whereas those grown in rich soil could be planted out in the garden to bloom again the following year. The idea that proper nurturing brings forth strong, healthy growth imprinted itself in all our minds, with no need for moralistic lectures.

A traditional extravagance was the annual purchase of amaryllis bulbs in different colors from John Scheepers, one for each of the children. One pot of three bulbs for the boys, and one for the girls. Once the roots had developed in a dark place the pots were moved into the light, where the flower stems grew so fast we could almost see it happening, up to a height of three feet or more. The flowers were spectacularly beautiful, and obligingly displayed their botanical anatomy in a way that was very easy to identify. (We referred to a poster purchased at a school supply store, from which we learned about pistils and stamens, calyx and anthers.) I found that learning something of the science of flowers did nothing but heighten our aesthetic appreciation for them. Science and beauty are far from mutually exclusive.

Watching the bulbs, the children learned that plants grow towards the light. They noticed that plants placed on the windowsill grew more slowly than those on the island, but that they were healthier and darker green. One year, unfortunately, they learned the meaning of the word "etiolated." I forgot all about our amaryllis, which I had left sitting on the water heater in a dark cupboard. When, with a sickening lurch, I remembered them and ran to their rescue, I was greeted by a tall, gangly excrescence of a livid yellowish-green. Placed in full sunlight the plants recovered somewhat, and did manage to put out a few small, distinctly sickly flowers, but it was a sad contrast to the glory of former years. Let's just say that "etiolated" turned out to be one of our more expensive vocabulary lessons.

It was fascinating to discover ways to watch root systems develop. Besides the hyacinth glass, my other favorites involved lima beans and radish seeds. To get a close-up view of a growing bean plant, we soaked six lima beans overnight in water. The next morning we lined a 32-ounce glass jar with a layer of paper towels, added about an inch of water (more if the towels absorbed it all), and carefully slid the beans between the damp towels and the glass. The children enjoyed the suspense of hiding the jar in a dark cupboard, encased in a cylinder of black paper to keep out any stray beams of light. A daily check of the beans soon revealed the root beginning to grow down, splitting the two cotyledons apart as it went. We marveled that the root always grew down, no matter which way up the bean was planted. How does it know which way is down? Best theory is that it's the statocytes, tiny root sensors that are highly sensitive to gravity, that inform the plant. But the rapidity with which a seedling changes the direction of its roots when turned on its side seems to belie this theory; if it is indeed the statocytes signaling cells in the root tip to change their growth rate, the change would be gradual to the point of imperceptibility. Like so much in nature, the process abounds in mystery.

A developing root must increase its surface area in order to absorb sufficient water and nutrients. Nowhere can this be seen more spectacularly than with the obliging radish. We soaked a clay flowerpot in cold water for several hours, as well as about a teaspoonful of radish seeds. We turned the pot upside down in a pie plate and added water to the depth of half an inch. Now for the tricky part: using an old pair of tweezers, we placed the soaked seeds on the top and sides of the damp pot. The seeds fell off. Patiently, we replaced them. We covered the pot with an empty coffee can, placed it in a dark cupboard, and checked it daily. Every day, more seeds fell off; every day, we reattached them. The good news: as the roots grew, the seeds fell off less and less often. Our travails were eventually rewarded by a halo of the fuzziest root hairs imaginable, on every root. We tried to estimate how much the roots' surface area had been increased—it fairly boggled the mind.

READING ALOUD

One cupboard in the kitchen was devoted to puzzles, current read-alouds, and building toys. A jigsaw puzzle would often fill that difficult "arsenic hour" before dinner, while building spatial discrimination and fine motor skills. Building toys of all descriptions were a regular hazard in negotiating safe passage across the floor. As tempting as it was to confine the mess to a computer screen and purchase virtual Lego, I'm glad I didn't. Manually manipulating real objects in three dimensions plays a vital role in brain development, and besides, it's a lot more satisfying to show off colorful 3-D creations to an admiring audience when they can be tripped over.

This cupboard was raided at reading-aloud time, which usually happened twice a day and formed the backbone of the children's education. I tended to gear the books to the eldest, and the younger ones were free to sit in. It was amazing to me how much they understood, even in difficult books. Rather against my better judgment, I found myself reading Charles Dickens' *Great Expectations* when Sheila was only two, and I wondered if the book meant anything to her at all. Right on cue, she removed her nose from her drawing to ask why Pip's sister was so unkind to him. Apparently she was following the action quite well. Given a steady diet of difficult books, she would undoubtedly have lost interest—but one thrown into the mix here and there seemed to whet her appetite for more.

The price of finding good books to read aloud was eternal vigilance. Notebook in hand, I scoured books such as Jim Trelease's *The Read-Aloud Handbook*, listing unfamiliar authors that looked promising and hoping their output was not marred by the unevenness that seems to plague some writers. Reading a variety of reviews helped. I tried to select a variety of books, not just fiction. I regret now not having read more biographies—for some inexplicable reason I thought they would be boring. How wrong I was! It is both fascinating and inspiring to read about the hardships and obstacles most great people have had to overcome. We tend to think that life should be easy, and strive to make it so for our children, but the truth is that most famous people have had to struggle, often against overwhelming odds, to become who they are.

I am reminded of a story about a butterfly enthusiast who witnessed a very rare butterfly struggling to emerge from its chrysalis. Only the tip of one wing remained trapped. Seeking to help, the man took a small pair of scissors and carefully snipped the chrysalis to free the wing. The butterfly spread its wings in the sun to dry. To his horror, the man saw that the part of the wing he had freed remained crumpled; it never became strong enough to fly. Apparently, struggle was necessary for the creature to be properly formed. The same seems to be true of humans. I'm not saying we should deprive our children or deliberately cause them hardships—no doubt life will provide them plenty—but by all means read to them about those who have faced difficulties and disappointments and overcome them. As Theodore Roosevelt said, "I have never in my life envied a human being who led an easy life. I have envied a great many people who led difficult lives and led them well."

It seems I was not alone in my suspicion of biographies: when Lorna selected a volume on the life and times of Franz Josef Haydn, she was thrilled to discover she was the first person to check it out in sixty years! The discovery gave her interest in music of the Classical era a considerable boost.

I never minded my children being busy while I read to them: listening to books is a predominantly left brain activity, so keeping the right brain occupied actually helps the child concentrate on what she is hearing. She might color, do a puzzle, or build quietly, my only rule being that the noise of her rummaging through the box of Lincoln Logs must not drown out my voice. If she preferred, she could simply daydream—there would be no comprehension test. Indeed, none was necessary: I found each morning that when I reviewed the previous day's reading before embarking on the next chapter, the children were invariably the ones helping me recall the action, not vice versa.

At some point in their development, all the children—boys included—enjoyed embroidery. I picked up Christmas ornament kits for next to nothing in July, and by late November we had several gems to add to the tree. Knitting too was highly popular. In liking to knit, Evan takes after the English grandfather he never knew, who used to relax by knitting fantastically intricate baby clothes whenever a close friend of the family gave birth. We probably looked like a scene from *Little House on the Prairie*, knitting and stitching while Mother read, but those were some of our happiest homeschooling times—and although Robin didn't play the violin like Pa, at least he wasn't moved to substitute the bagpipes.

I wondered if my tolerance for extraneous activity was hampering the children's concentration. Seeing Lorna intent on her jigsaw puzzle, seemingly oblivious to the world around her, I asked her if she was able to follow the story. She looked up, surprise written all over her face. "Well of course," she replied. "Why wouldn't I?" To her, it was incomprehensible that the puzzle might be considered a distraction.

As the children grew older, their listening activities included tracing maps of the countries we were reading about, as well as coloring photocopied pages from historically appropriate Dover and Bellerophon coloring books. Tracing maps was the mainstay of their training in geography, apart from the hours spent at the kitchen table admiring the world map. Over the years, we made salt-and-flour maps of the US, Israel, and Egypt, and once we fashioned the Far East out of mashed potato. I'm not particularly proud of this shortfall in geography education, but it worked for us, and the children's knowledge of the countries of the world is better than many. At least they've never asked if you need a passport for New Mexico, or wondered if you can drive to Hawaii, as did one applicant for the position of receptionist in Robin's office. And she was a college graduate!

To keep track of the books we read, I drew a rudimentary bookcase on a large piece of poster board, stuck it on the wall, and cut a generous supply of book spines of various heights and thicknesses from construction paper. Every time we finished a book, one of us wrote the title and author on a spine and stuck it on the bookcase. We all enjoyed looking over the books we had read—it gave us quite a sense of accomplishment. A very artistic friend of mine borrowed this idea; her bookcase was exquisite, her book spines elegant and varied. She made me positively ashamed of my childishly clumsy efforts. Hastily, I reminded myself that for our family the essential thing was not to make a work of art, but to get it done at all. I drew great comfort from Voltaire's dictum, "the perfect is the enemy of the good."

BATH TIME

Turning our bathroom into an Automatic Learning Center was as easy as—well, turning on a faucet. I capitalized on the fact that I had, as it were, a captive audience (show me the person who doesn't spend any time in the loo and I'll say you have a freak of nature). Up on the walls went my favorite calendars: one invited the children to tackle a daily math problem, with a small financial incentive to be the first with the correct answer, while in a different bathroom, guests were regaled with natural disasters—hurricanes, tornadoes, and lightning storms. It became quite a talking point.

The pile of books that lay within striking range of the seating area included random books of jokes, puns and oddities, crosswords, anagrams, the always inspirational *Book of Heroic Failures: The Official Handbook of the Not Terribly Good Club of Great Britain* (currently available, I am thankful to say, through Amazon), and *Brush Up Your Shakespeare!* by Michael Macrone. The latter offers "an infectious tour through the most famous and quotable words and phrases from the Bard." Through its pages we became familiar with several plays, as well as phrases that are in (semi-) popular use today, from the well-known "If music be the food of love, play on" (*Twelfth Night*) to the ever-handy, "Hoist with his own petard" (*Hamlet*).

But it was in the bathtub itself that things became truly exciting. A set of graduated stacking beakers encouraged the children to discover that a smaller receptacle could never hold as much as a bigger one, no matter how often they tried. Plastic measuring cups informed them that a half-cup measure would always hold two quarter cups. We held air under water using a clear plastic disposable cup, tilted the cup slightly, and laughed at the noise of the bubbles surfacing. *Which is heavier, water or air? That's right, water. Is it always? Yes. What would happen if it weren't? Where would the ocean go? The rivers? What would happen when we turned on the tap and put a glass underneath to catch the water?* Bath time was a good time to introduce the children to the three states of water: they're sitting in the liquid form, they can see the steam (gas), and the freezer usually had some (solid) ice cubes handy. We'd guess which would melt more quickly, an ice cube in the tub or one in a pitcher of cold water. *How about if we have another ice cube in a second jug and stir the water? Does the ice cube melt any quicker, or do we just get cold fingers?* We noticed that ice always floats, and thought about how disastrous it would be to aquatic life if it sank instead.

Clear plastic tubing was a great discovery, and considerably increased our arsenal of bubble-blowing techniques. We inverted a plastic cup underwater, so it was full of water, then used the plastic tubing to blow the water out, replacing it with air. *Now we have air under water; does that mean it has stopped being lighter than water? What happens if we tip the glass just a tiny bit? A tiny bubble comes out! What happens if we tip a glass a big bit? A big bubble comes out!*

A sieve in the bathtub steadfastly refused to hold water. *What happens if we line it with a dry washcloth and slowly add 1/4 cup of water? Where does the water go? Into the washcloth! How much water can one washcloth absorb? Let's find out. Suppose we line the sieve with a plastic bag: how much water goes through? None! It is all still in the sieve; plastic is impermeable to water. Even the tiny water molecules cannot penetrate the plastic.*

Possibilities for educating in the tub are numerous, and as enjoyable as they are manifold. Books with titles like *Science in the Tub* gave me a much fuller idea of the scientific potential of the evening bath, and these days, Googling "science in the bathtub" reveals a wealth of tricks to try. It's a softcore way of teaching some hardcore science.

NATURE: WHY GO ON A FIELD TRIP WHEN THE FIELD WILL COME TO YOU?

It was well before our exodus to Ireland that the children and I went on what was to prove easily the most influential field trip of our homeschooling career—influential not so much for what we saw, as for what we didn't see. I bundled the children into the car ("Why are we getting in the car? I don't want to go anywhere…I hate being in the car…when can we go home?") and drove thirty miles to Padilla Bay, a bird sanctuary that was renowned for the wide variety of species it attracted, especially during autumn migration, which was now.

Once there I put baby Fiona in her backpack and Andrew in his stroller while Iain slumped alongside, grumbling profusely. While I was admiring Iain's ability to "walk" without perceptible forward progress, Andrew found a cunning way to throw himself bodily to one side, tipping the entire stroller over and pitching him, howling pitifully, onto the stony ground, along with all of the paraphernalia designed to keep him happily occupied in the stroller. As I bent down to pick him up, Fiona seized the opportunity to give a mighty push with her legs and pitch herself headlong over my right shoulder, where she hung suspended by her safety strap, screaming into my ear and grabbing my hair by the fistful to give herself a sense of security in this world-turned-upside-down.

Somehow, order was restored, and we began the tour. Iain kept up a running commentary of negativity, though he seemed somewhat intimidated by the guide, a man of forceful demeanor. Under his leadership, we tiptoed quietly to a bluff. "Here," he whispered, "you will see flocks of migrating ducks, from mallards to widgeons. Nowhere else in Washington will you find this many species gathered in one place." Tingling with expectation, we peered around the rocky outcrop and saw…nothing. Nothing, that is, apart from a couple of sparrows hopping around desultorily, looking as bored as we felt.

"I can't understand it," said our (trusty) guide. "Usually you can barely see the ground for ducks. I wonder where they can be." Thus was established the first principle of Bernhoft field trips: Don't expect to see what you go there expecting to see. Don't go to a bird sanctuary and hope to see birds. Don't go to a fish ladder and hope to see salmon returning to their ancestral spawning grounds to lay their eggs, even if "this time last year, there were so many you could practically walk across the river on them."

After a few more hopeful sightings-that-weren't, it was time to abandon the birds in their sanctuary, wherever they might be, and strong-arm the hungry, fractious children into the car for the return trip. To them, the lesson was plain: field trips are a Terrible Idea, and should be resisted as stoutly as is humanly possible. Who was I to disagree with them? Back in our kitchen, I glanced out of the window while I made the tea. Finches and chickadees were squabbling over the contents of our solitary bird feeder, while sparrows and juncos hopped around beneath, cleaning up whatever spilled over. Early hummingbirds zipped around the hanging basket of fuchsias, while up on high, a bald eagle soared by. "You just drove sixty miles to see what?" I asked myself. "Birds, you say. And what, exactly, is that outside your window? Looks to me suspiciously like—birds!"

That trip seared itself into my memory. It was so very unpleasant, and the alternative, spending time and money attracting the birds to us, so very delightful, that it was retroactively awarded the title of Most Distinguished Bernhoft Field Trip Ever. Gradually, our balcony acquired several feeders. For the finches and chickadees there was shelled sunflower seed in a spherical feeder made of clear plastic, while the goldfinches enjoyed a thistle feeder that required them to hang upside down to eat. Woodpeckers found suet cakes irresistible; on one feeder the birds could hang upside down, while the other, upright one had a tail support that demonstrated how the woodpecker uses its tail for strength and balance as it ascends and descends tree trunks. We could also wonder at the distribution of claws: perching birds have three in front and one behind to hook over the branch they are sitting on; woodpeckers, who spend their lives creeping up and down trees, have two in front and two behind for greater stability. I found this hard to believe when I read it in a bird book, but was able to prove it to myself with not one, but four different types of woodpecker: the tiny downy, the almost identical but larger hairy, the roguish flicker, and the spectacular pileated, which dwarfed even our largest feeder.

It was blissfully easy to introduce the children to woodpeckers and their unusual feet in teachable moments that occurred quite spontaneously while the children sat on the kitchen counter admiring me making a cup of tea. (Now, that's my idea of a field trip: staying home and drinking tea.) A simple sugar-water feeder for hummingbirds rounded out our collection. The cheap, plastic type worked better than the more beautiful glass variety—not only was it easier to clean, but the brilliant red plastic "flowers" proved irresistible. Perhaps too irresistible—one year, a pair of hummingbirds overwintered in our Pacific Northwest garden, and we were treated to the unusual sight of hummingbirds trying to find nectar in our Christmas lights—but only the red ones.

From the National Wildlife Federation came abundant information about making our yard bird-friendly, and we also gleaned wisdom about "edible gardening" from our local newspaper. Within a couple of years, our yard was fairly bursting with good things to eat—supposedly for humans and birds, but our avian friends got most of the bounty. This was particularly galling in the case of the bing cherry tree planted in honor of our oldest daughter Fiona, who at age two had informed us she was too *bing* (big) to be called Baby anymore. The name Bing stuck, and now she even has a search engine named after her (good things come to those who wait). Every year, the cherries would be ripening beautifully; every year, we would look at them one evening and say, "Tomorrow, we pick." And every year, just after dawn, a black cloud of crows would descend, cawing lustily: it was the work of only a few minutes, but when they took off, every single cherry would be gone.

Some avian visitors were more welcome: each spring, our English ivy and serviceberries played host to the

black-masked cedar waxwing, and occasionally we would be
tantalized by a grosbeak seeking fruit on our feeders. I say
"tantalized" because by the time I put out half an orange for
it to feast upon, it had gone elsewhere and the orange was
left either to dry out or mold, depending on the weather.

I found that people who feed birds are also generous in
sharing their knowledge, whether through the library, our
county extension service, or the first-rate chain store Wild
Birds Unlimited. Our garden was a haven for wild birds,
complete with a birdbath for essential water. It took time
for word to get around in the feathered community that our
garden was the happenin' place to be, but once it did we had
a steady stream of regular guests, and we made sure to keep
our feeders well-stocked for their benefit. The most reward-
ing sight of all was the baby woodpeckers, clinging desperately to the balcony railings while their parents flew back
and forth with suet from the feeders. Even though the chicks
were horizontal, they still splayed out their tails as if they
were clinging to the trunk of a tree. Next to them perched
the baby finches, who encouraged their parents to feed them
by fluffing up their feathers to look cute and defenseless. This
actually made them appear to be a great deal larger than
their overworked parents, who fed them regardless.

You might think that I'd learned my lesson about the
inadvisability of avian field trips from our escapade at Padilla
Bay, but you'd be wrong.

One drear November morning, I took the children to a park ranger's demonstration about owls. The weather was cold and damp, the rain doing a passable imitation of conditions on the Scottish Isle of Skye: not so much rain "fall" as rain saturating the air, moving in every direction—including up. Our bearded ranger unveiled three somewhat scruffy-looking specimens that had been rescued from natural or man-made disasters, and embarked on a lengthy and somewhat lurid lecture on the Dangers Posed to Our Feathered Friends by Unthinking Mankind.

This was extreme emotional overload for Sheila, who at three had a very tender heart and needed no help whipping her owl-loving emotions into a passionate frenzy. She stamped up and down, huffing and puffing to vent her frustration. Finally, she'd had enough. In an impeccable English accent, she burst out, "Bloody hell, I can't stand much more of this!" and took off, storming furiously towards the car.

THE YARD

A garden, whether window box or estate, presents a fantastic opportunity for learning. In many ways, smaller is better. In a compact area one can amend the soil and grow concentrated beauty, instead of spending enormous amounts of time waging the damage control war that comes with a large garden. Nobody ever said that mass weeding and mowing were exactly fun. We had a daunting profusion of flowerbeds covered with either wood chips, groundcover, or weeds. The soil was simply dreadful—areas of sand interspersed with chunks of solid clay. Over the years I tried to intermingle the two, adding peat and plenty of stuff raided from friends with horses, and succeeded in producing two beds that would actually grow flowers.

Our yard was the setting for all kinds of natural events. One day, somebody dumped an ailing cat outside our house; we took it in, offered it food, and gave it a warm place to sleep. Sadly, the next morning we found it dead. I decided to give it a decent burial while enriching the flowers with natural fertilizer by burying it in the herbaceous border adjacent to our neighbors' front lawn. Unfortunately, the neighbors were at that time in the process of selling their house. Still more unfortunately, the real estate agent chose that very moment to show up with two prospective buyers. I smiled and waved a cheery hello, but quite frankly, it's not easy to look nonchalant when you're burying a dead cat.

My husband took time off from a particularly grueling political campaign to follow Winston Churchill's example and try his hand at bricklaying. Where Churchill built walls, however, Robin created raised flowerbeds to grow vegetables. It might seem quixotic to add more flowerbeds to our existing supply of weed- and woodchip-encrusted beauties, but with the soil being so dreadful it was easier to start from scratch. At least, so we thought. The man who delivered our "premium-grade garden soil" assured us it was "so fertile it would grow rocks." As it turned out, that was about all it would grow: it looked distressingly similar to the blue-grey stuff in our existing beds, only interspersed with a plethora of large stones. So it was back to the soil amendment business for us—a little more labor-intensive than we had planned, but we ended up with hip-level vegetable beds that were a definite improvement over the traditional "let's all bend over and get a backache" model. A visiting friend informed me that this technique, originally known as "lazybed" gardening, was introduced by Scottish crofters— "to raise the beds above the acid soil, you'll understand, not for their own comfort."

Lazybed or regular bed, planting is still a chore, and it was with wildly varying degrees of enthusiasm and commitment that the family set about the spring planting of vegetables. One year I made a motivational "before and after" book of photos. On one page stands the raised bed with its tiny tomato, bean, and sugar-snap pea plants beside orderly rows of infant onions, and carefully raked soil covering the carrot seeds; in the picture next to it, taken in midsummer, the riot of plant growth that had taken place is simply astounding— and at least in theory proved a great incentive come the following spring, when it was time to start all over again.

Sheila developed a passion for flowers at age three, when she encountered her first iris. I promptly purchased some choice rhizomes and coached her carefully to ask the nurseryman for "low-nitrogen fertilizer, please." He was duly

impressed and, with a twinkle in his eye, asked her to say it
again. That was too much—her blushing face disappeared
into the folds of her soft purple cloak, and nothing more
than a muffled squeak emerged. She had chosen her alle-
giance well: irises are amazing flowers. For most of the year
they present an exuberance of leaves that threaten to take
over whole chunks of the garden, but when they flower, one
would forgive them anything. Several flowers on each stem
unfurl in turn from bottom to top, each one a work of con-
summate beauty. They are most obliging about being picked,
and may be admired in minute detail as each flower unfolds
in a bottle on the kitchen table. Sheila's love of irises grew
to encompass all things botanical. To this day, she can be
relied on to brighten our kitchen with posies picked from our
garden. Her enthusiasm wilts with the flowers, however, with
the result that there are usually several bouquets in various
states of decomposition adorning our countertops. Yet another opportunity to observe entropy in action.

As Evan's tenth birthday approached, I asked him what
he would like to do to celebrate his double digits. He thought
for a moment. "Planting flowers is fun," he said. "Could
we plant some flowers?" We made a celebratory dash to the
nursery and chose a wide selection of our best-loved annual
friends; the rain held off long enough for us to accomplish
the planting deed, and we enjoyed them for the rest of the
summer.

I am exceedingly fond of marigolds. Sad to relate, so was something else in our garden. Every morning found more leaves and petals vanished, the remaining stumps covered in a tracery of slime that glittered rather fetchingly in the sun's early rays. *Slugs!* This meant war.

Surveying the arsenal of weapons available to me, I recalled a childhood visit to my Uncle Hugh and Auntie Beti in South Wales. Hugh was an avid gardener and had a novel way of dealing with his slimy foes: he picked them off his plants by night, and dropped them into a jar of salt. My eight-year-old, animal-loving heart had been outraged by his barbarity, but try as I might, as a callous adult I was unable to empathize very deeply with the slugs' mucoid fate. Nor could I find a better way; I disliked poisoning them, fearing the toxins would remain in the ecosystem long after their mission of destruction was complete. Besides, who's to say that commercial poison yields any more humane a death than salt?

The trail of vandalism left by the critters brought the bloodlust to my eyes like an avenging Viking warrior. Every night, I donned Wellingtons and gardening gloves, grabbed flashlight and slug jar, and made for my flowerbed. An erudite friend had penned Dante's "Abandon all hope, ye who enter here" in medieval Italian on my jar; it made me feel intrepid and cosmopolitan, though I doubt Dante had much of a slug problem in fourteenth-century Italy. And I can't say my modern American slugs were exactly impressed by the literary allusion; nevertheless, a good night would yield me upwards of twenty victims.

The slugs were to teach me a searing lesson about acclimation to depravity. *(Warning to those of a delicate disposition: what follows may be hazardous to tender sensibilities.)* I sallied forth to wage my nightly war and was rewarded with the gratifying sight of two slugs mating. Curled around each other with a passel of eggs between them, they represented a preemptive strike: hundreds killed at a single blow. I was triumphant! It was then I discovered *I had forgotten my gloves.* What should I do? Go back into the kitchen, tracking mud everywhere…who knows where I'd left my gloves…the house seemed an awfully long way away…I gritted my teeth, closed down the neural pathways to my fingertips, and barehanded the happy couple to their saline doom. "Ugh!" I muttered, "I'll never do that again!"

Except, of course, that I did. Next time I forgot my gloves, it was distinctly easier to overcome my abhorrence for slime; before long, I had dispensed with gloves altogether. I knew that what I was doing was repulsive, beyond the bounds of civilized behavior, but that didn't stop me. I imagined the twelve step meetings: *Hello, my name is Alison and I barehand slugs.* I did it anyway. It was not until the next season, after the long winter's hiatus, that I made the firm resolution never again to touch a slug without my gloves. I am proud to say I stuck to my guns. I was a reformed character.

In much the same way as I had become acclimated to the intrinsically repugnant in the garden, I noticed that it was easy to let our family's moral standards slide. Once I had breached the taboo of touching a slug, it became increasingly easy for me to do it: once I let my guard slip and we watched some program with more sexuality or violence than we were used to, that became the new "acceptable" by which future content was judged. Innocence is the most fragile of qualities, and once sullied can never be regained.

THE JOY OF COMPOST

In the Middle Ages, beggars often slept on the communal compost heap to keep warm. While our family never went so far as to relinquish our beds, I took enormous pleasure in the steaming signs of warmth emanating from our carefully mixed piles of brown and green matter. Even our license plate frame boasted: *Happiness is a steaming compost heap.*

I had been an enthusiastic fan of compost heaps since I was a girl, watching my father turn piles of dead leaves and kitchen scraps into rich, fragrant loam that grew the most abundant potatoes, the sweetest raspberries, the most fragrant climbing roses. Now it was my turn to enjoy the smells and textures of composting, and I found the process every bit as intoxicating as I remembered. My ally was the aptly named earthworm, which travels tirelessly between the various levels of soil or compost, carrying nitrogen on its slimy skin to nourish plants' roots. I decided to start a worm bin to encourage the little dears.

Great was my surprise to discover that worm bins are not designed to be inhabited by earthworms, but rather by red wigglers—thin, red worms that live in the top inch or two of soil, and may often be found under a layer of leaves or a large, flat rock. They can, however, eat close to their own weight in kitchen scraps each day, and turn them into castings and "worm tea," guaranteed to boost any plant's growth. Our green plastic worm bin made a good adjunct to the compost heap, which generated its own abundant supply of earthworms. It seemed poetically fitting when I learned that a worm has five hearts; they certainly brought a lot of heart to our gardening. Worms loved the compost, birds loved the worms, plants loved them both. And the more we learned about sustainable gardening—the antithesis of the single crop, chemical-based agribusiness that is ruining our farmland and our health—the more we came to appreciate the goodness of organic produce. Especially when, with the aid of entropy, lazybeds, and compost heap, we had grown it ourselves.

REQUIEM

To our enduring sorrow, the people who bought our house proceeded to cover our compost heaps and orchard with cement, and turn it into a home for their All Terrain Vehicles.

They ripped out everything we had so lovingly planted: fifteen mature fruit trees, hundreds of spring-flowering bulbs, twenty-seven species of rhododendron, innumerable delectable bushes and ground covers—all gone. *Poor hungry birds! Poor sad us!* Still, as the saying goes, "'tis better to have loved and lost than never to have loved at all." And even now, if I close my eyes I can still see the fritillaries growing through the verdant moss under the apple trees, beside the daffodils and Scottish bluebells…

4

PETS

DOGS

*W*hen we first moved to Everett, an important choice lay before us. On one hand, the glorious scenery of the Pacific Northwest invited us to keep our weekends free to uproot and go—hiking, canoeing, cross-country skiing, exploring new corners of the state. On the other hand, I had been raised with a dog, Robin with cats, and we both appreciated the stability and entertainment that pets bring to a home. To pet, or not to pet, that was the question.

Still vacillating wildly, I found myself at the library in the dog section. Specifically, I found myself transfixed by the spine of a book entitled *The Newfoundland.* "Hmm," I mused, "if I take this book home, it'll all be over. We'll end up with a

Newf." Unbidden, my hand reached up and plucked the book from the shelf. The die was cast.

Two months later, Phoenix came to join us. I didn't particularly like the name, but feared causing her an identity crisis if we changed it so late in life. She was three and a half months old, sixty-five pounds of exuberant, irresistible, totally untrained puppy. At least, I found her irresistible; Robin could be heard muttering darkly, "When can we get rid of her?" Even my dog-loving mother asked plaintively, "Are you sure this is a good idea?" as she regarded the small lake spreading over the hardwood floor from Phoenix's latest "sin of emission."

It was lucky for Phoenix that I had read that book so attentively; my heart was still swelling at the stories of bravery and downright doggy derring-do that lay within its covers. I alone recognized our latest family member's true potential. But even I had to admit that something had to be done about this chunk of canine mayhem. I knew her top weight would be around 125 pounds, and that she would be massively strong; I also knew that I was five months pregnant with my third child and not growing any more dynamic. I put two and two together, and figured out that the only hope of making her toe the line lay in training her to want to obey me.

Thus, with a certain degree of desperate urgency, the training process began. I have now trained two dogs, and can honestly say that I have learned more about raising children from my dogs than from any other source. Not that I've had to work all that hard on helping my children understand "sit," "stay," and "come" (though *understanding* and *doing* it are two different matters). Here are the most helpful lessons I learned:

1. Reward good behavior quickly. A good trainer is lavish with both treats and praise, bestowing them instantaneously.

2. Beware which behaviors you reward. When your dog whines for tidbits at the dinner table and you say "no" five times before giving in, you just taught your dog that persistent misbehavior will be rewarded. If your child whines for candy at the supermarket checkout line five times, and the sixth time you give in and buy it "just this once," you have taught her to ignore you the first five times you say "no."

3. Be careful which behaviors you punish. How many times have I seen a dog blissfully gallivanting around, completely ignoring his owner's increasingly frantic commands to "come"? When his people-radar finally kicks in and he runs enthusiastically to his owner, confidently expecting praise for being such a clever, obedient dog, what does he hear? "You bad dog!" He may even be hit. The irate owner thinks she is punishing the dog for staying away, but the dog knows better. He is being punished for obeying the command to come. The lesson received is, "When she's shouting *come* in that tone of voice, STAY AWAY."

Phoenix was there to greet the four younger children when each arrived home from the hospital. They all learned to stand by pulling themselves up on her thick coat—luckily, she was impervious to pain, and rewarded their efforts with nothing more unpleasant than great sloppy licks. Soon, she became famous in the neighborhood for her size and perpetual good nature. She was the ideal dog to see us through the baby phase: she enjoyed going for a walk but was perfectly happy to stay at home when I just didn't feel like it; she would blunder about the house, apparently oblivious to where she put her great webbed feet, but never once stepped on the baby; and she made a perfect backrest at a baseball game or at the beach. Oddly enough, given her heritage, she never took to the water. She would follow me out until the point where her paws were in danger of parting company with *terra firma*, give me an anguished look as if to say, "How could you betray me so?" then turn around and beat a hasty retreat to the security of dry land. The only exception was when I swam with her: she was thrilled to have her alpha dog lead the way. As the trusted leader of the pack, I could be followed anywhere—even into that menacing, moving body of water known as the Puget Sound.

Phoenix died of lymph node cancer just before we left for Ireland. When death seemed imminent we held a wake, inviting her many friends and admirers to come and say goodbye, bringing high protein, high calorie snacks (for the dog). The house was full of fans and well-wishers; they all signed one of the announcements I had printed and jotted down their fondest memories. On the day she died, Evan administered her last breakfast in the cool outdoors, where she was more comfortable. The vet came, and wielded her Needle of Oblivion as Phoenix lay in a gentle drizzle under the partial shelter of an overhanging bush, her head on my lap. A brief shudder, and she was gone. We buried her with full honors under the palm tree, in the august company of the first generation of stick insects and Fiona's frog. Robin played a particularly soulful lament on the chanter. The children wept as though their hearts would break—indeed, there wasn't a dry eye in the house—but the next day, life went on as usual. They seemed to have spent the full force of their grief in the rituals surrounding her demise.

When we returned from Ireland, I was eager to find a new dog. Not that I was lacking for company, exactly, but I needed an ally in the ongoing saga of Mummy's Disappearing Waistline and a motivator for daily walks seemed just the ticket. Wildly against my better judgment (perhaps it had something to do with the two glasses of champagne) I bid on a puppy at a benefit auction for EquiFriends, the therapeutic riding stable where Andrew rode every week. Rather to my dismay, I "won." The two days before we could pick her up were filled with misgivings on my part. *Buying a puppy of unknown origin, sight unseen? You've got to be crazy!* I tried to reassure myself that only nice people would support the EquiFriends auction, and that nice people have nice dogs, but I remained unconvinced.

The situation when we drove into the remote wilderness of darkest Snohomish County to pick up our auction indiscretion did little to reassure me. The "breeder" was a wild-eyed individual with a tangled mass of hair, apparently not on intimate terms with personal hygiene. Mutely, he gestured towards a barn that would have reduced even Virginia O'Malley to silence. Breathing softly lest the whole edifice come crashing down, we tiptoed cautiously past an enormous spider web— we had no desire whatsoever to disturb the black widow that lurked therein.

There, resting on a bed of filthy straw, were three puppies. Tail wagging, one immediately came over to check us out; one ignored us, while the third cowered in the corner. "We'll take that one," I said, pointing to the first, confident one. Our host shook his head: that one was already spoken for. Ditto its disinterested sibling. With sinking heart, I realized that our fate lay with the third puppy, the one cringing in the corner, whose eyes, one brown, one blue, regarded us with abject terror.

We called her Fritha, an Anglo-Saxon name which proved to be the best thing about her. True to her heritage, part Australian shepherd, part dingo, she related to our sheep (or the children, as we persisted in calling them) by snapping at their heels to round them up. She hadn't been with us long before the mere sight of her was enough to reduce the girls to tears. This made Andrew so angry that he kicked her; Iain and Evan studiously ignored her. Robin and I agreed this was not exactly what we were looking for in a dog. The final straw came when I was carrying her outside to do her doggy business, and she was so frightened by a perfectly ordinary garbage truck that she performed right down my front. Something had to give. I was deliriously happy to learn that the breeder would take her back, and even happier when the moment came to give her a farewell pat and drive away. Never had she looked more adorable than in the rearview mirror.

With my new, improved understanding of how deeply a dog's temperament is influenced by the characteristics of its breed, I swore off the champagne and set about some careful research. I wanted a dog who was smart and sociable, not stupid and neurotic like Fritha, and preferred one who would not carpet the floor wall-to-wall every time it shed, as had Phoenix.

A Portuguese water dog seemed the perfect choice. These dogs were originally bred to help Portuguese fishermen herd fish, and to retrieve broken nets and tackle; in World War One the British Navy used them to carry messages from ship to ship, and from ship to shore. The advent of on-board wireless, however, and its eventual acceptance by the reactionary "Old Guard" element of the navy, put an end to the dogs' usefulness, and by 1930 the Portie was all but extinct. Efforts to reintroduce the breed from a very limited genetic stock excited considerable scientific interest, which spread to America in the 1970s. So there was a homegrown science project just waiting for one of the children to develop an interest in genetics. (We're still waiting, by the way.)

I located a breeder, Renée, took the children to visit her new litter, and we were hooked. The puppies, of course, were impossibly cute, but what puppies aren't? Even Fritha had her moments. What captivated me were the three adult dogs sitting in a row outside the sliding glass door, heads cocked to one side, saying as plain as could be, "What's this? What's going on? Can I come and see? Can I? Please?" We chose a black, wavy-haired male, named Wings for the white mark on his chest, and I nervously produced our family profile to see if we were deemed worthy of owning such a noble beast.

Puppies need frequent human interaction if they are to grow into well-adjusted, sociable dogs. Fritha and her hermit-like, reclusive owner had more than amply borne out this truth to me. By contrast, these puppies were thoroughly domesticated. They had been handled lovingly many times a day since birth, and were well used to people, other dogs, and cats. Wings's emotional health seemed secure, and Renée wanted to be sure it would stay that way. Porties are extremely sociable dogs and do not take kindly to being left alone for any length of time. I assured her that, with six children being schooled at home, the likelihood of the puppy having any time at all to himself hovered somewhere around zero. We passed muster.

We had two weeks to prepare to bring the puppy home, two weeks to find a name that would be interesting and educational. How about something from mythology? At the time, I was reading the children the ancient *Epic of Gilgamesh*, and all were captivated by the character Enkidu. Half man, half beast, Enkidu is sent by the sun god to teach King Gilgamesh the meaning of love. *What a beautiful name for a dog,* I thought. The children had other ideas: they favored a name coined less than five thousand years ago, and came up with a barrage of more conventional suggestions—"I like Wings" and "What's wrong with Spot?" I was obstinate, and kept calling him Enkidu. I won out. Now every family member feels a personal connection with the earliest written story in the world.

Kidu was an unruly youngster, testing limits and trying my patience on a daily basis. Like wolves, dogs are pack animals; they need to know where they stand in the pack order if they are to be happy. Kidu had to learn that his place was at the bottom of the pack, below even four-year-old Evan. I picked up a couple of simple techniques which enabled every family member to assert their dominance: if Kidu showed aggressive tendencies such as growling, or worse yet, snapping, I would roll him on his back and have whoever he had threatened look into his eyes and scratch gently right where rib cage meets belly. Straightaway, his eyes half closed in blissful submission. If that failed, anyone with long enough legs would stand astride his shoulders, lift his front paws off the ground, and speaking in a very firm voice, admonish his nose. "You good dog, I'll give you an extra treat tonight!" worked just as well as "You bad dog, how dare you challenge Sheila's authority!" providing it was said in a sufficiently reproving tone of voice. Thus the family hierarchy was formed, with me at the top, everyone else in the middle, and Kidu at the bottom. Kidu knew his place, and was happy.

I took the business of training him very seriously for, as I had learned with Phoenix, training is equivalent to character formation. I asserted myself as alpha dog and he was not allowed to challenge my authority. While we all enjoyed playing tug-of-war with him, I never allowed him to win our battles: I had always to emerge victorious, holding the pull-toy. As he grew stronger and more determined, I discovered that blowing into his ear made him release his grip on the toy. How he hated it! Before long, he only had to see me reach for his ear and he would let go instantly.

This question of setting limits for dogs—and children—is one that interests me very much, because so many problems arise when limits and authority are unclear. Nine times out of ten, dog-training shows on TV feature owners who, wanting to be a friend to their dog, have abdicated their authority. In the process they confuse their pets, who find themselves rewarded for misbehavior and placed in a position of authority that represents a sudden and bewildering reversal of pack order. Small wonder they misbehave!

Limits are comforting to dogs and humans alike. I once heard about the headmaster of an Austrian school who, not wanting to inhibit the children's freedom in such a glorious mountain setting, tore down the fence around the school. Pupils were free to play as far afield as they chose, but greatly to his surprise, stayed very close to the security of the building. Only when the school installed a fence enclosing a fairly sizeable area were the children emboldened to make use of every inch of their playground: boundaries instilled confidence.

Just how disruptive it is for a dog to lose track of its alpha human was brought home for us later that year, when I took Fiona to British Columbia for a mother-daughter weekend on Keats Island, as a final celebration of her tenth birthday. Shortly after our arrival, Robin managed to track us down on the phone: "You've got to talk to Kidu," he said. "He's been tearing around every room in the house looking for you, and now he's running around the outside of the house, barking frantically. Tell him you're okay—tell him you're coming home the day after tomorrow." He held the receiver to Kidu's ear.

Feeling more than a little foolish in front of the other guests, I delivered the required message of reassurance in a happy, confident tone of voice. "It's okay, Kidu, I'm fine. I'll be home soon!"

Kidu looked at the telephone in astonishment: how could I possibly be hiding in something so small? Never mind, at least I was safe. He settled down to await my return.

The final educational area in which Kidu was to prove his mettle—or so I thought—concerned grooming. Porties have hair, not fur: they do not shed, as most dogs do, and thus are mostly non-allergenic. The disadvantage is that their hair, like ours, keeps growing and needs cutting every couple of months. While I realized that I would be the groomer, at least initially, I fully expected that each of the children would be eager to learn the gentle art of dog grooming, and that this lucrative talent would prove a life-saver when they went off to college.

It may come as no surprise to learn that I remained the sole groomer. The children, while periodically coerced into helping, were far from impressed by the grandeur of my vision and attained neither mastery nor even any real degree of competency. But I still think it was a good idea. It seems preferable to have a panoply of educational possibilities and let some of them fall by the wayside, than to have a more limited supply and use them all.

When Kidu was eleven years old, his heart gave out. Different vet, different flowerbed; same bagpipe chanter, same sorrow. Only this time, I read Gilgamesh's exquisite lament on the death of Enkidu, and we took comfort in the beauty of the lines that had been chiseled in cuneiform so very long ago. Five thousand years separated us from Gilgamesh, and the Enkidus we mourned were very different, but I still got goose bumps feeling that connection.

It was my last gift from Enkidu.

CATS

Once we had decided to tie ourselves down with a dog, Phoenix, it seemed natural to add a cat or two. A Siamese belonging to a nurse who worked with Robin had recently become a mother; the original plan that these kittens would be purebred had been foiled by an ardent suitor "from a good neighborhood." We chose a female who looked very much like her mother, even down to the kink in her tail that, legend has it, served to keep the royal ring in safety when the princess was bathing. Phoenix was enchanted by this fluffy new toy, and liked nothing better than to nestle the kitten protectively in her jowls, licking her in soggy bliss. We named her Pommie, Australian slang for an English person.

The ancient Egyptians used to worship cats as gods; cats have never forgotten this. Cats of my acquaintance had apparently taken this adage to heart; they were aloof creatures that sat on my lap when it suited them, allowing themselves to be stroked if, and only if, they felt like it. Nothing could have been further from my feline stereotype than Pommie. She rode on my shoulder, purring like an outboard motor. She came obediently to a finger snap, and even played fetch with the red and blue tops we brought her from the unfinished furniture store. I was thrilled! A cat that behaved like a dog—what could be better?

And then, one wintry morning, she hesitated at the kitchen door, unwilling to venture out. Perhaps she sensed some enemy—a coyote, possibly, or a hungry raccoon. Perhaps she was puzzled by the unaccustomed dusting of snow that softened the outlines of bush and tree and made the garden a strange, unfamiliar place. Giving her foot a dainty shake, she slipped out quietly to explore. We never saw her again.

We tried repeatedly to replace her. Tula and Snilders had the unfortunate habit of leaving their unmistakable autographs (perhaps that should be "coprographs," from the Greek *copro*, "excrement" and *graphein*, "to write"?) all over the basement, and were eventually relegated to an outside home. Substitute "the basement" for "the crypt" in my mother's favorite tongue twister, "The cat crept into the crypt, crapped, and crept out again," and you have in a microcosm the history of our feline family members. Why they chose to favor us in this way was never clear, but each one of them at some point disdained even the most pristine litter tray in favor of a dark, inviting corner of a closet.

A visit to the animal shelter yielded Choo Choo, a large ginger cat named by Iain in his train stage. Choo Choo, a one-man cat, adored Robin but terrorized Phoenix, who was easily ten times his size. The vast dog dared not walk past him as he lay, stretched laconically on the back of the sofa, one eye open a malevolent slit. Petrified, Phoenix eyed those claws, no doubt imagining the havoc they would wreak upon her nose if she ventured any closer. Choo Choo also scratched the children, which rather reduced his popularity with their mother. Robin felt a sense of masculine solidarity with him: Choo Choo was obviously misunderstood. If everyone were only nicer to him, he wouldn't have to scratch them—*quod erat demonstrandum*.

In an unguarded moment on a routine trip to the vet, I acquired Tom, George, and Muffin. Their owner had failed to pick them up after boarding them for a week, and they were to be euthanized that very afternoon. What choice did I have? I explained to them on the trip home that they would have to live on the balcony, but that this definitely beat the alternative. Not once did I pause to question their owner's motive in abandoning them. Not, that is, until later.

No problem with Tom, a slightly larger, more affable version of Choo Choo. George the tabby, however, was a different story. A female Jekyll and Hyde, she was ingratiating to the point of sycophancy as long as she was on the balcony. "I'm such a sweet, soft kitty," she would purr affectionately, "and it's so very cold out here…" But once in the house, she transformed into a creature with only one thing on her mind: "The cat crept into the corner, crouched, and…," well, you've probably guessed the rest. I'll swear she was motivated by pure vindictiveness.

As for the calico Muffin, she stole the other cats' food until she was too fat to jump off the balcony, then took to fertilizing my flower tubs directly. I retaliated by putting her out the front door after meals; she thus had to waddle all the way round to the back of the house and shimmy up the drainpipe before mugging her companions and helping herself to their dinner. Meanwhile Tom and George learned to attack their portions with gusto, and regained their lost weight. Muffin incorporated a leisurely pause to bask in the sun on one of her enforced trips round the house, and it was thus that a passing coyote found her. A tasty morsel, perhaps, but I hate to think what Muffin must have done to the coyote's waistline.

Word of a treasure trove of cat food on the Bernhofts' balcony, free for the taking, rapidly spread through the neighborhood. One evening, Phoenix's mighty barks alerted us to the presence of a raccoon family just outside our windows. Between splashing in the water dish and impromptu wrestling matches, the six little babies barely had time to eat—they paused only to grab another morsel of cat food between somersaults. Mother looked on with that "just five more minutes, dears, and then we really must be going" look, common to mothers at playgrounds everywhere.

The enchantment ended abruptly the morning I opened the breezeway door to find a belligerent raccoon hissing angrily at me from the top of a large bush. *No more Mr. Nice Guy,* he seemed to be saying, *I want my cat food, and I want it now!* That was the end of raccoon preschool at our house—but I missed it dreadfully.

Pobble, who had no toes, Attila, who had been misnamed Liebchen, Tom and Fat Alice, Kazu, Black Tom, all came and went. When we got Tissie, I really thought we had found another Pommie: she rode on my shoulder, came to a finger snap, followed me everywhere. Then she turned six months. Her personality changed overnight, and she completely ignored me for the next ten years. Then, gradually, she began to recognize my presence again, and has even been known to let me stroke her. But given her expanding waistline and her tendency to lie out in the sun in a formless puddle of succulent felinity, I fear a peckish coyote may soon mistake her for a jumbo hors d'oeuvre.

Good luck to his waistline!

5

Putting Their Best
Voice Forward

I *can't do that, but can I do something that looks a little bit like it?* Thus I mused, contemplating the theatrical productions that had played such a positive role in my childhood. I had loved it all: the costumes, the curtain, the camaraderie, as well as things that didn't begin with the letter *c*, like extemporizing in performances gone awry, and what one wag called "the smell of the crowd and the roar of the greasepaint." I wondered, *If we were to put on a little play in the basement this Christmas, do you suppose anyone would come?* I decided to find out, and thus Entropy Theatre was born.

Our first production was *A Christmas Mystery*, a nativity play in verse that I had found in a little-used volume at the library. Iain, at sixteen, was deep in the adolescent throes of learning to drive and had no time for such childish pursuits, while Andrew was aggressively disinterested in pretending to be anyone other than himself. So we looked to the Andrews family to boost our numbers. I had met Gale at the swimming pool when Sheila was a newborn, and our children, whose ages overlapped nicely, had become fast friends. Only Baby Melinda lacked a Bernhoft counterpart; unfazed, she cooed contentedly during rehearsals.

We heard about another homeschooling family, the Fundays (name changed for reasons that will soon become apparent), and recruited them, too. We found that they had idiosyncrasies all their own. Russell professed a desire to become a hit man for the CIA when he grew up, and practiced in the meantime by pelting his peers with pinecones at maximum velocity. By the third class, he had so terrorized the girls that they were scared to venture outside during break time. In a touching display of fraternal devotion, young Adam Funday eagerly followed in his big brother's footsteps. The family lasted only two plays, and no one was very sad when they dropped out. They did, however, provide considerable variety in our social landscape, and supply Russell for the unlikely role of Joseph. Let's just say there was little danger of him becoming typecast.

Now we had a cast—amateurish perhaps, but enthusiastic. Recruiting an audience was the next problem. There was only one performance, so parents and grandparents could be relied on to show up, and I augmented their numbers by talking to the neighbors on my daily walks with Kidu. My mother, as proud as a grandparent could be, spread the word among her friends, and promised tea and her finest Scottish shortbread as further incentive to attend.

The older children learned their parts easily and approached the stage with confidence. Not so Lorna and Evan. Lorna, who had refused to take part in the Saint Patrick's Day parade in Ireland because "somebody might LOOK at me!" was almost paralyzed with fright. She played the angel who opened the action. Shaking like an autumnal aspen in her glittering golden robes, she delivered the opening lines: "Now heed and harken gentlefolk, to you it shall appear/ How that the son of God was born all on a wintry year." She had not yet lost the English accent that all the children had at first; *appear* sounded like "appee-yah" and *year* like "yee-ah." Her part was eighteen lines long, and she exited the stage white as a sheet and gasping for breath. The audience loved it, gave her a sustained burst of applause, and the shy little girl transmogrified overnight into a veritable prima donna. We had an actress on our hands.

Not so five-year-old Evan, Shepherd #1, whose stage fright completely got the better of him. He hid himself in a remote corner of the basement, preferring the threat of unknown, potentially lethal spiders to the terrors of facing an audience. Fortunately Shepherd #2, Grant, knew Evan's part as well as his own and delivered all of the shepherds' lines as written, in first person plural. "See! We bring a ball for the king!" It might have struck the careful observer as strange that Grant was using the royal "we" when he was the only one on stage, but if the audience cared, they certainly didn't show it. Their response was warm and enthusiastic, and they eagerly insisted they would come to any further productions we might put on.

The routine was quickly established: two plays per year, one in December and one in late May or early June, combined with a short choir concert to total about an hour. I generally chose adaptations of the classics—stories that had stood the test of time and dealt with some of the great themes of literature: bravery, intrigue, deception, cowardice, downright evil and, above all, love. We wept at the desolation of Cyrano de Bergerac, we shrank with horror from the murder of Nancy in *Oliver Twist,* and we loved to hate Mme. Defarge in *A Tale of Two Cities.* The list of plays also included *Rip Van Winkle, The Scarlet Pimpernel, The Barber of Seville, Macbeth,* a couple of historical plays set in the Colonial era, and two Victorian-style melodramas that offered tremendous opportunity for overacting and generally having a riotous good time.

Most of the plays I discovered at the library, either in books or in magazines of newly written plays and adaptations of classics. I read through several contemporary plays that were supposedly "relevant to today's teens" and compared them with the classics. The difference was staggering. Plays made for teens seemed to trivialize the characters' emotions and experience, whereas the children responded powerfully to the greatness of Cyrano, the eerie menace of the three witches, or Sir Percy Blakeney's deceptive foppery.

There were exceptions: one time, I asked the students what they would like their next play to be about. "Pirates," said the boys. "Pirates and…detectives."

"Message received," I replied. "I'll do my best."

Imagine my glee when I found *Sabotage at the Savoy*, a gripping tale in which Sherlock Holmes and Watson investigate rum goings-on backstage at a performance of Gilbert and Sullivan's *Pirates of Penzance*. This was to be our most impressive production, with its imaginative sets and wide variety of characters and costumes, but in looking back on it four years later, eighteen-year-old Lorna asserted that the dialogue "lacked depth" and the plot was not "expertly conceived." Nobody ever said that about Dickens.

Our productions were fast outgrowing the limitations of our basement, whose two large rooms were connected by a wide entryway which served as the stage. An indoor wooden climbing frame provided the backdrop, and a large bed sheet draped across the middle of the inner room provided a rudimentary backstage area. It was perfectly adequate for A *Christmas Mystery*, but by the time we'd graduated to *The Scarlet Pimpernel*, with action occurring on both sides of the English Channel, we desperately needed something a little more expansive.

Nursing homes had been added to the list of performance venues, but I was always on the lookout for something a little more like a real theater. Then one day I found it. Since it was a public holiday, the Snohomish County division of the Washington State Music Teachers Association, of which I was a fully paid-up member, was unable to hold its monthly meeting at the public library. Instead, we teachers met at the Marysville Opera House, and as I entered the building my jaw literally dropped. Built by the Society of Oddfellows in 1907, the building had just been lovingly restored; its Wedgwood style ceiling and ornate plaster and paintwork took me back to English theaters I had known in my youth. But what riveted my attention was the stage…*complete with curtains!* My mind went into overdrive: *Do I dare ask? Surely it would be terribly expensive…certainly they wouldn't want to bother with such a small group as ours…* I screwed up my courage and spoke to the manager. She couldn't have been more helpful: the building was used mostly for weddings, but the dream behind the restoration project had been to see theater on the stage once more. Happily, and for a minimal cost, she accommodated us for four performances spread over three days. Combined with our traditional basement gig, this made for quite a respectable "run." The whole happy accident was like a fairy tale to me. How glad I was that I had summoned up the courage to ask!

My practice as director was to give the production a substantial push to start it in motion, watch as it gained momentum, then stand back and let the students take over. Our numbers had swelled to upwards of twenty, and to accommodate all this thespian talent I sometimes selected two plays—one for the older students, one for the younger. I added or deleted characters and scenes to make the plays fit our troupe, assigned the casting, directed the rehearsals, booked the Opera House, and coerced some hapless "volunteer" into designing and printing the programs. The most traumatic of these tasks was without a doubt the casting.

Once a student had cut her theatrical teeth on a small part, she was invariably ready for a big one. But why stop at any old part? Why not the leading role? My sense of fairness demanded that I should avoid nepotism by spreading the parts around evenly; my sense of justice said the big parts should go to those students who were reliable at learning lines and willingly volunteered the most hours; my sense of artistry dictated that the leading roles should go to the best actors. My job was made somewhat easier by the fact that the best actors tended to be the most enthusiastic, both about learning lines and helping out backstage. Lorna in particular could always be counted on to help me adapt the plays by writing in new parts (sometimes even whole scenes), and was quick to grasp the dramatic niceties of the whole. She spoke with the best vocal projection, and could be relied on to know every line of her own and everybody else's parts by week three. No need for a prompter when Lorna was around! Gladly, she agreed to take on the role of costumer. It galled us both that some cast members sat back while she did all the work, then grumbled when she was given the leading role.

The most tiresome problem I faced was those intelligent young people with more than adequate memories who thought it brilliantly funny to leave memorizing their lines till somewhere between the dress rehearsal and the first performance. This was especially galling as, apart from learning their roles, there was very little for them to do until the play hit the stage at the dress rehearsal. Here, even the most recalcitrant students came into their own, taking over more and more of the backstage grunt work until I was able to relinquish it all to their hands. Come performance day, I simply sat with the audience and enjoyed the play. I knew I was missing out on some of the best "disaster-narrowly-averted" backstage moments—a gun goes off at the wrong time, a nervous actor enters with entirely the wrong words, the saucepan lid/wooden spoon "clock" that has to chime the hour disappears, leaving an unpracticed volunteer to "bong" it vocally. But the confidence this autonomy gave the students made it all worthwhile.

As to sets, props, and costumes, I had read that the Royal Shakespeare Company frequently staged Shakespeare's plays with bare-bones sets and minimal costumes. *Aha!* I thought, *If it's good enough for the Royal Shakespeare Company, it's good enough for Entropy Theatre.* Our one-and-only backdrop consisted of a white sheet stretched over a framework that one of the dads made from plastic tubing found in the plumbing department. Ivy, an outstandingly artistic mother, could be counted on to transform this into a fireplace or a cave at a moment's notice. Our rehearsal schedule allowed for only one and a half hours per week, so time was at a premium. Wanting the actors to spend as much time on stage as possible, I encouraged them to mime rather than rely on props: we had already learned that by far the most efficient way to materialize a candlestick or a glass of wine onstage was to mime it.

Still, various cast members could be heard loudly lamenting our lack of visual hardware. As if on cue, enter three teenage boys. Nick Rudzis, Tim Evans, and the inimitable "Cow" Shea joined the cast, pronounced themselves adept with hammer, nails, and scrap lumber, and Entropy Theatre found itself staggering into the big time. The stage for A *Tale of Two Cities* was resplendent with a jail, which had the unfortunate habit of toppling over if anyone so much as looked at it the wrong way, and an only marginally sturdier sentry box. It was in *Sabotage at the Savoy*, however, that set fever reached its zenith: not only was Holmes's library resplendent in glorious Technicolor, but so was the stage at the Savoy Theatre, complete with a painted cardboard pirate ship, which didn't fall over even once.

It was the job of the wardrobe mistress to see that everyone had an appropriate costume. Only occasionally did we fall back on purchased costumes (for instance, Cyrano's nose); most of the time we relied on thrift stores, closets, and friends. Occasionally a mother would sew an authentic-looking costume for her child, raising the tone of the production considerably; but in general I was happy with something that more or less worked, something that was easy and fun to put together.

Being English, I was a stickler for pronunciation. In his goose-bump-inducing final speech, Sydney Carton's "better rest" definitely had two *t*'s in "better," and another one at the end of "rest." Americans tend to slur words together, and I repeatedly told my students to think of each word as a drop of rain on the windscreen of a car, distinct and whole unto itself. "Don't let the drops run together," I told them, "and beware the dreaded windscreen wiper." To teach them projection, I took them outside. We stood on the lawn while one person at a time recited their lines from behind a large piece of shrubbery. "Speak through the bush!" we exhorted one another. The phrase has become part of Entropy legend: to this day, "speak through the bush" is Entropese for "I can't hear you." I conjured up the figure of Maisie Witherspoon, eighty years old and somewhat deaf, sitting at the back of the balcony. "Can Maisie hear you?" The answer, all too often, was no. Maisie fared rather better when the actors used their head voice and resonated the sound in their nasal cavities, supporting the voice with deep breathing from the diaphragm. We had worked hard on breath control in singing, and the same principles naturally transferred to the spoken word.

Professional actors learn to project their voices sideways: they can talk to each other face to face on stage and still be heard. We lesser mortals have to look at the audience if they are to hear our lines. If Tim wants to give the impression of talking to Fiona, let them gaze at each other for a moment; Tim then turns to face the audience as he delivers his lines.

Everyone in the house will think he is addressing himself exclusively to Fiona, but every word is audible, even to Maisie Witherspoon. I drilled into the actors that audiences generally take a dim view of characters they can't hear; people don't much like to turn out on a cold, blustery winter's night (or any other sort of night, for that matter) and be forced to guess at what's happening onstage. Did we want inaudibility to be a hallmark of Entropy Theatre? Perish the thought! "Forget yourselves," I insisted, "project your character. Nobody's interested in you and your stage fright—they've come to enjoy the play. Let's give it to them!"

THE CURTAIN FALLS

The last performance at the Marysville Opera House before our move to California was a staggeringly emotional event. Such were the tears shed that I seriously considered putting up a sign: WARNING! FLOOR MAY BE WET. Sheila had had her appendix taken out on Saturday night, was discharged Sunday afternoon, sat through the dress rehearsal on Monday, and participated fully in performances Tuesday through Thursday. I was keenly aware that, without the miracle of surgery, she would be dead. Talk about thankful! I was also overwhelmed with gratitude for the four years of performances at that marvelous location. I never dreamed, when I scraped together the talent for our tiny production of A *Christmas Mystery* in the basement, that we would end up somewhere

as grand as the Marysville Opera House. Or that Lorna, barely able to eke out her opening speech in her first appearance,
would blossom into such an eager leading lady. Student after
student forgot their stage fright and grew in confidence as they
stepped outside themselves, going on to apply the skills they
learned to various activities in college and beyond.

CHOIR

Most new students' response to choir was lukewarm at best.
"It's okay, I'll just do drama," they hastened to assure me, and
were less than thrilled to learn that Friday afternoons came as
a package deal—if they wanted to act in a play, they had to be
willing to sing for the privilege. I think most of them came to
like it, though they might not have admitted it, and everyone
ended up being able to sing better than they could when they
started. Several of the students had no prior experience of singing, and one or two of them approached tone-deafness, being
unable to hit the same note as their neighbor even once, much
less carry a tune. But while I was frantically quizzing my col-
leagues in the Music Teachers Association, seeking ingenious
ways to help them, I found that the problem was somehow re-
solving itself: students were learning to sing simply by singing.

Relaxation and breathing are foundational to voice production, so every class began with stretching exercises to relax the
head, neck, and shoulders. Funnily enough, considering it's
such a universally popular pastime, breathing is almost never

done correctly; a typical breather uses only the top third of the lungs, and is unaware of the power lurking at the diaphragm. I had my students put their hands around their waist, fingertips touching just over the spine, and push their fingers apart as they breathed in deeply, through the mouth. This caused them to inflate the bottom part of their lungs as they lowered their diaphragm, giving them two lungs full of air for possibly the first time since their last temper tantrum. Now, supporting the air from the diaphragm, they hissed softly till all the air was gone. Suddenly, they had the basics of breath control. A few scales and arpeggios, and they were ready to sing.

Those who could not read music at all sat next to those who could. I regaled them with the legendary tale of Doris, who was reputed to have sung in my home parish choir for fifty years despite being unable to read a single note of music. She simply perfected the (gentle?) art of singing the same note as her neighbor, a fraction of a second later. Not even the conductor knew. She was stunned to learn, in her fifty-first year as a chorister, that notes written higher up on the page are sung higher in the vocal register. "Why did nobody *tell* me?" she wailed. In Entropy Choir, every student at least knew "up" and "down"; those who could already sight-sing improved, and those who couldn't soon learned to mimic their neighbors. One glaringly tone-deaf boy joined the choir; he eventually learned to sing by the natural method—peer pressure. "*Sol fa*, so good," one might say.

Books of songs are easy to come by, accompanists less so. Fortunately, I was able to accompany the choir on the piano myself, but I could also have bought a CD to use with a keyboard. I particularly liked the *Wee Sing* books and CDs. Folk songs have stood the test of time, being handed down from generation to generation simply because people enjoyed singing them so much, and those in *Wee Sing Fun 'n' Folk* are no exception. Many of the songs in *Wee Sing America* are work songs, sung by laborers working together to make their travails less arduous. It makes me realize how isolated most of today's workers are—whoever heard of a "Computer Programmers' Carol," or a "Ballad of a Bored Shelf Restocker?" It goes without saying that no one would want to recreate the abysmal conditions that produced the African-American spirituals or the songs of the Transcontinental Railroad, but it is worth noting that dreadful hardships have often caused humanity to dig deep into their souls, and find great beauty.

Eager to find an easy way for the students to sing in harmony, I explored the ancient realm of rounds. In a round, everybody learns the same melody, then sings it in parts, beginning at staggered intervals. Instant harmony! The oldest known round, "Sumer Is Y-cumen In," dates from thirteenth-century England, and judging by its complexity, must have been predated by many others which have been lost. (Generally, music was not written down until it had to be taken to a distant destination by someone who couldn't be relied upon to sing it when they got there.) Rounds, from the very simple to the highly complex, may be found in many songbooks; some of our favorites are in the *Waldorf* songbooks, which also contain a variety of appealing songs in one to three parts, listed in order of age suitability.

PPP

If Persuasive Poetical Pizza is the answer, what is the question? Try: how can I make my children want to learn poetry, recite Shakespeare, and give three-minute oral reports on any subject of their choosing, in front of an audience of their peers? Here's how it worked:

Once a month, students would stay late after class, which usually ended at 3:30. At four o'clock we would gather together for the program that someone (usually Lorna) had written out on a white board. There were typically between twelve and eighteen students with presentations to give, so by five o'clock we were more than ready for the arrival of the pizza delivery truck. Pizza and pop in hand, the children dispersed to various locations in and around the house for a time of food and socializing before their parents picked them up at half-past six. I explained to them that in this unsupervised time they were free to behave as they saw fit, but that this freedom would have to be curtailed in the event of any kind of trouble—and I was the one to define "trouble." They knew what I meant, and they fully rewarded my trust.

How I loved those Friday afternoons! They gave me a truly enjoyable way of getting to know my children's friends; I grew to love them, and they loved me right back. Hearing them say, "Your mom is so cool" was music to my ears—and it was so easy! All I had to do was let them know what was acceptable, and listen to what they had to say about the topics that interested them.

The content of PPP changed as the children grew older and was widely adapted to suit their ages and interests. The basic guidelines were as follows:

- Up to age ten—a poem by any author.
- Ages eleven and up—a passage of Shakespeare, at least as many lines as the child is old.

Sonnets were a perpetual favorite; at fourteen lines, their magic expired on birthday number fifteen, though not infrequently the teen responded by learning two sonnets. If students chose a speech from a play, they had to place the speech in context; this required reading the story of the play in a book such as Charles and Mary Lamb's *Beautiful Stories from Shakespeare*, and figuring out where in the action the speech occurs. Small wonder they preferred the sonnets!

One Friday, no fewer than three people had memorized Sonnet 71, which begins: "No longer mourn for me when I am dead/ Then you shall hear the surly sullen bell/ Give warning to the world that I am fled/ From this vile world, with vilest worms to dwell." Anxiously I searched for signs of listlessness or depression among the three, but to my relief all seemed well. It was just a coincidence—must have been a particularly rainy month. I encouraged the students to deliver their speech "in character." When Fiona gave Prospero's speech from *The Tempest*, beginning, "Ye elves of hills, brooks, standing lakes, and groves," she agreed (albeit reluctantly) to look as much like Gandalf as possible, complete with droopy hat and staff. She drew the line, however, at sounding like Ian McKellen.

Topics for the reports were gloriously wide-ranging, from the myths surrounding mistletoe to the history of toilets, from the yo-yo to Prohibition. We found that the more senses were involved, the more memorable the report. When her subject was chocolate, Fiona finished by offering pieces of baking chocolate to her classmates. Warning them that it was unsweetened, she said, "You can take as big a piece as you like, but if it goes into your mouth, it stays there." That was one report that was hard to forget—baking chocolate is horribly bitter! Another was Caitlin's spinning wheel, with the oily feel and distinctive smell of the recently shorn fleece she brought in. But what I remember most vividly is the succulent mealworm Kirsten offered as the culmination of her presentation, "Eating Bugs." Normally, I'm game to try anything once, but my gullet drew the line at that...

A three-minute limit was imposed after a few seemingly interminable, rambling orations on some vast and nebulous topic such as "The History of Filmmaking" or "Rock Music." Once imposed, the limit was self-evidently such a good thing that I wished I had thought of it before. The speakers appreciated the self-discipline it imposed, since they had to make a cogent argument in only three minutes; the audience liked it, because the pizza didn't have time to get cold.

Sometimes a younger child would ask for permission to give a report instead of memorizing a poem. By the age of ten, Evan had given reports on Light, Volcanoes, and Earthworms; each of these had consumed his interest, and his science studies, for some weeks. And sometimes a teen would ask for permission to memorize a longer, more challenging poem. Sheila learned "The Cremation of Sam McGee," by Robert Service, and has enjoyed tremendous mileage from it, riveting audiences of friends and acquaintances at late-night campfires. The line, "Then I took a hike, for I did not like/ To hear him sizzle so…" never fails to get a reaction!

Constructive criticism was encouraged, on the understanding that they would get as good as they gave. Some mistakes were almost universal, such as the tendency to begin a presentation: "So, umm, uhh, well, umm, uhh, right, so today I'm going to be talking about…" while shifting nervously from foot to foot and tugging distractedly at any handy article of clothing. "No *chevilles*," I'd say, "no redundant syllables. Think what you mean to say, look at your audience, and say it." The speaker should make eye contact with every member of the audience at least once, which meant that the audience needed to be paying attention and looking at the speaker. It was just as important to be a good listener as orator.

Various mothers told me how much their children had gained in confidence as a result of PPP, and in one case this was put to a rather unfortunate test. Louie, a ten-year-old friend of Evan's, was threatened by a vicious, unrestrained dog, and had to testify in court. He delivered his testimony in a clear, level voice that impressed everyone in attendance. Afterwards, his mother asked him if he had been nervous. "Not really," was his reply. "I just thought about Entropy, and it helped."

6

EDUCATING ANDREW

*I*t was May of the year that Robin, Baby Iain, and I spent in London, and we were visiting my mother in Bristol. Standing by the dresser in the bay window of my childhood bedroom, I watched with a sense of foreboding as the circle darkened in the bottom of the pregnancy test tube. I expected to feel joyful— Robin and I were eager to welcome a new child into our family—but couldn't shake the feeling that something was amiss. To calm my apprehension, I recalled what I had read innumerable times: a second pregnancy always feels different from the first, less exciting, less exuberant. I told myself that all was well.

Back in America, I was aware that this baby did not move as much as Iain had. "No worries," other mothers assured me, "you never notice the second baby moving as much, you're so busy with your firstborn."

At six months, I had an ultrasound. The baby looked rather small. "No worries," the doctor assured me, "you're probably a bit off with your dates." I went along with them, pretending all was well. But deep down, I knew something was terribly wrong.

Not trusting my intuition, I went ahead with the home birth we had planned as the only way to improve upon Iain's birth at an alternative birthing center in San Francisco. We summoned the midwives, Ira and Vicki, early one frozen February morning, one week before my due date. Labor was fast and intense. I did not see the baby come out.

The room fell silent. I asked if it was a boy or a girl; Ira said abruptly, "I can't tell, there's too much meconium."

Robin looked ashen. He told me later that he thought the baby was stillborn; what he could see looked a nasty purplish-green color.

"It's a boy," said Vicki. "We need to get him to the pediatrician."

Stunned, I climbed out of bed, showered, and dressed. The midwives were giving the baby oxygen, and his color was improving. We drove to the pediatrician's. She said, "I am very concerned that he may be a Down's." *What do you mean, he may be?* I wanted to shout. *Either he is or he isn't. He can't "may be."*

We drove to Everett General. The doctor there said, "I am very concerned he may have a heart defect. He needs to be transferred to Seattle Children's Hospital."

As they were readying him for the ambulance trip, we snatched a few minutes at home. I sat on the sofa, looking out of the window. There was Mount Baker, the snow-clad, dormant volcano that lay between us and Canada. Check. The waters of the Puget Sound, reflecting picture-book perfect, puffy white clouds in a luminous, pale blue sky. Check. Whidbey Island, which Iain insisted on calling "Wiggly Island." Check. *Would the new baby survive to call it anything?* The delicate outlines of snowdrops and early-flowering rhododendrons. Check. *Would I ever look at a rhododendron the same way again?* The scenery was unchanged from yesterday, but my life had taken a violent, earth-shattering detour. It was like being in a movie theater, and somebody had put in the wrong film; I wanted them to change it, now, while there was still time. It was like being on a train, and somebody had changed the points; we were going the wrong way, but could still see the tracks we had imagined we would be on—the normal baby tracks.

At Children's in Seattle, the worries mounted. They told us, "We are very concerned he may not live the night." We had him baptized.

Little Iain stomped around the waiting room, announcing, "I can't be good any more." (He'd been working on it now for over twelve hours.) With his English accent, it came out as an irresistible, "I cahn't be good any moah." Even in this numbingly grim situation, we found cause for a smile.

Later they said, "We have two words for you: normal heart." His earlier problems had been caused by a failure of the patent ductus to close—blood was still going to the umbilicus for oxygen, instead of the lungs. But this is a relatively common occurrence and did not account for his extreme distress. The doctors tried to offer some meaningful explanation but their words ran through my brain like water down an open drain. In my state of shock, I couldn't retain anything they said, and had to turn repeatedly to my husband for repetition and interpretation; his many years of medical training had equipped him to think clearly, even in the midst of personal catastrophe. We were relieved when the baby peed; evidently, his kidneys had survived undamaged. We were assured that the blood supply to his brain had probably never lacked oxygen, and thus his mental functioning had probably not been compromised.

But given that our baby's life was at stake, that "probably" was one too many. I was haunted by a nagging dread that our choice of a home birth had damaged him irreparably. *Would he have done better in the controlled oxygen environment of a hospital? Was that first hour of existence crucial to his well-being for the rest of his life?* I'll never know the answer to these questions: I have simply had to learn to live with them. I never attempted another home birth.

I tried to make sense of the statistics. My chances of having a Down's baby at thirty-two were, I was told, 1 in 850. The majority of Down's babies are born to mothers in their early to mid twenties, whose chances are 1 in 2,000 to 3,000. This apparent discrepancy arises because so many more women

give birth in their twenties than thirties. Doctors recommended amniocentesis for mothers age thirty-five or older because
at that age, the risk of conceiving a Down's baby is equal to the
risk of spontaneous abortion from the procedure. The numbers seemed to mean something, but I couldn't quite grasp
what. Eventually, understanding dawned: in statistics, the only
number that matters is the "one." Whether you're 1 in 2 or 1 in
2,000, if you're the one, it's 100 percent.

Andrew was six days old when he came home. During his time
in the ICU, he had forgotten how to suck. Combined with his
low muscle tone, that made nursing an ordeal in which I per-
severed only because I felt that this floppy rag doll of an infant
needed every health benefit I could give him. I resolutely refused to dwell on the contrast between this painful struggle to
get calories into him, and the exuberant ease with which Iain
had nursed.

SO WHAT IS NORMAL?

In the months following Andrew's birth, I must have read every book ever printed on the subject of raising a handicapped
baby. Desperately, I looked for signs in my newborn that he
would excel, that eighteen years later we would be applauding
tearfully as he graduated from high school. I read about the
benefits of early intervention therapy: if educated consistently
from a very young age, children like Andrew were performing

at 80 percent of normal by the time they were three. It sounded marvelous. *Eighty percent of normal, eh? Who's going to know the difference!*

We signed Andrew up at the Pediatric Diagnostic and Treatment Center near our home. They were pleased we had brought him in at such a young age, and were hopeful of excellent results. He was scheduled for therapy once a week. In each session, his therapists identified one age-appropriate activity he should be doing and wasn't, broke it down into tiny steps, and practiced each movement *ad nauseam*. When it was developmentally appropriate for him to roll from his back to his front, they first taught him to cross his right leg over his left and to raise his right hip. Once he could move to lie on his left side, they showed him how to complete the sequence of movements so he ended up on his front. Moving from front to back was easier: he stiffened, arched his back, dropped a shoulder, and flipped. It was so easy! But no, the therapists rebuked me, that wasn't right. He wasn't using the correct muscles. He must be taught to do it *properly*. We practiced again and again doing it the "right" way; Andrew was furious. *It's my body*, he tried to tell us. *I know what feels right to me.* But Kathy and Juliette were every bit as strong-willed as he, and eventually he gave in. *Just this once*, he seemed to say, *I'll do it your way. But don't expect me to make a habit of it.*

When Andrew was about eighteen months old, Kathy was greatly excited by the news that a family with a Down's syndrome son of the same age was moving to the area. This family had been living in the wilds of Northern California, with no access to early intervention therapy. Kathy was eager to see how much more advanced Andrew's gross and fine motor skills would be, compared to this baby whose only therapists had been a couple of totally untrained parents.

I, too, eagerly anticipated her assessment, but the weeks went by and none was forthcoming. Finally, I asked her outright. "Well," she said hesitantly, "I think Andrew is a bit better at rolling over, and he may be stronger at pulling himself up to stand."

Is that all? exploded in my mind. *Is that why I've been dragging my baby here for eighteen months, so he can possibly roll over a little more efficiently?* I was bitterly disappointed. The emotional toll of those months had been extreme; every week, just when it felt that I had come pretty close to accepting and loving my son unconditionally, came the dreaded Tuesday therapy session which rudely jolted me back to the reality of his limitations. Not that they didn't love Andrew and want the best for him—their affection was palpable—but their job as professionals was to turn the spotlight on his physical and cognitive shortcomings, and do everything they could to overcome them. Meanwhile, I struggled with an impossible dichotomy: the only way to find peace was by accepting Andrew's limitations, but as his primary caregiver, I had to spend half my waking hours doing battle with them.

I found out more about the meaning of "function at 80 percent of normal." Therapists identify ten things that a normal two-year-old can do—for instance, make a tower of three blocks—and train the developmentally disabled youngster to perform these tasks. When he can accomplish eight out of ten in a given period of time, he is said to be performing at 80 percent of normal. Unaccounted for is the missing, self-propelled desire to stack the blocks at all: left to himself, Andrew would simply hurl them around the room. In his eyes, that was what blocks were designed for. As his sense of self developed, he resented more and more the therapists' well-meaning efforts to change him for the better. (In later years, he added such gems as "there's no time for that now," "I'm busy right now," or even a cosmically despairing "there's no hope for it" to his arsenal of *bon mots* to get him out of any situation that threatened improvement.)

After the PDTC came the Little Red Schoolhouse, which he attended three mornings a week from the ages of two to three, then special ed preschool at the local elementary school. I was far less involved in his education at this point; it was a job for professionals. Lots of professionals. When the whole contingent—teacher, teacher's aide, speech therapist, occupational therapist, physical therapist, and a couple of assistants—was present, the ratio of pupils to teachers was one to one. It takes a village to raise a child; the more the merrier, right? Not necessarily.

THE JIGSAW PUZZLE

The reason I answer "not necessarily" has to do with jigsaws. When Iain was little and I had plenty of time to observe him, he loved to put together a four-piece puzzle featuring a tiger. He soon had the puzzle down pat and could put it together in a matter of seconds. I watched him fondly, basking in the re-flected glory of his genius.

But to my surprise and chagrin, he suddenly "forgot" how the puzzle worked. He put the first three pieces together effort-lessly, then regarded the fourth piece as if it had just flown in from outer space. A frown creased his brow. I could see him thinking, *What happens if I put it in this way…or if I turn it around and try it this way…or that way…*

The temptation to help him out was excruciating. I prac-tically had to sit on my hands and bite my lip to stop myself from reaching out and saying, "Here, you twit—it goes like *that*." But fortunately, I recognized that through trial and er-ror, a new, higher level of learning was taking place. He was figuring out for himself that a straight edge will never fit with a curvy inside edge, and that the picture will only match when the piece is a certain way up; who was I to get in the way of such a lesson?

In Andrew's classroom, puzzles were abundant; so too were attentive adults, ready to swoop down at a moment's notice saying, "Here—let me show you how it goes." This effectively prevented Andrew from learning in his own way, at his own speed, and gradually sapped his fragile initiative. Helpful adults abounded when it was the correct developmental time for him to learn to ride a bicycle, and strapped his feet to the pedals. He hated it, as anyone with any self-respect would, and steadfastly refused to cooperate. The only form of wheeled locomotion he ever deigned to use voluntarily was a variant of an early railroad car, which used a pumping arm movement to turn the wheels. In order to interest him in a bike, we had to remove those odious pedals altogether, and even then he regarded it with deep suspicion.

When at home, he stoutly resisted all attempts to educate him. He had his own goals mapped out, and if those consisted of sitting in the middle of the floor humming and throwing things into the farthest corners of the room, woe betide anyone who got in his way, whether literally or figuratively.

Every morning, the yellow school bus stopped at our gate to pick Andrew up. I learned to organize my day so that I had accomplished all outside trips before his return, shortly after noon. I found myself turning him into Public Enemy Number One: *I've got to get this finished before Andrew comes home.* The frantic early morning rush to get him ready for the bus was awful; early afternoons were little better, as we reintegrated him into the family and dealt with whatever unpleasantness had come up at school that day. However was I going to cope during the summer, when he would be home all day, every day?

His teachers wondered whether he would be eligible for summer services, available to students who were at risk of losing a significant amount of ground over the long vacation. Andrew did not qualify. Instead he spent the summer living alongside the family, obdurately refusing to join in anything that might in any way be construed as educational. I was mortified by my failure as a teacher, but in the battle of wills between me and my second-born son, there was no contest. He won by a mile: a mile made of solid granite.

I dreaded facing his teachers come September. I could not bear to be told how badly I had failed Andrew, how far he had regressed. I felt like a schoolgirl summoned before the headmistress. I gulped apprehensively. Then…surprise! I don't know who was more astonished, his teachers or me, but Andrew had not regressed at all. Quite the contrary, he had made significant gains—more than in any three-month period during the school year.

In other words, just sitting at home doing basically nothing, Andrew learned more than he did at school. He didn't have a television to watch, or computer games to fritter away his hours. As far as one-on-one educational interaction was concerned, forget it, but there was learning going on all around him as he sat in the eye of an educational hurricane. Whatever he had learned had been by osmosis. *Could it be that Entropy-style education works, even for Andrew?*

WE BRING ANDREW HOME

It was time to move Andrew from the sheltered walls of special ed preschool to the large, noisy world of regular kindergarten, with special ed assistance. But his teacher suggested we consider homeschooling him; she had noticed how uncomfortable he was in noisy situations, and thought he might do better in the peaceful atmosphere of home. *(Peaceful? Little did she know!)* We were delighted to oblige. I hoped that with time, he would regain his educational momentum, that he would rediscover the joys of personal initiative and start seeking out productive ways of filling his time.

When he was four, I had written an op-ed article about Andrew for our local paper, the *Everett Herald*. It described a happy, outgoing little chap with a zest for life and a great fondness for cracking jokes. However, Robin and I had noticed a falling-off in his enthusiasm, which we attributed to troubles at school: he seemed more introverted, even morose. Surely things would improve when he was safe at home with the rest of the family.

They say that life is what happens while you're waiting for something else. While Robin and I waited for Andrew's educational pendulum to swing back to the side marked "initiative," we instead noticed him becoming increasingly withdrawn. It was as if he were living in a fog; some days I couldn't reach him at all. Gone was the happy little boy who liked to laugh and come up with outlandish jokes; in his place was someone sober, even sullen, and silent.

Knowing that food allergies often lie at the root of behav-
ioral change, we looked to his diet for clues. In a desperate
bid to win the battle to get dinner for eight on the table each
night after a day spent homeschooling, I had instituted a weekly schedule. Friday nights were homemade pizza, Saturday
mornings, oatmeal buttermilk pancakes with cottage cheese
and applesauce. Both heavy on gluten and dairy products, the
two most common food allergens. Could this be the problem?

According to my reckoning, Andrew took in somewhere
approaching 80 percent of his week's calories on Friday night
and Saturday morning. If ever there was a boy who loved his
pizza, it was Andrew, and as for pancakes—bring 'em on!
To my dismay, I read that children often crave the very food
they're most allergic to. Robin discovered that for some people,
especially those with Down's syndrome, gluten and dairy products can have a narcotic effect. The reason Andrew was so out
of it was that his beloved pizza was quite literally making him
stoned. *Stoned! And right in my very own kitchen!* Overnight,
we removed wheat and dairy from his diet, and watched eagerly for results.

The dietary changes gradually restored his involvement in
life. He regained much of his sense of humor, and his expansive range of made-up words has enlarged the family vocabulary considerably. For reasons known only to Andrew, a video is
a "jigganut." I feel safe in asserting that we are the only family
on this planet that sits down together in the evening, not to
watch a DVD, but to "B-X a jigganut."

THEY'RE SO HAPPY, THEY'RE SO LOVING

Life was often frustrating for Andrew. He was blissfully happy whenever a new baby came along: he loved being a big brother, and would contentedly sit beside me as I fed his new sister or brother, "nursing" his realistic doll baby. "There you go, Baby," he'd say as he lifted up his T-shirt to suckle his doll on his diminutive nipple. But it became increasingly upsetting for him as each sibling overtook him developmentally, soon after their first birthday. He took it as a personal betrayal, and smart enough to know his Down's made him different, he did not like it, not one bit. "Down's kids are so happy," people told me, "they're so loving." I think they said it to make themselves feel better, not me. I think they hoped that by saying it, they could make it so. At any rate, I never heard it from the parent of an older Down's syndrome child.

Andrew's frustration and anger were never far below the surface, and sometimes found means of expression in antisocial behavior and bad language. The impact of his constant passion for rearranging the contents of the house was amplified by his zeal for throwing things down the laundry chute. This was not malicious, but compulsive: if any movable object was sitting around, minding its own business, Andrew was quite certain it should be relocated to the foot of the laundry chute. He lost no time in helping unite the object with its destiny.

ANDREW AND THE "WAVE"

Let any family member show particular interest in a specific book, and that volume disappeared. It might put in brief appearances before making its official return to the would-be reader, but looking for it in the interim was futile—it was like something out of *The Twilight Zone*. We learned to drop everything and seize a book on sight if "The Wave" brought it fleetingly to the surface; we also learned to swallow our frustration and instead marvel at Andrew's uncanny ability to drive his siblings crazy by losing their vital book-of-the-moment. Sometimes the volume would turn up under a bed, or in a bookcase with the spine turned to the wall, or at the foot of the laundry chute. Usually, elapsed time was measured in days, occasionally weeks. Once, it was considerably longer.

One April, I noticed that a library book had gone missing. No great surprise there, but as the weeks went by, and the Everett Public Library's almost inexhaustible patience began to run dry, I grew increasingly puzzled. I had checked every inch of the bookshelves at least three times, and investigated every potential hiding place I could think of, twice or more. The librarian grew restive; I paid for the book. Deciding that Andrew's room could use a change, I emptied his closet and bookshelves, removed all the furniture, and painted the entire room. No book. I reassembled his room. School began: we marked the passage of Labor Day, Halloween, and Veterans Day. No book.

And then one day, a week before Thanksgiving, I walked into Andrew's room and there, right in the middle of the floor, was the missing book! How was this possible? Where had it been for the past seven months? Tune in to the next thrilling installment of *The Twilight Zone* and find out.

For much of his childhood, Andrew perseverated with books, flipping obsessively through their pages, humming tunelessly. It seemed all he was interested in was the pictures and the satisfying feel of turning the pages. All that changed when, at the age of twelve, he caught the reading bug. Robin taught him using *Teach Your Child to Read In 100 Easy Lessons*, which he loved particularly for the silly stories. Decoding the words came easily to him and he read the pages fluently out loud. But it was, and remains to this day, impossible to test his comprehension—he thinks it's brilliantly inventive to answer a question with the wrong answer, and to set up a parallel, hysterically funny, universe peopled exclusively by ducks and Richard Simmons.

SOCIALIZING ANDREW

People wanted to be helpful. Hearing of my difficulties in raising Andrew, they hastened to assure me that their son, too, lost clothing, or strewed stuff around the house, or seemed incapable of telling clean from dirty. But what I needed was to have my problems heard, not minimized. I knew what it was like to raise a child who was not developmentally delayed, and now I was raising a son with Down's syndrome. The problems are altogether different.

My children's friends fell into two camps: those who made an effort to befriend Andrew and those who did not. The second group vastly outnumbered the first. Beyond a sneered "What's wrong with him?" few children asked any questions. I was always ready to talk, but nobody asked. I couldn't understand why parents didn't explain to their children that Andrew was different, and encourage them to include him in their play. If I hadn't been Andrew's mother, I like to think I would have sought out a mother with a disabled child and encouraged my children to get to know the disabled youngster, even if doing so presented challenges.

But time and again, I drove my other children to birthday parties and brought Andrew home alone. Only my close women friends were different; they greeted Andrew affectionately, asked him about his life and tried to make sense of his replies, and included him in their children's celebrations. To them I am eternally grateful.

It was all the more galling for me that Andrew's feelings were so often ignored when I saw how considerate he was of other people's welfare. He was always highly solicitous of his granny, helping her into and out of a chair and holding her arm as she walked (she was gracious enough not to let on that being held like that actually made walking more difficult for her), but it was on the sports field that he came into his own. Whenever there was an injury during one of our backyard games, trainer Andrew would be on the scene, crouching anxiously over the victim to take a pulse, or tenderly stroking the injured limb.

When he was seventeen, Andrew began attending the GOAL program at Everett High School. Gaining Ownership of Adult Life was designed to help developmentally delayed teens practice necessary life skills, from writing their name to riding the bus, from counting out money to navigating the streets safely. He graduated from this program when he was twenty-one; as we sat in the auditorium I recalled his infancy, and how I had dreamed of this day. We were three years late and he could not reliably write his own name, but still Robin and I wept as Andrew received his diploma. Mostly our tears were shed from pride, but we were more than a little fearful for the future. How would society treat him, one of the most vulnerable of its citizens? Untrammeled by worries beyond the here and now, Andrew simply reveled in all the attention. His face a mask of pure joy, he beamed as he stroked the golden sash on his chest, played with his tassel, and acknowledged his cheering fans. It was the greatest day of his life.

Today he spends his mornings with other developmentally delayed adults at the Ojai Enrichment Center. He used to devote his afternoons to long, solitary walks, returning home when he felt like it—after all, he was the Washington State Special Olympics Speed Walking Champion, with a medal to prove it. We had to rein him in a bit when Ojai sprouted some nascent gang activity and he fell in with a rather unsavory crowd (his social innocence is virtually unbounded.) Now his afternoons consist of personal hygiene, laundry, and bus trips to Ventura with his companion, Joanna—altogether a safer way of life, even if his waistline is losing some of its elegant trimness.

ANDREW LUMINOUS

All his life, Andrew has had a sixth sense about people, and his intuition has been unerringly accurate. He sees right through those who feign fondness for him, but a friend once made is a friend for life. Age is of no concern to him, and his heart is just as open to the homeless as it is to friends he has made at the library. He brings out the best in people, and anyone he meets emerges a better person for having known him, his family most of all.

One summer when we were at our family camp in Canada, a mother who had been observing our interactions said she had noticed how relaxed and loving we all were with each other. (I was feeling anything but relaxed and loving at the time, since Andrew was seizing any and every opportunity to disappear into the woods, so her comment really made me think.) She wondered if Andrew had a lot to do with it. "The other children see how you love and accept him even with all his limitations, and they feel secure that they'll never have to measure up to objective standards to earn your love. They know you'll always accept them, just the way you have him."

What a beautiful thing to say. What a perfect example of how Andrew, disabilities and all, sheds new light on the everyday. Over and over again, he reminds me what it is to be truly human.

7

ENRICHMENT: SOLITUDE, BOREDOM, HOUSECLEANING, & HUMOR

SOLITUDE

*W*hat is a section about solitude doing in the chapter headed "enrichment"? Solitude means being alone, and being alone means being lonely. And loneliness is the last thing we want to feel, is it not?

Not according to the Romantic poet William Wordsworth, who wrote in his poem "Daffodils" of his "inward eye / Which is the bliss of solitude." That phrase, "the bliss of solitude," strikes a strange note today. For Wordsworth and his peers, being alone was an enviable state, affording valuable time for introspection: he got to know the depths of his soul by spending time alone there. Not for him the fear of today's teen who, finding herself away from her computer and with a cell phone whose battery has just died, faces a moment of panic. How is she going to fill the next twenty-three minutes with only herself for company? The Romantics' bliss of solitude has today become a curse of solitude, to be avoided at all costs. University professors tell of students who cannot bear to be away from their friends for long enough to write a paper; even "studying" has become a group sport.

To me it was self-evident that young people are free to enjoy being with their friends only to the extent that they are also happy to be alone. If they fear solitude, they will be compelled to seek constant company—even with people they don't really like, doing things they know are, at best, a waste of time. Not for them the freedom of spending an afternoon lost in a good book, or lying on their back watching the changing shapes of summer clouds, or standing at the ocean's edge feeling the ebbing waves suck the sand from beneath their toes—listening only to the music of the waves and the mewing of seagulls. Not for them a quiet half-hour's introspection. I wanted my children to be familiar with the riches of solitude.

But aren't children who spend a lot of time by themselves the ones schools are trained to look out for—the geeks, the misfits, the budding mass-murderers? Isn't sociability a major index of mental health? Maybe so, but I look at my children and see young people who are gregarious and popular, who have flourishing friendships both on Facebook and in the flesh—in short, who have an enviable social life. And they are content to be alone.

They have experienced the bliss of solitude, and they like it.

BOREDOM: A SHORT HISTORY THEREOF

According to Peter Kreeft in *The Three Philosophies of Life*, there is no word in any ancient language for boredom. If there is no word for it, we can say with some certainty that boredom was not a problem to the ancients. Nor did the concept exist in America as long as labor was either creative—silversmithing, for instance, or coopering—or productive, like farming. (As for the common notion that farming is unskilled work, just ask anyone who has tried to grow and harvest any crop, and learn how "unskilled" farmers really are.) People who work hard to support themselves and their families are, by and large, happy. They know what needs doing and they know why they're doing it. Troubles arose when the Industrial Revolution of the early nineteenth century ushered in the soul-destroying tedium of noisy, repetitive, meaningless, production-line jobs. Workers were forced to move away from extended family and the land they'd grown up on, and take up residence in squalid slums hastily erected by unscrupulous factory owners. There, they found respite from the horrors of daily life in the bottle: for many, drinking was the only escape.

The stage was set for Charles Dickens—and the first recorded use of the word "boredom" in his *Bleak House*, 1852. Prior to this, the French aristocracy had come closest to the concept with *ennui*, which Merriam-Webster defines as "having too much time on one's hands and too little will to find something productive to do."

Meanwhile, factory owners and the burgeoning middle classes sought a less self-destructive form of escape. Finding themselves with time on their hands, plenty of money, and a wide choice of things to buy, they imagined they had discovered the recipe for happiness. Far from it. The equation: *time + money + shopping choices = happiness* may be the stuff of modern consumerism, but it didn't work any better in the 1800s than it does today. It left people feeling empty, unfulfilled. They needed something more…a way to fill those empty hours…that made no demands…they needed to be… entertained! Edison invented the phonograph in 1877, and it was rapidly followed by the radio, movies, and television. The entertainment industry had been born.

But go back to 1840 with talk of an entertainment industry, and you would have met with blank stares. Time off work was a pleasure, a time for passive receptivity to the world. Why would anyone want to fill it with things to do? There was even a word for it: idleness.

Kenneth Grahame brilliantly depicts idleness in *The Wind in the Willows*: Ratty spends his days "simply messing about in boats." Not doing anything particularly practical, it goes without saying, merely whiling the days away, with nothing in particular to do, and all the time in the world to do it in…until Mole bursts into his placid riverbank world, that is, and they have a grand adventure (the stuff of many a future story by a winter fireside) before returning to their solitary existences.

When I read this book out loud on the way to a skiing trip at Whistler, British Columbia, I paused to ask the children their thoughts on idleness and boredom. "I don't get bored," declared Sheila. "If I'm bored, I know there's something fundamentally wrong with my life." Truer word was never spoken— but she was not always so self-motivated.

Even Sheila at one point needed help coming up with ideas: she remembers being told to go outside and play, do a puzzle, read a book, or build something with Lego. Funnily enough, she does not recall my favorite rejoinder: "If you're bored, I've got a living-room floor that needs vacuuming." Periodically, I'd deliver an ultimatum to them all: "You've got excellent brains and a house full of things to do. If you can't find anything interesting to fill your time, let me pick something for you." That jogged their sense of initiative in a hurry—*anything* was better than some improving activity of maternal origin.

Boredom can be an excellent thing, if children recognize it as an opportunity to draw on their inner resources and find something meaningful to do, whether it be reading a book or indulging in a 3-D, Technicolor daydream. C.S. Lewis was bored for much of his childhood in Ireland; isolated from his friends by the ravages of influenza, and with just his older brother Warnie for company, there was little for him to do but dream up stories of an imaginary country peopled by ogres, witches, and talking animals. It's a sobering thought that, had Lewis lived in the age of television, we would probably not have *The Chronicles of Narnia*.

The key to avoiding boredom—having the will to find something productive to do—is the first victim of the entertainment mentality. I myself almost fell victim to the siren song of passive entertainment; it happened in England.

THE BBC: BRITISH BRAINROTTING CORPORATION?

When we moved to London for a year in 1983, Iain was eight months old, and I was looking forward to renting a TV and enjoying the British programming I fondly remembered from my youth. (In retrospect, it makes my toenails curl to consider the great swathes of my childhood that were wasted glued to The Box.) Inertia had its way, however, as it so frequently does; days, then weeks, ticked gently by with no sign of a telly materializing in our living room.

Robin and I evaluated our lifestyle: where would we find an hour or two a day to watch television? What were we willing to give up? Iain and I spent our days mostly on domestic matters—walking to the shops to buy that night's dinner, shoving the diminutive washing machine across the kitchen to the sink, where it discharged its load of dirty diaper water into the same sink we washed our dishes in. (I blench to recall this, but somehow our immune systems survived.) Every day I pegged the clean diapers out to "dry" in rain, wind, and snow. Whatever the weather, we fled the confines of our dark, dismal, and dingy flat to further our acquaintance with the neighborhood cats. Then there was the daily thrill of Daddy coming home and Iain "helping" him park the car in the garage, or dropping the car keys down a muddy grate full of slimy, stinking leaves (he only tried that once). More walks, this time to the "Bunny Park" with its avenue of stately horse chestnut trees, and tiny marmosets in an equally diminutive zoo. Home for dinner, and an evening of talking, reading, and playing together. All in all, there was no time for the telly, and nothing we wanted to give up to make time.

So it was not until we returned to America and took up residence in Everett that television first loomed on Iain's horizon: Robin installed a small set in the kitchen to watch football. (As it turned out, Iain had other ideas for Daddy's Sunday afternoons.) Meanwhile, I had heard about the wonders of *Sesame Street* and was eager to give it a whirl.

Iain's reaction, at nineteen months, was puzzlement; for him, entertainment meant being read to. Accustomed to following lengthy and quite complex story lines, he was bewildered by *Sesame Street*'s short, constantly changing segments. "Is this still *Sesame Street*?" he asked plaintively. "When will it be over?" Educational genius that he was, he had put his pediatric finger on the biggest problem with the format: by catering to children's short attention spans instead of challenging and stretching them, it effectively shortened them even further. It is a truism among educators that avid television watchers have trouble focusing on a story read out loud, or a radio drama, no matter how expertly tailored to the child's interests it may be.

Sesame Street was introduced in the sixties to familiarize preschoolers with letters and numbers in preparation for learning to read; since then, reading scores have declined steadily and drastically. Apparently, Baby Iain knew what was good for him.

THINGS TO DO

Here is a largely random list of things we liked to do instead of watching TV. It is by no means exhaustive, though some of the activities are pretty exhausting.

On hot days we would run through the sprinklers, either in swimsuits or fully clad, then air dry. We filled two-liter soda bottles with water and vied to see who could empty theirs fastest. Was it quicker to shake the bottle, swirl it, or simply hold it upside down? This frequently degenerated into a contest to see who could get their siblings wettest—no bad thing on a sultry August afternoon. We poked three holes in a soda bottle, one near the neck, one in the middle, and the third near the bottom, filled it with water, and observed how the weight of the water pressing down (aka "water pressure") caused the water from the bottom hole to squirt the farthest.

Another fine-weather activity was blowing bubbles. I made a bucketful of liquid by adding half a cup of Dawn or Joy dish soap (for some reason the brand matters) to a gallon of water. Adding glycerine, which the how-to books suggested would make bubbles stronger, only made ours more brittle. Anything was fair game as a bubble-blower, from strawberry baskets, which made a great frothing mass of tiny bubbles, to the huge bubbles of a bent clothes hanger. *Would a square blower produce cubic bubbles? Would an octagon create octagonal bubbles? How about a triangle, or a really flat oblong? What shape would they make?* I allowed the children to experiment for a long time—maybe a couple of years—before dropping the educational bombshell that a sphere is nature's most economical way of enclosing a given amount of air, and that a bubble will always find that most economical way. While they were contemplating their bubble creations, I raised the question, *Why, if bubble liquid is heavier than air, do bubbles go up?*

On cooler days we loved to read around the fire, play board games, do jigsaw puzzles, or build with construction toys. We baked bread and cookies, made gallons of applesauce from our orchard, and scoured the neighborhood for wild blackberries to make jam. When Andrew was in special ed kindergarten, his teacher suggested we fill a tub with those classic tactile delights, rice and cornmeal, to provide a more stimulating variant on the sandbox. Fondly imagining the hours of learning pleasure that would ensue, I added measuring cups, a sieve and colander. Think again! His greatest joy was to take cups of rice and cornmeal and hurl them into the farthest corners of the room. Not wanting to encourage a unit study on mice, I filled the tub with water instead and put it outside the front door along with the measuring cups. There it sprouted tiny creatures, which jack-knifed around just below the surface, looking distinctly menacing. It was not too much later that I figured out they were mosquito larvae. Not wishing to undertake a unit study on mosquitoes either, I hastily drained the tub and left the little darlings to die in the sun.

My favorite activity by far was walking. Twice a day, rain or shine, Kidu got his thirty-minute training walk, and I loved it when a child or two could be prevailed upon to come along. A baby snoozed contentedly in a front-pack, soothed by the rocking motion, then graduated to a stroller or backpack (the feeling of those little knees digging into my shoulder blades is one of the best things in the world). Later, a bicycle or scooter became the children's preferred means of locomotion. Later yet, the mature child might slow down to a mother's pace, and we could walk and talk together. We got to know the neighbors and their livestock, we knew in what order the trees blossomed in spring, when to expect the first crocus, who had the best show of dahlias, where to find the best fall color. Surely, there is no better way to get to know a neighborhood than to walk in it regularly.

Though we found so much to do at home, I still felt guilty that the children weren't involved in more organized activities. When I was expecting Sheila, Iain was nine.

Haunted by my looming immobility once the baby was born,
I filled Iain's schedule with extracurriculars—Boy Scouts,
swim team, music lessons. My days were absolutely packed,
between bundling the three younger children into the car
to drive him to and from practices, taking them all to the
library or on shopping trips. The "Am I being a good mother?" gremlin sat in stunned silence on my shoulder, filled
to satiety. *Of course I'm being a good mother, just look at the
evidence: I'm in the car half the day, I don't have time to cook
dinner, and what is more, I don't have a single moment I can
call my own. I deserve a medal!*

But I had a sneaking suspicion that something was out of
balance, that this wasn't really the best way to live, for me or
my children. When Sheila made her grand entry and all activities came to a screeching halt, I was vindicated: everyone
seemed better able to enjoy life—even Iain, who admitted
that he had felt rather harried under our frenetic schedule.
Now there was time to take in the small details that make
life so interesting, time to play games and talk to each other,
time to cook dinner again. The gremlin started up his old
line, "Do you really call yourself a good mother?" And I had
the confidence to reply with a resounding, "Yes!"

HOUSECLEANING

I tried to break it to them gently: at some point in their lives
the children would have to clean their own living space,

whether it was a room, an apartment, or (in their dreams) a mansion. Dirt management might not be the most enthralling way of spending an afternoon, but one thing is certain: it's a whole lot more fun if you know how to do it right. For many years, Thursday afternoons were spent in the raucous and frequently argumentative pursuit of domestic cleanliness. Rewards were several: a somewhat cleaner house, the confidence that comes from knowing how to clean, an awareness for the rest of the week that the hardest part of cleaning is tidying up all the rubble before you can even start, and best of all, the weekly reward of dinner out. We patronized local ethnic restaurants which in themselves were educational—Mexican, Thai, Indian, Vietnamese, and Chinese. The whole family is now adept with chopsticks, and all are aware that the curries of southern India are hotter than those of the north, for the intriguing reason that, being closer to the equator, food in the south spoils more quickly; curries must be more pungent to cover up that succulent, gone-off flavor.

How well I remember one particular Thursday when Iain was twelve and I was visibly pregnant with Evan. Mexican food won the popular vote that day. As was my custom, I bridged the difficult gap between ordering and the food's arrival by reading aloud—I believe it was *Tuck Everlasting,* by Natalie Babbitt. The mealtime itself was to us perfectly ordinary, but it made a big impression on someone: when the time came for the bill, we were informed that the solitary diner who had just exited had paid it in full. We were stunned, deeply touched, and greatly encouraged by this vote of confidence from a total stranger.

This incident was an unexpected gift, a memory to be treasured and savored. It helped me persevere through the weekly grind of instilling some degree of order and sanitation to the house. True, we could have paid somebody to come in and clean (and we sometimes did) but I liked to encourage the financial principle of keeping our money within the family wherever possible—an idea that makes even more sense in today's economy.

The children were all masters of prevarication; requests to empty the dishwasher or wipe down the counters were routinely put off with "I'll do it in a minute." With greater maturity came more sophisticated delaying techniques: Evan once gave a big smile and a cheery "Right-ho" when asked to take the laundry out of the dryer. Only later did I find that he had dumped the clothes straight onto the floor ("You never said, *and put them away…*") and that one of the cats had evidently mistaken the pile for a novel variation on a litter tray. (Could *Amelia Bedelia* possibly have been inspired by a teenage boy?) I ordained the only acceptable response to a request: "I'd be happy to." It could be said cheerfully, with a smile; it could be said dolefully, with a sigh; it could be groaned, or muttered, or shouted, provided it was said. And acted upon.

I discovered "The Clean Team," a California-based company run entirely by men, that takes an almost frighteningly methodical approach to house cleaning: their DVDs demonstrate how to move through the house with military precision, cleaning each room from left to right. Sort of like an orderly swarm of dirt-eating locusts. To encourage a sense of professionalism, I invested in Clean Team aprons all round as well as their organic cleaning products. Now the children knew what to do, when to do it, and had the requisite tools. I won't say that the war was won, exactly, but at least the battle lines were drawn. Today, the girls tell me with incredulity about roommates who "literally don't know how to vacuum a floor." I'm glad I made housecleaning part of the curriculum at Entropy Academy.

HUMOR

England. The morning sun was just beginning to melt the ice drawings I had made on the inside of my windows the night before, when I was awakened from a deep sleep by a dream. In it, I was drawing a cartoon of a man on a windswept beach, giving a box to a girl. From the box erupted an angry-looking bird. The caption read, "He gave her a nasty tern." I was ten years old. It was my first pun.

They say the pun is the lowest form of wit; I retort that at least it *is* a form of wit and thus spices up the pablum of everyday speech. To my mind, anything that helps us get through the day with a bit of a laugh, or even a groan, can't be altogether bad. The house was always overflowing with books of puns, word play, and jokes, from knock-knock jokes to oxymorons.

This latter category includes phrases that seem to be contradictory but on second glance reveal a deeper truth: Mark Twain famously observed that "it takes a heap of sense to write good nonsense," and he claimed that his long-suffering mother "had a great deal of trouble with me, but I think she enjoyed it." (Sounds like my kind of woman!) Who can resist the wisdom of Robert Zend: "People have one thing in common: they are all different," or the self-deprecating wit of Robert C. Benchley's, "Drawing on my fine command of language, I said nothing." And Sir George Savile perfectly sums up my feelings about education when he says, "Education is what remains when we have forgotten all we have been taught." All these examples come from *Oxymoronica* by Dr. Mardy Grothe, which is currently my favorite book in the world; over two hundred pages of gems.

Some of the funniest people I know are also the smartest, and often those who deal with adversity best are those who can find something to laugh about in their distress. The British sense of humor frequently bamboozled their German attackers in World War Two. A cartoon from the 1940s shows two English soldiers standing in a house next to an enormous hole in the wall.

"W-w-what made that hole?" stammers one soldier.

"Mice," says the other.

The cartoon was circulated to the German troops with an explanatory note: "This is an example of the so-called English sense of humor," the German caption informs. "The hole was not, in fact, made by mice but by an explosive ordinance device."

The British ridiculed the literal-mindedness of their antagonists, cracking jokes and singing as they waited out the long nights of the Blitz bombing raids over London, huddled for safety in the London Underground stations. Class distinctions disappeared.

In one story, a submarine is sunk and a lowly private bobs to the surface, finding himself alongside Admiral Mountbatten, Right Honorable Earl of Burma, Viceroy of India and second cousin once removed to Queen Elizabeth II.

The Cockney sailor cheerfully observes, "Scum always rises to the top, dunnit, sir?"

Lord Mountbatten's reply was not recorded, but he seems to have taken the comment in good part; later he observed, "Sailors, with their built-in sense of order and discipline, should really be running the world."

Who will argue with that?

Evan showed early signs of a precocious sense of humor. Sitting on his potty not long after he was toilet trained, he was asked by Fiona what he was doing. He looked enormously pleased with himself. "Making snowflakes," he said. Fiona howled with laughter—his output at that moment was about as far from snowflakes as it is possible to get. I fear her reaction encouraged him; it was not too many days later that his sense of humor struck again. He and I were in the orchard, ruminating on the glories of our steaming compost heap. It was a cool, crisp morning in early spring, and I found the signs of warmth emanating from the piles of rotting vegetable matter deeply satisfying. Evan's cheery voice roused me from my reverie: "Close your eyes and open wide, and something nice will pop inside."

Wondering dimly what edible substance could be found in an orchard in springtime, I trustingly "opened wide" as instructed. Into my mouth popped—a snail shell! Evan was laughing so hard he almost fell over, and once recovered from my shock, I joined him. Fortunately, the shell was unoccupied: not being French, my salivary glands would definitely not have been titillated to find the occupant *chez lui*.

For his fifteenth birthday I gave Evan a copy of Stephen Colbert's *I Am America (And So Can You!)*, inscribing it in the spirit of Dr. Grothe: "Because being funny is a serious business." Colbert's take on reality is irreverent, idiosyncratic, and very perceptive, and I hope some of it rubs off on Evan. I don't wish him to encounter great difficulties in his life, but if he does, he'll have a first-rate coping mechanism: a healthy sense of humor.

8

My Educational Philosophy:
Konos, Reading & Math

*C*onsiderably less grandiose than it sounds, my "educational philosophy" was born of desperation. I had to find some way to silence the infernal gremlin that spent its days crouched on my shoulder, informing me what a lousy excuse for a homeschooling mother I was. Gremlin fodder was in abundant supply — whole days were governed by "the tyranny of the dirty diaper"; in a contest between the most interesting academic argument and the baby's least interesting output, the diaper always won.

Had there been the option of an online K–12 education designed and administered by professionals, I would probably have jumped at it. Lucky for me there wasn't. I would most likely soon have given up, frustrated by the lack of creativity, by the time-consuming tedium of merely making sure that each child followed the day's appropriate online lesson. Homeschooling entropy-style presented the constant creative challenge of finding the best way to meet each child's educational needs. Herculean on a good day, Sisyphean on a bad, the task seemed not infrequently insuperable; but without it we would have missed out on the single most formative and enjoyable aspect of our family life.

Compounding my feelings of inadequacy was the problem of homeschooling magazines. These abounded with stories of families that sounded a lot like ours, except that they had more children, baked all their own bread, made their own clothes, accomplished a bewildering array of extracurricular activities, and volunteered thirty hours a week helping the homeless (I exaggerate only a little). It was a happy day for me when I realized my error: I had been assuming that these families were doing everything we did, *plus* all the things they wrote about. Hesitantly, I began to entertain the notion that if I too wrote down all the things our family accomplished, the gleaming magazine families might in their turn be impressed. True or not, it was a comforting thought to hold on to.

When asked "How do you do it all?" I was quick to admit that I really didn't know. Homeschooling is anything but easy: knowledge must be imparted in a somewhat orderly fashion, while at the same time, dinner must be cooked, arguments adjudicated, exercise enforced, and a safe passageway cleared across the living-room floor. Oh yes, and don't forget the laundry. When baby number five, Sheila, was born, I found myself with a nine-year-old and, thanks to Andrew's developmental delay, four children under the age of five. Nothing can describe the bedlam. I gamely made up a week's lesson plan for Iain, sticking it on the fridge with cheery magnets and high hopes; a month later I took down the now-obsolete schedule, stricken with pangs of guilt. What more proof did I need? I was a failure!

And then, something rather wonderful happened: recognizing that if he left it to me he'd continue to live in a state of abject ignorance, Iain took his education into his own hands. He would come to ask me what he should do next, take one look at a scene which could well have been propaganda for the Zero Population Growth movement, shake his head knowingly, and go figure it out for himself. Fortunately, I'd had the foresight to make sure that the relevant books were readily available; he alternated long hours, nose in a book, with equally long hours thinking deep thoughts about baseball while rearranging his pop can collection. I've often wondered why I was so lucky. Part of the reason is that there simply wasn't much else for him to do—no TV, no video games—and part that he saw his parents spend what little free time they had reading, and discussing what they read.

To preserve my dwindling reserves of sanity, I came up with a list of Basic Educational Requirements (BER). And when I say "basic," I really mean it. My bare bones list answered the question, *What must a child have learned by the age of ten if he is to be on a pace with his school-educated peers?* It was a shockingly short list, consisting of being able to read, write (by which I mean formulate words on paper, not be a budding novelist), and understand the four math functions: addition, subtraction, multiplication, and division. Middle school may be viewed as a time for consolidation of basic skills; if a child enters high school with only my BER under his belt, he will be adequately prepared to tackle ninth-grade curriculum. I gathered from public school educators that a distressingly high percentage of students who go through conventional kindergarten through eighth grade do not measure up. Not only that, they have all too often had their love of learning squelched.

This is no mean feat. A baby is born inquisitive and primed to learn; she does not have to be taught to walk or talk. A young child is thrilled to recognize letters on a cereal box or count to ten. How is it that so many schools kill that innate enthusiasm, and how could I maintain the exhilaration of learning? Only one thing was certain, I had to cover the three R's, the meat and potatoes of education. This could, for the most part, be accomplished using a variety of entropy-style methods, which I outline in the relevant chapters of this book. Then came the fun stuff—gravy, or for vegetarians, chocolate sauce. The gravy could be tremendously exciting, interesting, mind-expanding, even life-altering; but if we didn't quite get to it, the earth would still orbit the sun, and night follow day.

I frequently pondered Yeats's dictum that education is not the filling of a bucket but the lighting of a fire. There is a trick to lighting a fire, as any Boy Scout knows: put on too much tinder, and the flames are smothered; put on too little, and the fire will not catch. The same thing applies to education: load the child down with workbooks requiring mindless regurgitation of information, and the love of learning is smothered; make too few demands, and watch them fritter their brainpower away on absolutely nothing. The trick of finding the right balance is an elusive one, and differs from child to child.

Lorna posed an extraordinary challenge in this regard: given material that was too hard or too easy, she would literally wilt. All the strength drained from her body and she would collapse, her head hitting the table with a resounding thud. Not until the following morning could she be persuaded to crack open a schoolbook again without collapsing in a heap, a pitiful cry of despair on her lips. Once, I made the seemingly innocuous request to "copy this out in your best handwriting." Oops, bad choice of words. I could see her muscle tone diminish before my very eyes. Frantically, I hastened to assure her that "it doesn't have to be your *best* handwriting—*any* handwriting will do," but it was too late. Wailing, "But I don't *have* a best handwriting!" she was drifting gently to the floor like a discarded silk handkerchief. Nothing would persuade her to endure further instruction that day. My only comfort was she could be relied on to spend the next several hours with her nose buried in a book; she was getting an education even if it wasn't the one I had intended for her. *Perhaps she needs professional help,* I thought. *I'd better start making inquiries.* Fortunately, seeking professional help takes time, and while I was still wondering how to go about it, Lorna solved the problem by herself. Wilting attacks became fewer and farther between, she learned to manage her perfectionist tendencies unaided, and today is as focused a scholar as you could hope to meet.

KONOS

There are two extremes of homeschooling styles: on the one hand is unschooling, where the children are left to roam free in the hope that they'll bump into enough educational paraphernalia that they learn what they need to. On the other hand is "school at home," complete with desks, uniforms, bells, and copious lesson plans. Typically, I'd start the school year closer on the continuum to school at home, with ambitious ideas both of the learning objectives I was going to accomplish, and how I would achieve them. Such educational zeal lasted, if I was lucky, about two weeks. There ensued a slide towards the—shall we say, less-structured end of the spectrum; sometimes this was gradual, sometimes virtually instantaneous. Either way, it was inevitable, and once I accepted that pandemonium followed every industrious beginning as surely as night follows day, things started to improve. If I was going to work with entropy, I needed a system that was both detailed enough to keep me on some kind of track, and flexible enough to accommodate the tyranny of the dirty diaper, afternoons when math and science were best taught by making cookies, and days when the prevailing mood was, to put it politely, "a little off." I found just the system I needed, sitting unused on my bookshelves.

I had discovered *Konos* curriculum when Iain was only six. It is a Christian unit study–based system that makes abundant use of life's spontaneous teachable moments and encourages co-oping with other families one day a week. My first truly memorable co-op moment came back to me. I had taken both ends out of a tin can and stretched a burst balloon over one end, fastening it on with a rubber band. A piece of broken mirror was glued to the balloon, and the contraption held so that sunlight reflected off the mirror and onto an outside wall. The balloon vibrated in response to sound, and the reflected light danced on the wall. My fellow *Konos* mom, Karen, took turns with me singing, bellowing, and shrieking into the can. We sang high—the reflection on the wall quivered rapidly. We emitted a "moo" at the bottom of our register—the result was a slow undulation of light. Karen and I were thrilled, and chortled, "Acoustics 101—this is what homeschooling's all about!"

Iain and his friend Paul, on the other hand, looked bored out of their minds. *Mothers*, they seemed to be saying, *you can't take them anywhere.* When we paused to draw breath and invited the boys to join in, we were met with incredulous looks. "You want us to do *what*? You've GOT to be kidding!" They endured another minute or so of maternal lunacy, then: "Can we go play now—*please*?" If in the teachable moment there lurks the concept of an "eager student" I fear our first effort was a failure. Still, somewhere in the boys' collective unconscious percolated the idea that short sound waves create higher pitches than long ones. We would come back to that later.

Reviewing the intervening years, I noticed that almost every memorable activity had come about when we were following one of the many, varied suggestions in *Konos*'s pages. The curriculum worked for the whole family, was stimulating for me, and was really, truly, FUN!

Why had I ever tried anything else? Teachable moments were everywhere: on a trip to the ocean, I took a full-size garden spade and dug holes at intervals between the water and the high-tide mark. We discovered different types of worms, gathered in bands running parallel to the water (biology). Subsequently, we noticed birds congregating according to the preferred type of worm (more biology). Between bouts of bird-watching, we built a medieval fortress sandcastle (history), while Robin and Iain painstakingly rerouted a stream running to the sea (physics). This became something of a ritual for them, even though they knew that their efforts, like our sandcastle, would be obliterated with the incoming tide (oceanography).

Konos is organized around character qualities; its main focus is the kinesthetic, hands-on learning that had proved so memorable to Iain and me. This is augmented by auditory and visual learning modalities, resulting in a curriculum that covers every elementary subject apart from math, phonics, and formal grammar, in every learning style. Kinesthetic learning is vital for every young child—no toddler ever learned to walk strapped in a chair, watching a marching band on TV. For a preschooler, learning is all about experimentation. In later years, firsthand experience is not as important; the children learned the states and their capitals without visiting each one, aided by geography songs, flashcards, and jigsaw puzzles that utilized sight, sound, and touch. The best advice I ever heard about learning styles was to discover your child's style, and use it whenever that child encounters a challenging concept. A variation on the steady diet of visual learning that comprises most traditional curricula is often all that it takes for the light bulb to go on.

The girls and I began our *Konos* studies with "Attentiveness: listening closely and watching carefully." Evan was at the age when destruction was his specialty, so we did our best to cater to this particular talent. We made a model ear under the dining-room table; Evan crawled through it and ripped it to pieces. Meanwhile, Sheila turned the pages of a see-through book about the ear, Lorna researched causes of deafness, and Fiona studied the Reticular Activating System—the part of the brain that filters out some sounds and allows others to pass through. We discussed how much harder it is to hear "please empty the dishwasher" than "who'd like ice cream?" and agreed it must be the RAS at work. Lorna and Fiona sat outside with their eyes closed for ten minutes, noticing how much sharper their hearing became when they

couldn't see. We read a story about a blind girl who was un-
beatable at hide-and-seek; her ability to sense another's presence in a room was virtually infallible. Was it her finely tuned
hearing that aided her, or another, "sixth" sense?

Konos gave us plenty of opportunities to learn through art.
The abstract concept that blue plus yellow equals green came
to life when Sheila gradually added blue pigment to yellow,
and observed the transformation from chartreuse to forest
green. Fiona, who was studying the eye at the time, informed
her that it was the cone cells in her retina that enabled her
to see colors, while the rods that helped her see in the dark
perceived only shades of grey. We took different-colored items
outside at night: sure enough, it was impossible to tell green
from red in the dark. Rods are at their densest towards the edge
of our vision; to get a good look at a particular star, it worked
best if we stared slightly to one side of it.

In the course of studying sight, we discussed symmetry,
which was not at first an easy concept for Sheila to grasp. But
once she put a big blob of paint on paper, folded it in half,
rubbed it thoroughly, and opened it to make a mirror pattern,
there was no stopping her—she was off to the garden in search
of symmetry in flowers.

The glory of a real-life cow eye came to our kitchen courtesy of a helpful butcher. We were awed by how completely
each part of the eye depends on the others: there is no reason
for a light-sensitive retina without a contracting iris to meter
the amount of light that strikes it, no cause for an iris without

a lens to focus the beams of light, and neither is of any use at all without an optic nerve to relay messages to the part of the brain which just happens to know how to invert the image and interpret it. Charles Darwin's modern-day apologist, the "devout atheist" Richard Dawkins, has written that "the universe we observe has precisely the properties we should expect if there is, at bottom, no design, no purpose, no evil, no good, nothing but blind pitiless indifference."

Thus the atheist has no choice but to believe that each element of the eye had to evolve to its perfected form independently, simultaneously, and for no apparent reason.

Small wonder the "pitiless indifference" that underlies Dawkins' universe is blind.

READING

Once I discovered *Teach Your Child To Read in 100 Easy Lessons*, literacy was a breeze. Two-year-old Lorna would bring the book upstairs first thing in the morning and hop into bed with me for her "reading lesson." On the other end of the spectrum, Robin used the book to teach Andrew when he was twelve; to this day he can sound out words phonetically, though his pronunciation leaves something to be desired and it's hard to know how much he understands.

Iain's best friend, Tristan, is just about the most interesting, thoughtful, well-read, and entertaining conversationalist I know.

He was four when I met him, and was stoutly resisting his mother's early attempts to introduce him to the alphabet. Resistance became something of a *modus operandi* for Tristan, and he didn't learn to read until he was twelve. It was fortunate that he was homeschooled. Although he drove his mother to distraction (which may have been part of his motivation), he was not labeled a slow learner, nor placed in a special ed class, nor targeted by remedial reading teachers. Self-esteem intact, he finally deigned to put vowels and consonants together and launched into *The Lord of the Rings* trilogy. Within a year he was systematically working his way through the *World Book Encyclopedias*, reading fluently, and with considerably more enthusiasm than many of his peers who had been drilled in phonics since they were five.

Over the years I have regaled numerous worried mothers of late readers with Tristan's literary rags-to-riches story, usually over a nice, comforting cup of tea—a combination that has proved, on the whole, quite satisfactory. I reassured anxious mums that boys' brains develop later than girls' (most late bloomers are male), and that a late start in reading is no indication of a shortfall in overall intelligence. Sometimes it took several bouts of tea and reassurance to see a particularly worried mother through, and occasionally—very occasionally—professional help was necessary, for instance, if the eyes weren't focusing properly. But for the most part, early reading problems are self-correcting.

Once the children could read, they had no shortage of material. A library book basket sat in the living room next to the comfortable sofas, and with it another basket in which I placed new books, mostly published by Scholastic, along with a notebook for the children to jot down title, author, and their impressions. The books were there to be read or not, impressions recorded or not. Looking through the log the other day, I found one name signed meticulously against every single title: Lorna's.

WRITING

Let 'em at it! In Entropy Academy, the best way to teach writing was to give the children a variety of writing tools, plenty of paper, and leave them to it. The only way I could hinder the process was by pointing out their mistakes—particularly the reversal of B and D, P and R. The boys were particularly prone to letter reversals (though the girls did it too) because a vital connection is made later in boys' brains. I found that casually modeling the correct letter formation was the most productive way to teach; sooner or later the neural connection was made, the child noticed his error, and the problem disappeared. Andrew had particular problems learning to form letters; at his therapist's suggestion, I had him draw large letters in trays of shaving cream or cornmeal. There were major battles over the shaving cream; he hated getting his fingers messed up with the stuff, and flatly refused to recognize it as a writing material. In the end I gave up trying, and he learned to write letters in his own time, using a pencil.

As to the question of what to write, my children were never keen on creative writing of any kind apart from voluminous personal correspondence to their friends, to which I was emphatically not privy. Iain stoutly resisted all my attempts at making him write until he was ten, when Robin took him and Andrew on a Custer Battlefield/Oregon Trail field trip on the way home from visiting Grandma and Grandpa in North Dakota. I drew the battle lines, and literally forced him to write a paper on Custer's Last Stand. It was sheer torture, but I didn't give in. When he had finished, I don't know which of us was more surprised to find that he had quite enjoyed it. Flushed with success, he turned out another paper…and another…and here he is, many years later, still turning out papers by the yard, and still quite enjoying it.

With Evan I took a path of far less resistance: copying chunks of his favorite books. Robert Lawson's *Rabbit Hill* got a lot of wear, as did Walter R. Brooks's *Freddy the Detective* and Michael Bond's *Paddington*. All of these tickled Evan's funny bone, so he was happy to copy whole paragraphs with minimal complaint. For my part, I was pleased that he was writing good prose (even if it was not his own) and learning to spell correctly by copying. Since then, his spelling has benefited most from his understanding of word etymology through studying Latin and *English From the Roots Up* by Joegil Lundquist, which covers both Latin and Greek roots. Louie and Michelle joined Sheila and Evan to form a mini co-op for *Roots* studies; having a peer audience certainly egged them on to develop a prodigious vocabulary, while their mother Eileen and I looked forward all week to our time together. We tackled problems as diverse as how to encourage good handwriting in an age of e-communication, whether fermented food was worth the trouble, and, most compelling of all, how to make a killer latte. Best of all, we laughed—at jokes, at life, at nothing at all. To paraphrase Dickens: "It was the best of times, it was the best of times."

I fully intended to set aside a special "Family Reading Time" every day, when we would sit and read our own books together, sharing interesting or amusing snippets as they arose…but all too often this fell by the wayside. Perhaps the problem was that it never quite became a habit, and so required jump-starting every time. Perhaps Family Reading Time would have benefited from a pithy acronym like "FRT" (pronunciation *ad lib*). I can see us explaining our bumper sticker *MAKE FRT HAPPEN!* to total strangers, using the opportunity to wax eloquent on the benefits of the whole family curling up together with a good book, or several.

Hindsight is a wonderful place!

MATH

Miss Pooley had all the grace and winsome charm of a fire hydrant. Her short, grey hair was swept back severely to reveal what, in retrospect, were merry, twinkling eyes. I'm sure she had a kind heart, possibly even a sense of humor, but she never showed either in her dealings with me. She had a way of answering my questions in middle school math class that made me feel like a complete idiot for having asked. Problems written on the board were a series of meaningless squiggles understandable only to those who were "good at math"; I could make neither head nor tail of them, and was therefore "bad at math." The whole business seemed mysterious and occult. Somehow, I managed to scrape through fairly advanced levels of math without ever recognizing the correlation between the digit 5 and the number of protuberances on a hand or foot. Whether I was absent for the kindergarten lesson on one-to-one correspondence or had a mathematical learning disability, I do not know, but it amounted to the same thing: like Winston Churchill's Russia, math was a riddle, wrapped in a mystery, inside an enigma.

The scene shifts: now I am the teacher, Iain the pupil. Using David Quine's aptly named *Making Math Meaningful*, we are finding out how to take twenty-seven away from fifty-three. We have toothpicks, singly and in bundles of ten. I lay out five bundles of ten and three ones. "Can we take seven away from three? No. So let's split up one of the five bundles of ten—now we only have four tens—and add it to the three to make thirteen. Can we take seven away from thirteen? Yes!"

Eureka! I've got it! For thirty-five years I'd been wondering why Miss Pooley made me cross out the five to make four, and add a one to the three. Finally, it made sense! Math was no longer an enigma understandable only to a chosen few: it was the branch of logic dealing with numbers. To say I was ecstatic would be an understatement—I couldn't sleep for a week.

Imparting my mathematical revelation to the younger children was easy, largely thanks to Ruth Beechick's brilliant book, *A Easy Start in Arithmetic*. This is part of a trio which also covers beginning reading and writing; they are tiny books, worth their weight in gold. Beechick explains that teaching math must begin by giving the child plenty of real-life experience with concrete numbers. *We usually set four forks and knives at the table; how many do we need if Grandma and Grandpa are coming to dinner? Let's count out four, plus two more—that's right, that's six.* She also suggests practice in estimating: *How many cars are in this parking lot? About sixty. How many of them are red? About eleven. Are there more black cars, or white?* Take a handful of marbles and estimate how many. Pour out some M&M's and see who can estimate the number most closely; the winner gets to eat one. Using a ruler, mark off one foot along the corridor. Estimate how long ten feet will be; how about twenty feet? *How tall is Daddy? How high are our doorframes?* I had us guess first without looking, then look and estimate, and lastly check with a tape measure. *How tall is Shaquille O'Neal? Would he bang his head if he came to tea? How much would we have to shave off our doorframe so*

he could walk in without stooping? All this estimation seemed
a little frivolous to me at first, but the solid grasp of numbers
it imparted was truly impressive—and vital even when calcu-
lators are used, or else answers can be off by several orders of
magnitude without the student knowing.

The second stage of understanding numbers is conceptual.
I'd say, "What is four plus two?" and Fiona, thinking of four
forks, mentally added two more to make six. At this stage we
played "the age game": *If Iain is twelve and you are six, how old
will he be when you are seven? How old will you be when he is
sixteen? When he is ninety-nine?* The game fascinated the children, who played it anywhere, anytime. Little did they know it
was sowing the seeds of algebra.

The third and final stage of math education looks like this:
$4 + 2 = 6$. Problems ensue when this is made the first and final
stage of mathematical understanding, when the child might as
well see @+#=&, in true Miss Pooley fashion. Concrete and
conceptual understanding must come first if the numbers are
to mean anything beyond third grade. I bought the occasional
book featuring worksheets of easy math problems, and allowed
the children to do some if they wanted to; it made a pleasant
diversion, but I never confused it with teaching them math.

More pre-algebra training: "I'm going to put ten raisins on
the table and cover some with my hand," I told Sheila, "you
tell me how many I'm hiding." By the time she was six, Sheila
could figure out that if she could see seven, I must be hiding
three more. In another version of the same game, I'd say, "I'm

going to put some raisins on the table and cover up four. See if you can tell me how many there are altogether." Sheila sees five, adds the four she knows I'm hiding, and guesses nine. I unveil the four to reveal…she's right! Later, the number under my hand will be known as x, and bingo! Instant algebra.

I read glowing reviews of a computer program, *Quarter Mile Math*. Apparently, the reviewer's children voluntarily spent hours practicing their math facts, achieving an astonishing level of mastery. Naturally, I assumed mine would do the same, and promptly purchased the program. Unsurprisingly, it didn't work out quite as expected: I personally found it tremendous, and had lots of fun sharpening my math skills, but the children used it only under extreme duress. If *Quarter Mile Math* was calling them in their free time, they were deaf to its invitation. This pattern was to become all too familiar: throughout my homeschooling career, my habitual assumption was that what works for someone else's children would work just as well, if not better, for mine. It very seldom did. I ended up spending far too much money on educational gizmos that were seldom used, but other mothers were more than willing to take my castoffs, and the cost compared to one week's tuition at a private school was infinitesimal.

Mathematical manipulatives were invaluable teaching tools and some of them became enduring favorites, pulled out repeatedly to concretize an abstract math fact, or simply for fun. A basket of pattern blocks graced a corner of the living room; these geometric shapes, about a quarter of an inch thick and made of brightly colored wood or plastic, made brilliant, quilt-like patterns that we found utterly mesmerizing. No one ever suspected how much geometry was being sneaked in—I never really understood thirty-degree and sixty-degree angles till I started messing around with pattern blocks. This basket was a magnet to visitors of all ages, from hyperactive young boys to hypoactive adults; young or old, all sat in stunned silence, beguiled by the beauty of their creations.

Once I discovered Cuisenaire rods, I was hooked. They are an extraordinarily effective way of demonstrating and understanding number concepts. The rods are perfectly proportioned and color-coded—the "one" cube is white, two is red, three light green, etc. One-centimeter rods come in storage trays with books of problems and puzzles to tax even the sophisticated mathematical brain. More conducive to building, and the free play that is so important to learning, are the two-centimeter rods. They are satisfyingly bigger—eight times so—a fact that continues to surprise me even though I know on paper that one cubed is one, while two cubed is eight. The younger children made a staircase of rods from one to ten then added a white rod to each step, proving over and over that any number plus one equals the next number. Such an obvious thing to adults, such a mystery to the young child! Later, they explored what happens when a red (two) is added to each stair, and were fascinated to find that the staircase remains perfect.

I used the rods to teach the commutative property of addition and multiplication. It was easy to see that $4 + 6 = 6 + 4$ when we laid two "trains" side-by-side — one made from purple 4 added to dark green 6, the other from dark green added to purple. To demonstrate that $3 \times 4 = 4 \times 3$, we made a train of three purples, and laid it alongside a train of four light greens. If ever the children forgot this property, a quick trip to the rod box soon reminded them. Eventually, I only had to move towards the Cuisenaire cupboard to hear, "Oh, it's okay, I remember."

It was challenging to see how many ways we could make an orange (10) using two rods. Soon, a pattern emerged: one rod would grow shorter, the other longer; $10 + 0, 9 + 1, 8 + 2, 7 + 3, 6 + 4$, and after $5 + 5$ the pattern continued, to form a mirror image. I showed them how to do a similar trick with their fingers. To demonstrate prime numbers, I asked *which rods can be equaled using two or more rods of the same color, excluding white?* Take a light green 3. No two rods of the same color are equal to a light green, so it's a prime number. The only thing that equals one light green is another light green, or three ones. How about a purple 4? Two reds are the same length as a purple 4, so it is not a prime number. Yellow 5; no two rods of the same color equal five, so it is prime. Dark green 6 can be made with two light greens or three reds. Not a prime number. Black 7 cannot be made with two identical rods, and is therefore prime, while brown 8 is the same length as two purples or four reds.

In this way, the children (not to mention their mother!) came to a visual and tactile understanding of prime numbers, as well as factors. Estimation was covered too, by laying an orange rod on the floor and trying to guess how far four more would take us.

Simpler than a Cuisenaire rod, not to mention less expensive, is the humble sugar cube. *What is one, cubed? It already is a cube. What about two, cubed? Let's see...it takes four sugar cubes to make two into a square, and four more to make a cube, so that's eight. Let's try with three squared, that's nine, and cubed—that's a whopping twenty-seven. Four squared, let's count it, sixteen.* By this point, I generally lost them or ran out of sugar cubes. And by the time the relevant child had gained the maturity to count out sixty-four sugar cubes, the concept was already learned.

When Evan was four, the whole family spent three months in Pennsylvania. Far from our cupboard of math manipulatives, I decided to improvise with candy. "Runts" are versatile, fruit-shaped candies that come in several different colors. Evan had enormous fun organizing them into families by shape and color; he sat enraptured for half a morning. Unfortunately, I was a little too enthusiastic with my reward system, and his digestive system rebelled—one candy per correct answer might have been more merciful than three. Suffice it to say that Evan hasn't been able to so much as look at a packet of Runts since 1998.

Family Math is full of intriguing games that can be played with minimal equipment, and makes a versatile adjunct to any math curriculum. Best of all, the book contains "hundreds boards" to photocopy—simple 10 x 10 grids just waiting to be filled in. We started by writing in the numbers from one to one hundred, and put it on the wall to admire. On the next sheet we filled in all the multiples of two, noting the orderly columns. Once it was up on the wall I pointed out that all the numbers we had filled in were even, the empty boxes odd. We paired things up: raisins, M&M's, plastic dinosaurs. If there was one left over, the number was odd. If there were none left over, the number was even. I got them to consider infinity: *Think of the largest number you can imagine—is it odd? If it's odd, add one to make it even; now it's even, add one to make it odd…*and so on, *ad infinitum*—literally. What a productive way to while away a few "odd" moments!

Hundreds boards reveal unexpected patterns in math. These can be made more intriguing, not to mention downright beautiful, by using a different color for each number's multiples: for instance, the children colored threes in red, fours in blue, and purple where they overlapped. On another sheet, they entered the square numbers: 1, 4, 9, 16, 25, etc., noticing how the difference between any two consecutive squares is always the next greater odd number: the difference between 25 and 36 is 11; between 36 and 49 is 13; between 49 and 64 is 15, and so on. Maybe it's because math was such an abstruse mystery to me for so long that I was so tickled by discovering all these patterns. I have since been even more tickled to discover mathematicians who regard mathematics as an art, not a science, and who revel in its beauty. Such sensible thinkers are likewise fans of pattern, and see it everywhere, especially in nature: the Fibonacci series, for instance, can be seen in the proportions of a snail shell, the swirl of seeds in a sunflower, or the very DNA from which all living things are made. *Numberphile* on YouTube is aptly named, featuring mathematicians who are quite simply crazy about numbers and their mysteries.

Sheila was very proud of "her patterns." When Granny came for dinner, she was immediately dragooned into admiring Sheila's multicolored hundreds boards. My mother put on a good show, exclaiming with wonder at the purple tens that finished each line, always joined by the pink fives. She never realized, or so she claimed, that the multiples of nine would make a striking diagonal across the page. I fear Sheila lost Granny when she tried to explain the glories of square numbers, but considering that Granny's age at the time was greater than nine squared, I think she could be excused a little haziness on the subject.

One of the nifty things about math is its consistency: $2 + 3 = 5$; $2,000,000 + 3,000,000 = 5,000,000$. When we couldn't get our heads around a problem involving large numbers, I frequently restated the problem using tiny numbers. Once the procedure was clear, we could apply it to the more complex problem, secure in the knowledge that what is true of small numbers is also true of large.

I took every opportunity to teach the same concepts in different ways. Building on their experience with the rods, the girls furthered their grasp of the commutative properties of multiplication in the context of a dolls' tea party: *if two dolls each have three cookies, how many will they each have if they want to share with a friend?* Fiona patiently explained to me that if two dolls have three cookies, then three dolls will have two cookies each—in other words, that 2 x 3 = 3 x 2 = 6. Later, we doubled the number of cookies and proved that 3 x 4 = 4 x 3 = 12.

When we came back to the US of A after our year in Ireland, I made a horrible mistake. At a homeschooling picnic/curriculum exchange, I was dazzled by a glossy, colorful, fourth-grade math text and chose it to use with Fiona that year. I had been warned against such things, but it was so shiny, so inviting, and best of all—it was free! Fiona and I waged bitter war over that book all year. I pushed; she pushed back. I pulled; she pulled against me. I simply could not teach her. Finally, close to despair, I asked her why she was having so much trouble. After a moment's thought she told me, "I already know all this—I learned it at school in Ireland." I was speechless. *WHY DIDN'T YOU TELL ME?* I bellowed silently. *DON'T YOU THINK YOU MIGHT HAVE MENTIONED THIS BEFORE?* All that actually emerged from my mouth was a horribly strangled, "Oh, I see." I turned the recrimination against myself. How could I have been so…so *stupid*? My world heavyweight math gremlin gave me a very serious talking-to: no homeschooling mother worth her salt would have been such an idiot as to waste an entire year of math instruction, all for want of asking the right question. Why hadn't I entertained the possibility that third-grade Irish math education might be ahead of American? I berated myself for months, and long after that had a sick feeling in my stomach whenever the thought of Fiona's math crossed my mind.

But the story has a happy ending. Using Saxon Math, amplified by the *Key To* series, Fiona came to love math and today it is her favorite subject. True, she didn't get to calculus in high school, but she has since had a marvelous time with an online college calculus course that she took just for fun. I haven't heard from the math gremlin in quite a while, and I can't say I miss it.

9

Tools For Life:
Logic, English, & the
Four Levels of Happiness

*N*othing is certain but death and taxes." Really? I propose a
third, equally uplifting contender to the list: problems. The
only lifetime guarantee I could offer the children was this—
from the cradle to the grave, we will face problems. Some
are trivial, some sensational; some are inconsequential, while
others appear insuperable. Big or small, funny or sad, problems are inevitable, and we will be infinitely happier if we are
prepared for them, with a game plan at the ready. Enter our
best friends and allies in the war on problems: a logical mind,
a good command of language, and the ability to prioritize our
lives to find happiness.

LOGIC

Put simply, logic enables us to sort out the various components of a problem, evaluate their validity, and, weighing the pros and cons, arrive at a solution. The first underlying truth of logic is the principle of noncontradiction: something cannot both be and not be at the same time. When Fiona's frog died, it could not simultaneously be alive. If the three-letter animal in a cross-word is *dog*, it cannot also be *cat*.

Cause and effect comes next. The dominoes are lined up and Evan pushes the first (cause), observing the ripple as the rest topple in turn (effect). Lorna comes home from a sleepover at her best friend Camille's house with raccoon eyes, her mouth jammed wide open in a perpetual yawn. When capable of speech, she admits that they stayed awake till 3:00 a.m. The effect of this particular escapade: no sleepovers for a month. Thereafter, they were permitted only if I could not tell from her behavior the following day that she had been allowed the privilege of an overnight stay. She could choose whether to get enough sleep, or simply behave as if she had. That was definitely a consequence I could live with!

Sometimes, cause and effect is merely embarrassing: I normally allowed the children to choose their own clothes each morning, with some pretty hilarious "mix-and-not-match" results. Looking through the yearbooks, the girls howl in horror, "I can't believe you let me out in public wearing *that*!"

"Nobody died," I counter, and the mortified children learn that decisions have consequences.

One fine spring day when Iain was four, an impromptu trip to the zoo beckoned. It had been an exceptionally cold winter, during which Iain had insisted on wearing only T-shirts (and pants, I hasten to add). Despite my warning that the temperature was likely to escalate into the seventies—which translates in Seattle to "roasting hot"—he insisted on wearing his very warmest sweater, refusing to be swayed even when I told him he'd have to carry it himself when he got too hot. Sure enough, the mercury rose. Seeing little clouds of steam emitting from his ears, I relented and offered to carry the chunky woolen garment. But no. Bright red and sweating visibly, Iain was bound and determined to stand by his sartorial decision. I was very proud of him!

Tempting as it was for me to solve the children's problems for them, I soon recognized that my goal of producing autonomous problem solvers was best met by helping them think their own way to a solution. If six-year-old Lorna was invited to a birthday party by one friend and the roller-skating rink by another, the quick fix was for me to decide for her. Instead, I helped her make up her own mind by asking: "Can you do both?" (Principle of non-contradiction—if she does one, she cannot also do the other.) "Which friend would you rather spend time with? Which friend have you spent more time with recently? Who else will be there? What will they be doing at the party? How badly do you want to go skating? Is there anybody else you could go skating with?" Halfway through the interrogation, Lorna announced her verdict, inspired no doubt by a growing suspicion that my apparently interminable questioning would, indeed, never end. The party won.

Even though it was the more inconvenient choice for me, my reaction was to congratulate her on making a decision, and to help her stand by it. After all, ten years down the line the birthday party or roller-skating would have faded into oblivion, but her ability to make a good decision and stick to it would still be standing her in good stead.

Of all the children, Fiona found the decision-making process the most elusive, if not downright threatening. As her thirteenth birthday drew near, I suggested taking a group of her friends to an Everett AquaSox game (a minor league baseball team affiliated with the Seattle Mariners). She winced as though I'd stuck a pin into her. "Is there something else you'd rather do?" I inquired. "*Anything* else?" The agonized look intensified; I could see she was starting to think about her Froggy. "I don't know-wuh," she wailed, and promptly vanished. I found her huddled in the dark, undemanding security of her closet. She ventured out only after I promised not to mention anything as inflammatory as planning a birthday outing again.

Fiona turned out to have an extraordinary affinity with logic; it was a world where, once she'd figured out the premises, things behaved in a comfortingly predictable fashion. Nothing like the chaos theory of real life! She found that prioritizing, a skill acquired in the rarefied air of pure logic, helped her to solve her own, apparently insuperable, personal problems. Questions posed in the subjunctive helped too: instead of the threateningly direct, "Do you want to take some friends to an AquaSox game for your birthday?" I tried, "If you *were* to have a birthday outing, what might it look like? Anything like, say, an AquaSox game?" Putting the first step in a theoretical mode took the immediate pressure off and enabled her to think more clearly.

When faced with the major decision of whether to transfer to a different college for the final two years of her undergraduate career, she sought assistance from her most reliable ally, logic. Armed with lists and flow charts, she made her choice within a couple of days, and with no recourse to the darkest recesses of her closet.

BUT I DON'T KNOW LOGIC!

How did I train the children to be better logicians than myself? It was ridiculously easy: all I did was buy them books of logic puzzles for birthdays or Epiphany, and let nature take its course. Just two days ago, Fiona unearthed a book of false logic puzzles from four years ago, and stayed up half the night with it. These puzzles are completely beyond me, something along the lines of: *You land on a planet where half the population tells the truth only in the morning, and the other half tells the truth only in the afternoon. You do not know what time of day it is. You must ask two people one question each to find out the name of their president.* Totally imponderable to me, totally enthralling to her.

On car trips, or simply to fill in the odd ten minutes, we'd crack open a book of lateral thinking puzzles—stories to be read by one person, who also looks at the solution, while the others ask questions to figure out what has happened. *Jack and his sister Jill come home to find George and Amanda dead on the floor. Even though they suspect Terence, they do not call the police, or even reprimand Terence.* No, Jack and Jill are not cold-blooded sociopaths. Careful questioning reveals that George and Amanda are goldfish, Terence the cat.

We were startled to realize how many assumptions we made, and how they colored our understanding. *Stella is standing in the school playground. She has no raincoat or umbrella, nor is there a shelter of any kind, and yet she remains perfectly dry. How can this be?* The answer, quite simply, is that it is not raining. We hear the word "raincoat," and assume the skies have opened. Along the same lines: *Jason is standing in the rain. He has no umbrella or raincoat, and yet his hair is not wet.* Having ascertained that he has no other form of protection from the rain, we turn our attention to the second part of the sentence: *and yet his hair is not wet.* Could it be "not wet" because he doesn't have any? Yes, indeed—Jason is bald!

As we became more proficient at thinking logically, we explored syllogisms: if A is true, then B is also; if B, then C; therefore, if A, then C. For example, all cows are mammals; all mammals give birth to live young; therefore all cows give birth to live young. False syllogisms, which use data incorrectly to draw erroneous conclusions, provided a nice twist:

- Ted has cold, wet feet. A duck has cold, wet feet. Therefore, Ted is a duck.
- All cows eat grass. All cows are mammals. Therefore, all mammals eat grass.
- God is love. Love is blind. Ray Charles is blind. Therefore, Ray Charles is God.

Anyone can tell that these statements are false, but the fun comes in figuring out where the logic tripped up, and then trying to explain it to somebody else (Venn diagrams help).

A book reserved for car trips was *The Fallacy Detective* by Hans and Nathaniel Bluedorn. Each chapter defines and illustrates a specific fallacy and the reader must decide whether or not the additional examples demonstrate that fallacy. Our recognition skills became finely tuned to fallacies, both at home and in the media (especially during election time). How blatant politicians can be! *I don't believe what you say, because you are a liar. I know you're a liar because I can't believe what you say* (circular reasoning).

Lorna crawls ingratiatingly into my lap, "Mummy, I know I'm your favorite child."

"How do you know that?"

"Because you love me the best."

There are times when the lecture on circular reasoning can wait for another day.

The old political trick of simply calling one's opponent a liar is an *ad hominem* argument: if you can't argue against the message, attack the messenger. *Senator Sketchy has come up with a bold plan to solve the nation's economic woes, but how can he know anything about economics when he has just left his wife of twenty-seven years?* On a domestic level, our *ad hominems* tend to be even less subtle.

Sheila: "Evan, please put the tennis rackets away."

Evan: "Why should I? You didn't hang up your towel when Mum asked you to—besides, you're fat."

By moving in the same sentence from a truthful *ad hominem* (about the towel) to a lie (Sheila is anything but fat), Evan has made verbal retaliation well-nigh impossible. Squealing incoherently, Sheila launches an uncoordinated physical attack; to Evan's glee, all thought of putting away the tennis rackets is forgotten.

By far the most popular fallacy in our family is the red herring: a topic is introduced that appears relevant to the subject at hand, but actually leads away from it. Thus a discussion about what flight Lorna should take back to Philadelphia is derailed by Robin telling us about the nutritional perils of a Philly cheese steak. It's all about Philadelphia, but it hardly helps Lorna get to her first class on time.

THE BUTTON BOX

My grandmother's ancient button box helped me teach classification, first of all informally—placing the buttons in piles according to color, size, or number of holes—then later, using Venn diagrams. Buttons could be distinguished by various criteria: *does it have a shank, or holes? Is the button flat, or does it have a rim? Is it textured or smooth? Shiny or dull? Solid- or multi-colored? Is the edge smooth or notched?*

Venn diagrams consist of overlapping circles: one circle could contain red buttons, for instance, the other, buttons with two holes. In the space where they overlap go red buttons with two holes. If I add a third circle for buttons with a rim, the overlapping area in the center would contain red buttons with two holes and a rim. Often, one of us constructed the Venn diagram with string or embroidery hoops, while the other tried to deduce the organizational criteria. These might include the important "not" category of logic: one pile of buttons was blue, the other red, black, yellow, and green. *These buttons are blue, those are not blue.* Lorna countered with her own two piles. *These buttons have four holes, those do not have four holes.* I was consistently amazed at how sophisticated a young child's logic could be; the non-threatening familiarity of the box and its contents seemed to give their minds the freedom to soar.

Feeding the box was easy. I found buttons on old clothes, at fabric stores, and more cheaply, on otherwise undesirable items of clothing at thrift stores. I once bought star-shaped buttons that proved so ridiculously hard to use that they were soon relegated to the button box. Had I given in and bought the multitude of buttons that tempted me, the button box would have become a button bucket. Playing with the buttons was good preparation for Attribute Blocks (by Learning Resources), a set of five shapes in two sizes, two thicknesses, and three colors, which reinforced and extended our classification skills. Lessons using Attribute Blocks clarified my own powers of logic; the more lucid my understanding, the more effortlessly I was able to impart my knowledge. We put our classification expertise to the test by playing the game of *Set!* in which we raced to find a SET of three cards where each feature (color, shape, number, and shading) was either all the same or all different on each card. At first, I won easily; it was not long, however, before the nimble mind of even the youngest child could beat me hollow. But then, homeschooling has never been about preserving the maternal ego—if it were, I would have given up years ago.

INTRINSIC AND ACCIDENTAL PROPERTIES

Intrinsic properties describe the essence of a thing; accidental properties can change without destroying what the thing is. A rose bud is intrinsically a rose, but only as the petals unfurl and reveal its color, shape, and scent are the distinctive accidental properties revealed. The flower wilts and dies, but the bush, pruned down to brown stumps for the winter, remains a rose. Next summer it will produce, not zucchini, but more roses. Seeking a way to bring this lesson home to teenage Fiona, I hit on something very close to her heart: her baby brother.

An egg leaves the ovary and begins its journey down the fallopian tube. As it travels, it meets with a whole host of at-tackers—an army of sperm, all determined to inflict an in-trinsic change upon the egg. One succeeds. As it penetrates the egg, its tail falls away to join the millions of unsuccess-ful sperm left outside. The egg undergoes an instantaneous electrical transformation, rendering it unavailable to any other suitor. The sperm's head invades the nucleus, merging its bundle of genetic material with that of the egg to become a single cell, containing all the genetic material necessary to make an adult human being. Male or female, redhead or bald, poet or engineer, it's all contained in that single cell. Dividing and replicating itself many billions of times, it will make two of some things—ears, lungs, kneecaps—and one of others—nose, spleen, spinal column. Its intrinsic qualities will never change: it will always be the same person. It will grow so large that it has to live outside its mother—another accidental change. The delighted parents welcome it into the world. By gum—it's Evan!

Evan goes on growing. We look at him and wonder how his accidental properties will unfold: will he be a musician, a scientist, an athlete, a couch potato? We can tell that his eyes will be brown, likewise his hair, but will he be taller than his father or the same height as me? Will he be good-natured, or have an acerbic wit? No matter how intently we stare, we cannot see the adult that Baby Evan will become. All we know is that twenty years from now his baby pictures will look just like him. Reminding myself that those years will pass almost before I know it, I re-immerse myself in his babyhood.

Evan walks, he talks, he develops a wicked sense of humor and a profound sense of self, which Freud would call his ego. He shaves off his eyebrows with his daddy's razor. *Never mind, they'll grow back.* But, Fiona wonders gleefully, what if he shaves his head, joins a gang, and starts beating up old ladies—are these still accidental changes? Going still further, I muse, *What if he starts smoking crack and becomes a changed personality? What if he becomes a sociopath, a serial killer? Surely that would change his intrinsic nature?*

The answer, as I discovered with some research, is no. He would still be himself at some level, still capable of repentance. The only possible intrinsic changes are conception, at which point a human being comes into existence, and death, when he ceases to be. In the years between, all change is accidental. No living person can ever become anything other than a person. Even the most degenerate drug addict is, at some level, the human being his mother loved.

When Fiona was seventeen, she and I visited London. On the sidewalk outside Westminster Abbey, I fell into conversation (about the weather—what else?) with three rather striking young men. Impaled with studs too numerous to count, rainbow-colored hair raised in a crest of spikes, the leader of the three looked intently into my eyes and said, "Yes, you can take a picture of us…if you wouldn't mind giving us a pound… for expenses, like." Judging by his sallow skin and the three rotting teeth protruding from diseased gums, the main expenses of his life were run up at a meth lab. I have a photo of them with Fiona, who looks absolutely horrified; one of them is giving the camera the "V" sign—and in England, it doesn't mean peace. But, I insisted to my incredulous daughter, the person I saw when I looked into those eyes was good. Lost, perhaps; maybe downright depraved—I'd certainly never invite him home for a cuppa—but in some way lovable. And I'm not even his mother.

ENGLISH

George Bernard Shaw spelled "fish" as follows: GHOTI. That's *gh* as in *enough, o* as in *women,* and *ti* as in *action.* What can you do with a language as crazy as that? Love it, that's what.

In order to explain why our language and spelling are so unusually—how shall I put it—*various,* I invited the children to take a brief time-travel trip to Britain, BC. We found it peopled by Picts and Celts, all running around merrily fighting each other, painting themselves blue with woad, and hurling stirring epithets in Pictish and Celtic. Then we conjured up the Romans, who may have squashed rather a lot of local color, but brought the blessings of flushing toilets, under-floor heating, and straight roads. Oh, and a whole passel of words, many of which remained in our language after the Romans left in 476 AD. When the Angles and the Saxons arrived, soon after, with their Germanic languages, they liked what they saw and decided to stay (I think it was the woad that attracted them). So successful was their invasion that today "Anglo-Saxon" is virtually synonymous with "English."

Barring a few Viking invasions, everything went along swimmingly until King Harold was unfortunate enough to receive an arrow in the eye at the Battle of Hastings, 1066. So began the Norman Conquest. The Normans were basically Vikings who had invaded northern France and stayed long enough to develop a taste for frogs' legs and red wine. They insisted that everyone in the English royal court speak French and drink wine, but had little influence on the common people, who stuck rebelliously to their mead, beer, and Anglo-Saxon tongue. Even today there are relatively few English words that come from French roots, and most of them have to do with *gourmet* cooking and fancy food. Traditional English fare—bubble-and-squeak, toad-in-the-hole, and the legendary spotted dick—has distinctly Anglo-Saxon roots, as do most strong, monosyllabic British epithets, none of which are fit to print here.

With a linguistic history like this, it's small wonder that English is such a porous language and adapts so swiftly to new influences. Nor is it any surprise that the spelling is so seemingly chaotic. Take the word "chaos," for instance. Why should the CH be hard and sound like the letter K, while the CH in "champion" is soft? We asked the same question of the words "chord" and "chocolate," then moved on to examine "chip" and "chivalry." By this time the children were clearly over-whelmed—or was it just plain bored? Either way, my scholarly explanation fell on deaf ears; nobody but me seemed to care that words with Greek roots have the hard CH sound (charac-ter, echo, chorus) while in French-based words, CH sounds like SH (chef, machine, parachute). Instead, the inconsis-tencies of their native tongue were inciting interest in their father's linguistic heritage: Icelandic. Now, there's a language that knows how to behave—indeed, has remained largely un-changed over the past thousand years. For some reason, this treeless piece of real estate, several hundred miles north of Scotland, has failed to stir the hearts of would-be invaders suf-ficiently to goad them into action; accordingly, the language, like the population, has remained static. No weird aberrations in spelling here!

HOW CAN I TEACH SUCH A DIFFICULT LANGUAGE?

Children learn to speak by emulating adults, by saying "ba-ba" and having an enthusiastic caregiver mirror it back to them so they can join in the excitement and say it all over again. This mirroring is vital: I learned from Andrew's speech therapist that children of deaf parents, left in front of the television, nev-er learn to speak, no matter how many words they are exposed to. I wanted my children to speak in cogent, well-formulated sentences, so I modeled it constantly in my own speech. I'm not averse to baby talk in small quantities—there is a difference between a toddler and a grad school physicist, after all—but children, even tiny babies, seem to enjoy being talked to respectfully, as one sentient being to another. Just plant the seeds of correctly spoken English into the burgeoning mass of neurons and synapses that is an infant brain, and that amazing brain will reap the harvest of a lifetime of verbal fluency.

Not that it all has to be serious: Bernhofts love to play and make up new words. Perhaps they take after their mother—when I was asked how I had enjoyed my first day at kindergarten many years ago, I responded, "I liked it quite well, but I found it very aggrannoying when people kept intersturbing me." I also found it jolly "aggrannoying" that both my parents laughed at me and told their friends, who laughed too. I couldn't see what was so funny. It seemed to me a far more satisfactory word than either aggravating or annoying, while "intersturbing" had just the right blend of interrupting and disturbing. Like a pod of whales, our family developed its own distinctive *argot*, or slang, to which we have all, at some point, contributed. We get some pretty queer looks when we forget which words are peculiarly ours, and which belong to the world at large.

If speaking proper English seems to happen automatically when properly spoken English is modeled, what about written English, with its complex grammar and spelling? The most effective way I know of teaching grammar is to read good books aloud, the more the merrier. The children learned to recognize correct grammatical constructions by ear, while developing an indelible feel for the beauties and subtleties of the language. Some of them only studied grammar "by ear," while others engaged in more formal study, but there was no appreciable difference in their ability to communicate effectively. Iain, in all his years of studying English, has never diagrammed a sentence in his life, and neither have I, despite being educated in England. A pity, in retrospect; I now find it rather fun, and would have enjoyed sharing this extreme linguistic precision with the children. I do not think, however, that it would have made them better writers.

Reading aloud might seem like a panacea, but it's not much help when it comes to spelling. Thanks to my English accent, the girls grew up believing that Tolkien's orcs were actually *awks*, while to six-year-old Iain, King Arthur's magical sword was *Excalibuh*. I found that spelling is best learned by reading extensively, which teaches how correctly spelled words look, and by writing, which teaches how to recognize words that "look funny."

Even with this soft-core approach, the children not infrequently despaired in their quest for mastery of the twenty-six unpredictable rogues that form our alphabet. They were only somewhat appeased by my explanation that standardized spelling is a relatively recent innovation, for which we have Noah Webster to thank. His dictionary had the effect of freezing a fluid language mid-flow, into somewhat predictable patterns. To curb any resultant wave of enthusiasm for idiosyncratic spelling, I pointed out that the same word may be found spelled five different ways in one Shakespeare play. With no possibility of sight word recognition, we can be sure there were no speed-reading courses in Elizabethan England. Every single word had to be sounded out according to complex rules that had not quite been formulated yet. Fun? Maybe, but not for long.

A nifty puzzle impressed the importance of punctuation: Use commas, inverted commas, and periods to make sense of the following: *Jill where John had had had had had had had had had had the teacher's approval.*

Jill, where John had had (written) *"had," had had* (written) *"had had." "Had had" had had* (received) *the teacher's approval.*

It was most entertaining to read the string of eleven "hads" in a dreary monotone, then articulate the second version as distinctly as possible—*Masterpiece Theatre* on steroids, perhaps.

I discovered an abundance of fun to be had with word games, readily found in library books (though nowadays a plethora of games are accessible online). We had a few standby favorites. "I went to *(place name)* to buy some *(edible substance)* to feed my *(animal)*"—working our way through the alphabet: "I went to *Albania* to buy some *artichokes* to feed my *albatross*. I went to *Belgium* to buy some *beer* to feed my *borzoi*. I went to *Constantinople* to buy some *catnip* to feed my *chinchilla*," and so on. Sometimes, we'd go through the alphabet several times; if the number of people playing was a factor of twenty-six, we'd skip a letter so no one ended up with the same letter twice.

We could always—well, almost always—get everyone roped into a game of "Spot the Homophone." I'd choose two homophones (words that sound the same but are spelled differently) and make up a sentence, blanking them out: "Let's *blank* at my house and eat *blank*." (Meet and meat.) "Always ride on a *blank* if you want to *blank* dragons." (Sleigh and slay.) Sometimes my word choices would cause violent argument: "Don't bear a *blank* if you can't park in the *blank*." I may be the only member of the family who believes that *grudge* and *garage* can, at a stretch, sound identical.

Another game we enjoy to this day is "Make the Adverb Fit the Crime." *I have a fever, she said hotly. I work at a prison, he said guardedly. The power's out, she said darkly. The plane can't take off, he said flatly. I like French food, she said saucily. Yes, I perform amputations, he said off-handedly.* (As you can tell, it's hard to stop once you start.) Sometimes, the verb alone can carry the extra meaning: *I'm taller, he groaned* (grow-ned). *I must learn the Heimlich maneuver, she choked. How can I catch that mouse, he mused* (mew-sed).

But mostly, we just enjoyed words. When Lorna was three, we walked up the road to a tiny park which enjoyed a superb view of the Puget Sound and the distant Olympic

Mountains. "Look," I said, as I held her up on the fence to see better, "look how smooth the water is…and the mountains are all jagged." She rolled the word around her mouth, savoring it slowly, exploring its edges. *Jagged.* It is forever Our word, conjuring up as it does that limpid twilight, the feeling of the cold air on our faces, my hands encircling her waist, the sound of the other's voice. "What's in a word?" asked Shakespeare. *All the world, William, all the world.*

THE FOUR LEVELS OF HAPPINESS

The welcoming committee was in place. Iain had hidden the dessert so it was difficult, but not impossible, to find. The girls stood poised to seize the clerical collar and hold it hostage for the evening. Evan chortled with glee at the prospect of being "hooshed" into the air in a maneuver known as the "rocket." Dinner was prepared, and I had Flanders and Swann's immortal "Hippopotamus Song" at the ready on the piano. Our copy of *Froggy Gets Dressed* had been located, and awaited its obligatory group recitation. We were ready to greet Father Spitzer.

Not, perhaps, a typical way to greet a Jesuit priest; but then, Father Spitzer is far from a typical priest. I like to describe him as a cross between Albert Einstein and Winnie the Pooh: an incredibly brilliant physicist/philosopher/theologian, with an incurable fondness for condensed milk. Hence Iain's efforts to "hide" the seven-layer bars so Father Spitzer could only indulge in a small sample before the onerous business of eating the main course (and, if we were feeling particularly brutal, a salad for good measure—the palindrome, "Egad! Alas! A salad age!" might have been penned expressly for Fr. Spitzer).

After dinner, after the singing, recitations, and mandatory game of hide-and-seek (here, parents and children enjoyed a distinct advantage, as Fr. Spitzer is legally blind), came the main business of the evening—we brought forth our most piercing questions about the Meaning of Life, and our guest beguiled the hours with his answers. Iain was nine when these sessions began, and manfully willed himself to sit upright, propping his eyes open with matchsticks when necessary, not wishing to miss a word of the discourse. Thus it was that we first heard the material that was to assist Robin and me so much in forming our children's moral natures, and that would later be published by the Center for Life Principles as "The Four Levels of Happiness."

Aristotle came up with three levels of happiness around 500 BC.; his ideas were refined by Aquinas in the Middle Ages, and brought to the modern world by Father Spitzer, who added the fourth level. As a way to understand mankind's search for happiness, it was both easy to comprehend and profound; the more I thought about it, the deeper its applications to our lives became.

The four levels follow a roughly chronological path—each one satisfies for a while before leading to a crisis, when it no longer suffices. Level One concerns the gratification of the senses: a small baby is in Level One bliss when she is warm, dry, well fed, and held in loving arms. She needs nothing more. But we live in a culture that values competition, and most young children quickly learn competitive strategies. As she grows, she becomes aware of herself in relation to others; physical comfort is no longer adequate, she wants to be *more* comfortable than her friend, have the *bigger* cookie, the *trendier* dress. This is the crisis of Level One, and it leads naturally to Level Two, happiness derived from personal achievement and ego gratification.

Children at this stage see one of their peers doing something—playing a violin or kicking a ball—and they want to do it too. In fact, they don't just want to do it, they want to do it *better*. The tricky balance I tried to maintain was simultaneously encouraging this drive to excellence while at the same time reassuring the child that he is loved and accepted just the way he is. Levels of ambition vary, from the straight-A student, the Olympic gymnast, the Eagle Scout, to the child who is perfectly happy knitting, making pancakes, or cutting out paper snowflakes. I felt it was important for each of our children to excel at something, and was determined it should be more constructive than playing on an Xbox or hanging out at the mall.

The quest for Level One happiness never goes away: people always tend to be sad when they're cold, hungry, or in pain. Similarly, Level Two carries on well into adulthood; it is the drive behind the quest for a bigger car, a more luxurious home, more money, more trophies…the list goes on and on. It says, "The most important thing in the world is me, my achievements, and my stuff." Crisis Two hits when the new Boy Scout comes into town with more badges, when the brand new luxury car is superseded in the showroom by the latest technological marvel, when all that remains of the five-star vacation that was the envy of all your co-workers is a half-unpacked suitcase and a pile of credit card bills. Even the super-wealthy feel a gap that money simply cannot fill; as Maurice Sendak put it, "There must be more to life than having everything." Crisis Two is resolved when a person begins to explore Level Three happiness—seeking the joy that lies beyond the acquisition of stuff, by doing good things for other people.

Performing a kindly act for a neighbor, a friend, or any cause beyond ourselves, seems to be the best cure for the blues; Level Three activity gives us a warm feeling that all the self-indulgence in the world cannot match. This helps explain why so many people give to charities, volunteer their time at schools and nursing homes, and reach out to give total strangers food for a Thanksgiving feast. They are looking for love, truth, and beauty. They want to make the world a better place.

As a nation, we tend to look for happiness in the "sex, drugs, and rock 'n' roll" mindset of Level One, or the meaningless materialism of Level Two—transient pleasures that leave us feeling dissatisfied or even depressed. Glossy magazines exhort us to "Take time for yourself," when a Level

Three approach, "Take time for someone else," would be infinitely more productive. I tried to find ways to engage the children in altruistic Level Three activities: we sponsored a child in Africa and put her picture on the fridge; we collected clean, used blankets from our neighbors and took them to a shelter for the homeless; we visited the elderly in rest homes. I was careful not to overwhelm young minds with problems too great for them, or too upsetting; when the twin towers fell, I watched one jumper fall through the air and the TV was off. International terrorism is way beyond our family's sphere of influence, at least for now, and I didn't want to risk plunging our more sensitive offspring into depression. Not to mention myself.

Even altruism has its limitations; Level Three also has its crisis. There comes a point when we humans are drawn to Level Four: not just to manifestations of truth and beauty, but to Truth and Beauty in their perfected form. When we look at a glorious sunset, or Monet's *Water Lilies*, or listen to one of Beethoven's late quartets, the yearning we feel is not simply for beauty, but for the author, the absolute source of that beauty. Beyond any appeal to our senses, beyond ego gratification, beyond the common good, God waits for us in silence.

Children may be far more in tune with Level Four than they are given credit for. Mysteries of faith that perplex adult minds can be readily embraced by the young, for whom so many things in life are mysterious. I made sure to have inspiring reading material available at home, as well as fine art reproductions and music. We went as a family to Mass at least once a week; there we met the Author of truth and beauty Himself, and had time for contemplation. Given only sufficient time and silence, I knew the children would absorb these riches into the very depths of their souls.

My children are light years ahead of where I was at their age as regards spiritual matters. Not for them the absurdity of relativism; they know that Good and Evil exist, and that the world has an underlying order that can be appreciated, and analyzed systematically. As a young girl, I found Beauty always unattainable, always incomprehensible, and thus it was in my mind associated with grief. I like to imagine myself, aged around ten, listening to Fr. Spitzer as he answered the profound questions that troubled my young heart. How very much happier I would have been. I was glad to have provided that opportunity to Iain, and to the younger children in their turn.

Fr. Spitzer was our stalwart ally as we went about the daily business of forming our children's characters. The Four Levels of Happiness helped us delve into the meaning of many a book: how could Gatsby's love for Daisy, ostensibly so Level Three, fail to bring him happiness? Given that Daisy is married to another, does Gatsby really want the best for her? In what ways was he "great"? And what about Robin Hood — if it's good for us to give our time and treasure to help those less fortunate, is Robin in line with Level Three principles when he robs the rich to help the poor? And how, if at all, does this differ from the actions of the pigs in Orwell's *Animal Farm* when they oust the humans and take over the farm?

But it is the personal Spitzerean anecdotes that we recall most fondly. At Lorna's fourth birthday party, two-month-old Baby Evan was nestled securely in Fr. Spitzer's arms. Evan reached up and touched Father's slightly unshaven cheek. A look of amazement spread over Evan's face. He squinted quizzically at his hand, touched his own face, and reached out to touch the priestly cheek once more. Fr. Spitzer's voice quivered with excitement as he breathed, "Look! Look…*He's discovering his ego!*"

That's one for the baby books—philosopher style.

10

SCIENCE

*O*bservation is the key to science: observation, and asking, "Why?" The Ancient Egyptians noted that headaches were miraculously cured by chewing willow bark, but apparently lacked the scientific methodology to investigate why.

It was not until the nineteenth century that scientists thought to ask, and their curiosity was handily rewarded by the discovery of salicylic acid, and thus aspirin. Egyptian architects fashioned right-angled triangles by tying knots in rope; their angles were so precise that the pyramids are still standing, more than four thousand years later. But the Egyptians are not credited with discovering geometry. That distinction belongs to the Greek, Euclid, who proved Pythagoras' theorem in Book 1, Proposition 47, of his *Elements*. (Thank you, Fiona.) Similarly, while the Egyptians were aware that the annual flooding of the Nile coincided with the movement of the stars, and even worked out how to predict the yearly inundation, it was the Greeks who codified the study of stars into a science and called it astronomy.

My goal for the first eight grades, then, was to turn out little Ancient Egyptians—curious, full of wonder, and excited about the world around them. Ready, in short, for the Big Fat Greek Takeover of high school science. "Wow!" moments abounded in everyday life: observing a lunar eclipse, seeing a rainbow in a drop of dew, watching a pencil appear to bend in a glass of water. Before long, my proto-Ancient Egyptians were starting to figure out "how": how a catapult flings a marshmallow farther than even the strongest human can; how a pulley helps to lift a heavy weight; how a prism splits a beam of light into a rainbow. "Why" could wait for high school.

SEEING STARS

Living in an urban area, our view of the stars was considerably obscured by the astronomer's bane—the glare of street lighting. A family camping vacation in the wilds of north central Washington afforded a splendid opportunity to explore the heavens. On a bitterly cold September night, Iain and I dragged our sleeping bags to the middle of a field, lay flat on our backs, closed our eyes for two minutes to acclimate them to darkness, then opened them wide. *Wow!* Who would believe that the Milky Way would be so—well—*milky*? Billions of stars, mind-boggling in their distance and immensity, cut a brilliant swathe across the sky. We recognized a few old favorites—the Big Dipper, the telltale "W" of Cassiopeia—and noticed that Scorpio had chased Orion out of the sky for the winter. We reflected on how small our terrestrial problems seemed by comparison with the vastness before us. (Later, when I repeated this observation to Fiona, she heaved the most piteous sigh: "Mine don't!") But mostly we were content to look, and to wonder. Back home, Iain and I stuck silver stars on the inside of a black umbrella to make familiar constellations. The point where the spokes came together was the North Star, and we twirled the umbrella slowly to show the younger children how the stars revolve around the North Star. I pointed out that only at the North Pole would the North Star be directly overhead; in the Southern Hemisphere, stargazers look for the Southern Cross, not the Big Dipper. We looked at a globe, counted the countries south of the equator, and wondered why so very much of the Southern Hemisphere is water.

THE MARVEL OF WATER

Many of the mysteries of water were familiar to the children from hours of experimentation in the bathtub. Outside the tub, we had fun demonstrating that water has a skin: Evan filled a medicine-dropper with water, and I asked him to guess how many drops he could drip on a dime before the skin broke and the water overflowed. We were amazed—his record was seventeen! He reinforced the lesson, accidentally but emphatically, when he did a mighty belly flop at the swimming pool. The memory of his stinging belly is enough to remind him that water does indeed have a skin, and that, encountered at speed, it can feel distressingly akin to a brick wall.

An early lesson for Iain and me was that science experiments, like field trips, almost never turn out as expected. We spent fruitless hours trying to float a needle in a glass of water. Abject failure. And yet, if water has a skin, it should be possible…Years later, it finally hit me: the needle must be thin, and bone dry. A fat needle, or one that is slightly damp, will sink every time (at least we proved that much). My joy was unbridled when I discovered that if I put the thin, dry needle on a small piece of tissue, the paper absorbed water and sank, leaving the needle floating triumphantly. But back in the Dark Ages of experimentation, the infallibly sinking needle meant that Iain's usual response to my cheery, "It's time for an experiment" was to roll his eyes and groan, "Do we have to?" I was comforted when Robin described his high school experiments as typically ending in failure; indeed on one occasion he all but blew up the new, state-of-the-art science facility. And still, he went on to become a surgeon.

Science experiments were best tolerated when approached with a casual, "Let's just see what happens" attitude. Books with subtitles like *Easy science experiments using equipment you'll find around the house* were often exactly that and, much

to my surprise, frequently worked. Still, I was immensely relieved to discover that experimentation is far from the be-all
and end-all of science: observation, accurate measurement,
and classification play a part too. These I could handle.

CLASSIFICATION

We had learned the basics of classification from the button
box; trees provided a more organic way of furthering our studies. *Are the leaves evergreen or deciduous? If they're evergreen,
are they coniferous or broadleaf?* We learned that broadleaf
evergreens abound in the tropics, and that although broadleaf evergreen rhododendrons and azaleas thrive in the mod-
erate cold of the Pacific Northwest, in the truly frigid wastes
of Fargo, ND, only the narrow-leafed conifer will survive the
winter.

   In a conifer, how many needles come off in a bundle?
Whether in single needles, pairs, threes, or even up to seven
in a bundle, there will never be any variation on the same
tree. Some evergreen cones hang from the branches, others sit
upright on them. Deciduous leaves may be simple or compound. Simple leaves come off the tree one at a time, with a
distinctive horseshoe at the stem, where the leaf parts company with the twig. Compound leaves look like many separate
leaves but all fall off together, and only the main stem has the
distinctive horseshoe shape. Every year we were joined by our
friends the Henry family on a quest to find the season's most

spectacular leaves; a surprisingly noisy and energetic affair, this involved a lot of running and not infrequently tears. There followed the agonizing business of choosing the best from the overflowing grocery sacks we brought home, and relegating the rest to the compost heap. The very finest were preserved by ironing between two sheets of waxed paper; the results graced a glass bowl on the dining-room table till they were ousted by Christmas decorations.

Another annual tradition was the "leaf family." Parents and children each chose a leaf of appropriate size, and all were stuck onto the same sheet of construction paper. Heads, arms and legs were drawn on *ad lib*, the finished product covered in contact paper and put up on the kitchen wall. Next to it was another sheet of construction paper on which a variety of seed heads illustrated different methods of seed dispersal. Some were windborne, like the dandelion; some, like the poppy "pepper-pot," were shaken by wind or passing animals. Some stuck to animals and were brushed off far from the parent plant, while others were in the fruit eaten by birds or animals, deposited some time later along with a small packet of fertilizer. Weeding the garden together brought us into contact with all these differing types, as well as a particularly pernicious weed whose ripe seedpods never made it to the wall because they exploded at the slightest touch. Making a leaf family, collecting seed pods, deciding at what point a flower becomes a weed—all these activities had a common goal: opening the children's eyes to the wonders of the natural world around them.

PURCHASED SCIENCE KITS

Informal projects were augmented with kits from Stratton House, a company that caters expressly to homeschooling families. Each kit consists of a parent guide, a set of reproducible lessons, and all the equipment needed for two or more children to complete the lessons with minimal parental involvement. Thus were made some of our best science memories. In the astronomy unit, the Henrys joined us in discovering a very concrete (pun intended) way to demonstrate the incredible vastness of space. Jasmine and Camille, together with Fiona and Lorna, paced out the relative distances of the planets from the sun, whose enormous circumference was represented in part by an arc that completely filled the width of the quiet road in front of their house. The girls drew in the planets with colored chalk. The boys, Brent, Paul, Aaron and Evan, stayed on track with the girls for a while, but were derailed somewhere around Jupiter by some tantalizingly squishy blackberries, and even squishier bugs. Tamara and I amused ourselves by figuring out how far away the nearest star would be on this scale, and were astounded to learn that it would be in Portland, Oregon, some two hundred miles away. This insight into the immensity of a light-year has stayed with us to this day.

I became aware of TOPScience when Fiona was in middle school. A brilliant resource, this non-profit provides a host of fascinating science activities that use items even I could find in my kitchen. Parents will be reassured by simple but effective organizational principles that help them monitor academic progress. Looking over their website makes me want to round up random children off the street so I can have the fun of teaching this again. I can hear it now: the muttered "Watch out for the lady in that house—she's seriously crazy!" as the sirens grow louder, coming to take me away…

Usborne science books proved an inexhaustible source of education—and entertainment. One evening when everyone else was still eating dinner, I crumpled a piece of paper into an orange-sized ball; standing on a bar stool, I dropped the paper and an orange from the ceiling. Just as Usborne had predicted, they hit the ground at the same time. I forget now what exactly this proved, but it was a "Wow!" moment concerning wind resistance that piqued our interest to find out more someday.

For the most part, however, it was in seizing the teachable moment that the bulk of our science learning lay. Sometimes we went in search of the TM: an unusually low tide uncovered a treasure trove of deepwater flora and fauna at the beach; but sometimes it found us: small birds would fly into our breezeway and need help finding the exit. Several had to be nursed back to health in a shoebox first, and those that didn't make it yielded a close-up investigation of down, contour, and flight feathers, as well as types of beak and claws.

And one teachable moment that flew in through an open door didn't have any feathers at all…

FIONA AND THE BAT

"Mummy, there's a cweetchah on the cushion!"

Divining that three-year-old Fiona meant "creature," I glanced over. "No there isn't," I said absent-mindedly, "it's a banana skin."

She began to cry. "Mummy, it's a CWEETCHAH!"

I walked over to investigate the shriveled black object stuck between the cushions in the eating nook. "No, look. It's a bana...a ba...Oh! It's a *bat*!"

I treated our visitor with the utmost respect, having that very morning read in the newspaper about a well-intentioned teacher who, wanting to prove to her kindergarten class that "bats are our friends," had taken one in for show and tell. She encouraged each child to touch the webbed forelimbs that make it the only mammal capable of sustained flight, while the bolder students allowed the bat to crawl over their skin and nestle in their hair. Unfortunately, the bat turned out to be rabid. Each one of her students had to be given a free but excruciatingly painful rabies shot. Somehow I doubt that the experience made those children look on bats with increased trust and affection.

Having no desire to subject either my children or myself to such a fate, I took the cushion outside and thumped it on the balcony railings. The bat clung fast. I thumped harder. The bat's grip tightened. It took all my strength, but finally I dislodged the creature, and it hit the cement ten feet below with a rather wet noise.

Hot on the trail of the most exciting teachable moment of the decade, I scuttled down the outside stairs and regarded my victim, which was lying face down, unmoving. *Was it dead?* Taking a garden trowel, I carefully flipped it over. It glared at me from tiny, malevolent black eyes, opened its mouth to reveal two rows of razor sharp, blood-stained teeth, *and hissed at me*!

I have no recollection whatever of ascending the stairs. First thing I knew I was slamming the kitchen door behind me, shaking with fear, my heart hammering like an express train. Once I could draw breath, I squeaked (most unconvincingly), "Who wants to go and look at the nice bat?" There were no takers. Later on, when the thing had breathed its last, I pinged it unceremoniously over the bluff.

I think of it as "the teachable moment that wasn't."

TO THE ZOO!

Living close to Seattle allowed us access to the Pacific Science Center, as well as the zoo and other museums. The science center was a terrific place to soak up hands-on science, and "hands-on" meant that it was not soon forgotten. Scooping up water with Archimedes's screw brought to life the advance it represented over the cumbersome *shaduf* of the Egyptians. Even young Evan could turn the handle and watch the twisting corkscrew carry water up to the irrigation ditch. On road trips, we visited science museums in different cities and compared them to the PSC. Each one had something new to offer.

In the course of many years of zoo trips, I made two observations. The first is that many families take babies and children who are too young to enjoy the animals, burn out in the ensuing mayhem, and then fail to take older elementary, middle, and even high school students, who would have a far more mature and educated appreciation. The second point has to do with timing. A graph of animal activity reveals that virtually all creatures are busy early in the morning and again in the evening, with a gradual slide towards torpidity at noon. Visitors, by contrast, are few in the morning and evening, and most numerous at noon, when the majority of the animals are asleep. So "go early or go late" was our motto. Easy to say, hard to do: what about rush hour? How much idling in traffic listening to the sweet, familiar music of children whining, was I willing to tolerate, on the off chance we might catch the penguins in watery action? Going with another family helped with the traveling woes, and a back-to-school trip with the Henrys became a September tradition. Even if we didn't get there till lunchtime, and found most of the animals sound asleep, I consoled myself with the thought that a sleeping tiger is better than no tiger. It is also vastly superior to a virtual tiger, no matter how good the graphics.

SCIENCE IN THE KITCHEN

All the growing of plants and sprouting of seeds that went on both in and out of the kitchen taught the children worlds about science, as did cooking. Especially bread. I never lacked for an enthusiastic helper when it was time to bake, and each child in turn learned that yeast needs three things to thrive: water, food, and warmth. *What do people need to thrive?* Water, food, warmth—and love. Studies in Russian orphanages found that even when babies were kept warm and adequately fed, they failed to thrive in the absence of a loving touch. Maybe a little TLC wouldn't hurt the "yeasties" either: water just the right temperature, a pinch of sugar for food, and being left to rest undisturbed in a warm place (sounded pretty idyllic to me). We chose strong bread flour for its high gluten content, and noticed how stretchy the dough became as our vigorous kneading strengthened the gluten. One year, I ran out of strong flour to bake my traditional huge recipe of Christmas bread. A special trip to the store seemed far too much like hard work, so I made do with what happened to be on hand: low-gluten all-purpose flour. Never again! Even after the dough was kneaded the regulation 150 times, and a half-dozen stiffly beaten egg whites folded in, the yeasties were evidently on strike. The loaves were as sorry a sight coming out of the oven as they had been going in.

The only means of transporting live yeast across the continent during the Westward Expansion was sourdough. As part of a history unit, Fiona and I mixed together a cup of flour, one of water, and a quarter teaspoon of yeast, leaving it to sour for several days, loosely covered, on a counter. A second batch was made without commercial yeast, and left uncovered to be colonized by naturally occurring, "wild" yeast. The image of us lassoing wild yeast, rounding it up, and herding it into our bowl of starter had Fiona and me in stitches.

We baked loaves from both starters, after taking out enough dough to start up the next batch of bread, five days down the trail. I wondered if our family's appetite for bread could possibly keep pace with two sourdough starters, but the wild yeast batch soon turned rancid, and was summarily discarded.

Quick breads are leavened not by yeast, but by baking powder. This combination of an alkali (usually baking soda) and acid (typically cream of tartar) gives off carbon dioxide when mixed with a liquid. The gas bubbles introduce air into the bread just as the yeast bubbles do, the main difference being that yeast takes some time to work, while baking powder works instantly. "Double-acting" baking powder keeps working longer, but even so, without the strengthened gluten of yeast bread, quick breads are crumbly when cut.

To demonstrate how acid and alkali combine in a chemical reaction, I had the children make three small piles of baking soda. To the first we added water, which is neutral. No bubbles. To the second, we added water and a solid acid such as cream of tartar, and noted the resulting fizz. In the third pile, the addition of an acidic liquid—buttermilk or lemon juice—caused an equal exuberance of bubbles. We deduced that if a recipe for biscuits contains buttermilk, some of the acidic baking powder needs to be replaced by alkaline baking soda. We also realized that if, in the course of making butter-milk pancakes, we found we were out of buttermilk, we could "sour" the milk with a little vinegar or lemon juice.

A child who has helped cook chicken at 350°F and at 500°F will not be surprised to learn that heat accelerates rate of change, nor will one who has watched potatoes cook at a hard boil versus a gentle simmer. Those same potatoes can demonstrate osmosis: we left a potato in a bowl of water tinted with food coloring for a few hours, then cut the potato in half to see how the color had been absorbed.

While we had the food coloring out, I put a stick of celery in a jar of red-tinted water. Once the color had tinged the leaves, Evan carefully cut across the stalk and found that the vesicles carrying water up the plant were dyed bright red. One Fourth of July we made a white carnation patriotic by splitting its stem three ways and putting each end in a jar of red, blue, or clear water. Capillary action never looked prettier.

On Tuesdays, we enjoyed a snack that reinforced our knowledge of the Earth's structure: Earth Balls. A chocolate chip formed the core, and this was surrounded by peanut butter play dough representing the mantle. (To make the play dough we smooshed together one cup of peanut butter, half a cup of dry milk powder, and honey to taste—about 1/4 to 1/2 cup.) Each ball was then rolled in finely crushed graham cracker crumbs, which approximated the Earth's crust. Looking at a cross section diagram of the Earth, we realized that our "crust" was about one hundred times too thick, but it tasted good, and we never forgot the sequence: core—mantle—crust.

The center of the Earth is both liquid and solid: liquid, because the heat is so extreme that it melts even the hardest rock; and solid, because the pressure is so colossal that matter is super-compressed. How can something be at the same time liquid and solid? We never tired of answering that question with cornstarch and water. Made into a paste that could be thick or runny according to the whim of the moment, the cornstarch feels solid when tapped with a finger; but let that finger rest on the surface awhile, and it sinks into a pure liquid. All five fingers together can pull up an angular chunk, but once that chunk is airborne it will slip between the fingers and pour back into the bowl in a steady, liquid stream.

Just before we left Ireland, we held a fair to use up our excess homeschooling supplies. We had a grand time, with three-legged races, sack races, and a multitude of craft activities. The most popular attraction by far was the "Treasure Hunt at the Centre of the Earth." In the bottom of a huge bowl of corn-flour (as cornstarch is called there) and water, I hid numerous European coins that predated the bland uniformity of the euro. Children and adults alike shrieked with surprise at the changing consistency of the mix as they retrieved liras, marks, francs, and pesetas—and no matter how messy they got, their clothes had only to air dry and the cornstarch brushed out harmlessly.

INERTIA

Objects at rest tend to stay at rest. This was amply demonstrated every morning by those of our children who had attained the status of teenager. *Objects in motion tend to stay in motion* presented more of a challenge: eggs, cooked and uncooked, made the principle clear.

Liquid has more inertia than a solid, and an uncooked egg is mostly liquid. Spun on the countertop, a raw egg's movement is reluctant and uneven, while a hard-cooked egg, by contrast, spins fast and furious. This technique is a foolproof way to test whether a stray egg in the fridge is raw or cooked.

If it's raw, we found a handy way to tell how fresh it is: the air pocket at the blunt end gets larger as the egg ages. We put a fresh egg in a bowl of water; it sank. We took it out, and left it at room temperature. One week later, the blunt end tilted upward in the water. Another week, and it pointed straight up; seven days after that, the whole egg hovered near the surface. At this point we handled it with the utmost respect. The year Andrew broke the floating egg was memorable, but in entirely the wrong way: the smell of rotten egg pervaded the house for days. We also discovered that fresh is not always better: when hard-boiled, a day-old egg was virtually impossible to peel. It was infinitely easier with one that had aged a week or two.

According to one story, Christopher Columbus also knew a thing or two about eggs. A dinner guest belittled Christopher's accomplishment of discovering the New World (which Columbus believed to his dying day was China): "Anyone could have done it," the scoffer said, "anyone who kept sailing till he reached shore, that is." Columbus picked up an egg. After spinning it to make sure it was hard-boiled, he offered it to his detractor. "Here," he said, "balance it on its end." Try as he might, the guest met with nothing but failure: no matter how carefully he balanced it, the egg started to roll the second he let it go.

Columbus retrieved the egg, tapped the bottom sharply on the table, and stood it on its crushed shell. Outraged, his guest rose to his feet. "That's ridiculous!" he expostulated. "Anyone could do that."

"Yes, indeed," replied Columbus evenly, "anyone could. *But I did.*"

So, science includes experiments, classification, observation, and a little lateral thinking. Cooking was the universally popular science lesson: each child took turns helping to make dinner, and with it, memories. In the process, family traditions were passed on, and each child became a more than competent chef. To this day, when any of the geographically distant children come home, our normally rather humdrum cuisine is elevated to gastronomic heights; and at Thanksgiving the kitchen positively bursts with noise and gaiety as the children prepare a sumptuous feast.

The only unpopular thing about science in the kitchen is the volunteer experiments in putrefaction that lurk in the back of the fridge. If it's bread mold it could, theoretically, lead to a unit study on penicillin. A greenish-purple slime, however, is best relegated to the garbage quietly, and without fanfare. I wrote this limerick when Iain was seven:

> *There was a young man from View Ridge*
> *Who had to clean out his mum's fridge.*
> *It not only was slimy,*
> *But greasy and grimy,*
> *And full of green things that went squidge.*

Those "green things" might have been teachable moments on steroids, but it would take a stronger stomach than mine to make use of them.

11

MUSIC

*P*aul Mace was a close friend of the family in my growing years, and a remarkable cellist. Later, he married, and the couple was soon expecting their first baby. Every night, the father-to-be unwound after work by playing a movement or three from the Bach unaccompanied cello suites. Every night, his pregnant wife put her feet up and listened, smiling as she stroked the belly in which an energetic infant did calisthenics. When the baby was born he was a colicky little chap, but there was one thing he would invariably quiet down for: Bach unaccompanied. Apparently, music training begins before birth; a baby hears the same music as his mother, and learns to associate a particular piece of music with the unalloyed bliss of floating in the full-service, watery sanctuary of the womb.

There is no twenty-four-hour "womb" service in the crib, however—it is an altogether more hostile, more demanding environment. Food is not piped in automatically, neither is water, nor oxygen. And all these strange, harsh sounds! I tried to make the crib a quiet, safe oasis—no garish toys with their obnoxious, battery-operated noises; the noise pollution of our world will catch up with Baby soon enough. A wooden rattle makes a satisfying clacking sound, and soft toys with equally soft squeakers provide a comforting first discovery of cause and effect. The younger children all fell asleep to the strains of a wind-up music box inside a soft animal. What happy memories we have of sitting around campfires, listening to the contented sounds of Baby drifting off to sleep to the strains of "To Market, to Market, to Buy a Fat Pig."

BABY GOT RHYTHM

Nothing spells "freedom from siblings" quite as clearly as a stinky diaper, and I came to look forward to changing time as the only reliable alone time I had with the baby each day. Together, we built up quite a repertoire of songs, rhymes, and fingerplays, and sometimes, in a desperate attempt to keep a fractious baby amused in a shopping cart, I'd whip out a few ditties in the supermarket line. More often than not I found I'd made the sales clerk's day, not to mention the other shoppers'.

Sometimes other people made the music. Baby and I sang along with Raffi and John McCutcheon, or danced to classical marches and waltzes. Wanting the older children to appreciate how intimately we are hard-wired for rhythm, I showed them how to locate the pulse on their wrist, with its steady duple rhythm—*one, two, one, two, left, right, left, right*. A Sousa march was just the thing to get our military juices flowing; harkening back to his days as a military policeman, Robin would "Present—Baby! Right shoulder—Baby!" and go marching off, Baby squealing with glee as she drooled down his back.

Triple time was rather more complex and required a stethoscope to reveal the heart's triple beat: *THUMP bu-ump, THUMP bu-ump, ONE two-(three) ONE two-(three)*. For sheer enjoyment, nothing beat a classic waltz, preferably by Johann Strauss—it was practically impossible to listen to the *Blue Danube* without dancing. I got some precious piano practice time working my way through the waltzes of Frédéric Chopin while the children danced. They didn't really care what went on in the right hand, just as long as the left hand's regular ONE-two-three, ONE-two-three never faltered. I liked to imagine I was a privileged pupil of Chopin in nineteenth-century Paris, playing for her *enfants*. What a glorious dream!

Evan was dragged into these impromptu dance lessons whether he wanted it or not. On one occasion Lorna resorted to outright bribery, so great was her desire to perfect a socially polished younger brother. She promised him a dollar of her own money if he would but join her in dancing Chopin's Waltz in C-sharp minor. He acquiesced, and she was true to her word.

TEACHING MUSIC IN THE HOME

Researchers have found that playing an instrument stimulates the brain more profoundly than performing even the most complex mathematical calculations, so the very young child who learns a musical instrument is doing marvelous things for his developing brain. For beginners as young as three, or even two, the Suzuki approach has proven highly successful. But the cost of Suzuki lessons is high, both financially and emotionally. The parent must act as cheerleader, not only insisting that practice is done but also making it fun. I have known parents who can do this, and I take my hat off to them, but I emphatically do not count myself among their number. I needed a far less taxing way.

Accordingly, I augmented our random dance sessions with simple percussion instruments—tambourines, claves, finger cymbals, jingle bells—and as the children marched or waltzed, their improvised music naturally kept in rhythm. It was then a simple matter to write a few rhythmic patterns on index cards to show how notation relates to sound. Sheila has no memory of learning to read music. Words, yes; but, "I just grew up knowing how to read music."

While working with the non-family piano pupils that I squeezed into my schedule, I realized that children don't develop a sense of rhythm from simply listening to music—they also have to move to the beat. This is true even for listeners of traditional, tonal music, but the problem is compounded when tastes run to the more avant-garde: one pupil who had been raised on modern jazz had a desperately hard time keeping a regular beat. Analyzing meter in songs we heard on the car radio helped—and counting along to help the performer keep time—but mostly it was the rhythm of physical movement that kept us in good metrical shape.

If the children learned to keep rhythm by dancing, they learned to sing by singing. And where better to practice than in the car? I kept a supply of popular CDs on hand; sometimes the children would sing along enthusiastically, sometimes they'd just listen, and sometimes they'd groan, preferring silence, or their own random chatter. No matter—over the years, the effect of all that music added up.

AN EAR FOR AN ERA

Singing in the car was one thing; however, learning to appreciate the subtleties of classical music quite another. Wide dynamic ranges meant either that eardrums were ruptured by the *fortissimos*, the *pianissimo* passages were inaudible, or I risked life and limb by driving with one hand glued to the volume control. My search for a way to ensure that we listened to classical music at home, on a regular basis, ended on the Christmas that Robin and Iain made me a jigsaw puzzle board. From then on, we'd take the felt-covered, wooden-rimmed piece of plywood out after lunch and listen to music for an hour or so while working on a jigsaw.

The puzzles that appealed to the widest age range were 750-piece ones with distinctive images—the sort that, if we studied the picture hard enough, allowed us to figure out where any given piece belonged. Not for us the double-sided monsters with virtually identical pictures of rosy red apples on each side! Sheila, however, once tackled single-handedly a 1000-piece jigsaw of the Sistine Chapel, and was justly proud of her accomplishment. Satisfying and soothing, jigsaws provided another way to familiarize ourselves with great art and a wide variety of music. When I was organized enough—which was distressingly seldom—we concentrated on one musical era per month, rotating through medieval/renaissance, baroque, classical, romantic, and twentieth century.

Driving in the car, I'd flip the radio on to the classical music station and play "Guess the Period," and later, "Guess the Composer." Baroque was easy: the harpsichord was a dead giveaway. We learned to recognize the terraced dynamics—blocks of loud and soft—of Bach, Handel, and Vivaldi, contrasting them with the delicate phrases and gradual *crescendos* and *diminuendos* of Mozart and Haydn. The clarinet, introduced during Mozart's brief lifetime, instantly became his favorite woodwind, and he wrote some of his most hauntingly beautiful melodies for the instrument. Whenever we heard a clarinet, we knew we were in the Classical period or later. We listened for the aural scaffolding of classical sonata form, and the second-inversion tonic chord that signals the "look at what I can do!" bravura of the classical concerto's cadenza. Beethoven ushered in the stormy unpredictability of the Romantic era, with its high drama and greatly expanded symphonic orchestra, while music of the twentieth century sounds—well, "weird" might be a good adjective to begin with. So deeply ingrained did the habit become of listening intently and asking "Who wrote this, and when?" that whenever Sheila heard unfamiliar music wafting out of one of the practice rooms at her music school, she stopped to analyze who the composer might be.

IT'S 1900—NOW WHAT?

Many years ago, my two-year-old brother Ian was riding his tiny tricycle around our living room while my father listened to Igor Stravinsky's *Rite of Spring* on the gramophone. This ballet had literally caused a riot when it premiered in Paris in 1913, and an outraged American critic wrote, "He that could write the *Rite of Spring*/ If I be right, by rights should swing." Little Ian pedaled along, listening intently, then stopped dead in his tracks: "What's gone wrong with the gramophone, Dada?" Little did he know that he was echoing the sentiments of some of the most sophisticated musical minds of a half-century earlier.

"Serious" composers of the first half of the twentieth century had rather a hard time of it. Convinced that tonal music was dead and gone, they felt constrained to write atonal music with no identifiable tunes, which appealed to an extremely rarefied subset of the human race, often not including the composer himself. Arnold Schoenberg, a leading exponent of atonal music, created the dodecaphonic system, which organized the twelve musical tones according to principles that are intentionally inaudible, but treat each note equally (think of it as musical socialism). He was happy to revert to writing tonal music with singable melodies when he left behind his European angst and moved to sunny Southern California.

Other composers turned out music that audiences actually wanted to hear: slaves on the Southern plantations created the blues; Scott Joplin penned his immortal ragtimes; and Dixieland jazz delighted the multitudes. The invention of the phonograph meant that music was no longer restricted to those fortunate few who could either perform it at home or afford to patronize public concerts. Music was for everyone, and it meant money—big money.

An album of Vera Lynn's greatest hits recently topped the charts in Britain, more than seventy years after her heyday during World War Two. The nostalgic lyricism of songs such as "We'll Meet Again" captures the ethos of the time perfectly—in a way that the anguished minimalism of Schoenberg's compatriot, Anton Webern, cannot begin to approach. Besides, who has heard of Webern, anyway? At their best, popular artists have a way of speaking to their times that melds music and history into a symbiotic whole. How can we understand the twenties without the Charleston, or the sixties without The Beatles?

Music has enormous power over the unconscious mind; as pianist Karl Paulnack puts it, "Music has a way of finding the big, invisible moving pieces inside our hearts and souls and helping us figure out the position of things inside us." Nowhere is this emotional wrenching more vivid than at the movies. *ET* or *Star Wars* relies on music for their dramatic impact almost as much as did the operas of Richard Wagner, one hundred years earlier. Wagner was the first to capitalize on the power of a musical phrase (*leitmotif*) to evoke a specific character, event, or emotion. James Horner was just one of many contemporary movie composers who used this technique to haunting effect. Whenever we saw his name in the credits, we would try to listen attentively. This is hard to do, so effectively does music slide past the conscious mind to work directly on our feelings. Shifting harmonies speak the language of emotions, melodic fragments pique our intellects, while rhythm speaks directly to our physical bodies. These three elements combine to dictate the moviegoer's reaction to events on the screen. We watched the terrifying scene in *Wait Until Dark* where a blind Audrey Hepburn is being stalked by a murderer, with the sound turned off. Funny thing—no suspense! We also found that, devoid of a soundtrack, the most passionate love scene seems screamingly funny.

STARTING LESSONS

Some teachers advocate starting lessons as early as three years old, while others recommend waiting till the child can read fluently, aged seven or older. I have taught piano beginners aged four to fifty-four, and found that it takes about six months to teach the average four-year-old what a keen ten-year-old can learn in as many days.

But—and it's a big but—music is not about product, but process. It stimulates the growing brain in a unique way, and young music students frequently excel at reading and math, as well as social skills. This musical advantage may arise because playing an instrument requires the creative use of three senses simultaneously: hearing, sight, and touch. (One mother proudly told me that her son used these three senses playing video games—hardly what I would call creative activity!) Music also teaches delayed gratification: *I practice today in order to sound better tomorrow.*

Precocious youngsters bring their own problems. When Lorna taught piano as a high schooler, two of her pupils were sisters, ages four and six. The four-year-old could do anything Lorna asked of her, with infinitely greater facility than her sister, and look impossibly adorable while doing so. And she knew it! She soon realized, however, that she could get by well enough with minimal practice, and her exuberant talent began to fizzle. Meanwhile her sister plodded steadily along, eventually emerging by far the stronger player; yet again, the tortoise beats the hare.

Being a pianist myself, it seemed natural for me to start teaching Iain when he expressed an interest in the piano. I soon discovered the importance of scheduling. His lesson was on Monday, but week after week something would turn up to bump it to Tuesday. Then somehow Tuesday didn't work, so how about Wednesday? Or maybe Thursday—oh, let's just leave it till next Monday. Iain's pianistic progress, predictably enough, was vanishingly slow. I resolved to fix a regular time and stick to it as closely as if I were paying an outsider. Gazing sternly into a mirror, I practiced saying, "I'm sorry, Iain can't play this afternoon; he has his piano lesson." Somewhat to my surprise, other parents took me at my word and it worked—both for him, and later for the girls. But I had other things to worry about with them.

I graduated from England's Royal College of Music with a degree in piano teaching, and spent years studying pedagogy with the Music Teachers National Association of America, so I don't think accreditation was the problem. But somehow, approximately 50 percent of the lessons I gave my girls ended in a maelstrom of tears and desolation (mostly, but by no means exclusively, limited to the students). I never understood it—my other pupils loved me, but Lorna and Sheila could be guaranteed to turn on the waterworks every time, no matter how patient and forbearing I tried to be. Fiona, thankfully, not so much, though even she had her moments. Once the basics were mastered, I was happy to turn them over to another teacher, whose many inspiring qualities included not being their mother.

Thinking that my daughters' lachrymosity might be connected to the pressure of my expectations, I decided to aim really low with Evan. My goal was that, at the end of the year, he would know a little bit more about playing the piano than he knew at the beginning, and by jingo, he did! The saying is true: "If you aim at nothing, you'll hit it every time"; but unfortunately, this really wasn't fair on Evan. While we had no tears, we also saw slow progress, and today he is nowhere near as accomplished a pianist as his inborn talent would allow. (As a happy footnote, he sidestepped his mother's pedagogical deficiencies and taught himself to play the guitar quite proficiently with no help from anyone.)

When the children were young, I allowed myself to bask in the illusion that there were infinite years ahead for them to improve technique and learn more repertoire. The sad truth is that childhood is a precious, non-renewable resource, and twelfth grade comes all too soon. With it, the door to learning an instrument swings shut, usually forever.

HOW NOT TO BEGIN VIOLIN

When Fiona expressed an interest in starting the violin, I was faced with the immediate prospect of finding an instrument and a teacher, and driving her to lessons each week. There was also the small matter of money. I was happy to find a teenage girl nearby who was a competent violinist, very sweet-natured, and didn't charge much. *What a find!* I thought, and chose to ignore her lack of teaching experience, even when she quibbled about the smallest musical detail and kept Fiona working on the same measure for weeks. We stuck with her for two years before upgrading to a more advanced teacher. That was when I found out what a terrible price we had paid for those two years of "bargain" lessons. Fiona had developed serious technical problems that an experienced teacher would have nipped in the bud. As it was, it took many frustrating years of practice to unlearn what she had so diligently learned incorrectly. The "affordable, convenient" lessons proved to be time, energy, and money down the tubes—Fiona would have been better off starting from scratch, two years later.

What I should have done was to interview a couple of teachers by phone, find out when their student recitals were, take Fiona to be impressed and inspired, and entrust her musical education to the very best I could afford. A nascent music gremlin threatened to take up residence and grow sleek and fat, but I banished it emphatically. Instead I opted for a more positive outcome, and the younger children benefited from her experience. Lorna on cello, Sheila on viola, and Evan on violin all had excellent teachers from the outset.

PERFORMANCE OPPORTUNITIES

What is music if it is not performed? I manufactured opportunities for the children to play in public by having regular family concerts in our home—monthly at first, then, as the repertoire became more complex, every two or three months. My mother, proud Granny that she was, went into overdrive: inviting friends and neighbors, making pots and pots of tea, and baking piles of Scottish shortbread. We didn't have the MGM lion roaring to get the program underway, but a Portuguese water dog jumping through a hula hoop brought the house down every time—and Kidu loved all the attention! The family performed, and basked in the compliments. The older children gained experience in printing programs, and they all learned to stand still and look the audience in the eye while announcing their pieces. They also learned the courtesy of bowing to acknowledge applause; it may feel awkward and embarrassing, but it's the performer's way of saying, "Thank you for listening."

Our visitors loved everything about the concerts, and their enthusiasm encouraged the performers to overcome any initial reluctance. As Sheila argued so adamantly, *nobody else's* mothers made their children play concerts on Sunday afternoons—why did *their* mother have to be so *strange*? Between family concerts, chamber music, and youth symphonies, the children had plenty of opportunities to perform, as well as to taste the enormous pleasure of making music with other musicians, both at and away from home.

INSPIRATION

Nothing inspires a young performer like being exposed to greatness, whether in the artist or the instrument. When I was eleven, Rachmaninoff's touring piano—a twelve-foot concert grand—spent a few days in Clifton Village, the part of Bristol where I grew up, and I was privileged to be given the opportunity to play it. I can still remember the thrill of entering the room where it sat waiting, and the overwhelming joy of hearing the first Brahms Rhapsody emerge under my very own fingers from the keys that Sergei Rachmaninoff himself had played. Just for a moment, greatness lay within my grasp. For string players, opportunities are relatively abundant: it is not uncommon to run into an Amati, Guarneri, or even Stradivarius violin, which a breathless youngster may be permitted to touch. So blood-curdlingly competitive has music performance become, that instrumentalists who belong at Carnegie Hall or the great concert halls of Europe may be found in the most surprising venues. Some years ago, the "heroic virtuoso" Mark Salman played all twelve of Franz Liszt's dazzlingly difficult *Transcendental Études* (which Salman learned—and memorized—in three months, in response to an associate's challenge; an extraordinary feat!) at Snohomish County Public Utility District #1 Auditorium, to an audience of maybe 120.

Not only are stellar musicians performing for audiences one-tenth the size they deserve, but they are invariably delighted to talk to their audience, especially youngsters, when the music is done. What to say? "Thank you" is always a good place to start, followed by something that shows you've been paying attention—"The waltz made me want to dance" or "I loved how angry you made the Beethoven sound."

Nor was our choice of concerts limited to classical music. Everett Civic Music, part of the national Civic Music

Association, put on eight concerts a year in a wide variety of styles, ranging from symphonies, soloists and chamber music, to classic rock, jazz, Viennese café music, ballet…We had enormous fun making new musical acquaintances, and were inspired to seek out more bargain-priced or free concerts within a few miles of home.

PRACTICE DOLDRUMS

No matter how great the inspiration, progress in playing an instrument does not follow an orderly, straight line leading upwards to mastery. Rather, it is a series of ascents interspersed with plateaus of varying duration. Every performer has endured the frustration of long periods when even the most diligent practice seems to lead to no improvement—indeed, hard-won gains may appear to be slipping away. So it came as no surprise when I heard anguished cries of "PLEASE may I try the tuba?" or simply, "I really want to give up the violin!"

My answer to the first question was invariably no. It is only too tempting to "instrument-hop," reaching the same plateau on each instrument before switching to another. When Fiona brought me a well-reasoned letter outlining six compelling reasons I should let her switch to bassoon, I pointed out to her that in four semesters she could take four instruments to the level of the first plateau—or persevere on her violin and gain a fair degree of mastery. As to the second question, Evan repeatedly begged me to let him give up the violin, and words cannot express his jubilation when I finally saw the light around eighth grade—the age most students quit. He has never regretted it, and I recognize now that the violin never really floated Evan's boat. His time is far better spent with his guitar.

Sheila is a different story. Between the ages of eleven and twelve she must have beseeched me a hundred times, often with tears coursing down her cheeks (assuming she had any left after her piano lesson), to allow her to give up the viola. And believe me, Sheila can be *extremely* persuasive! I am horrified to think how close I came to giving in; but instead I straightened my backbone and braced myself for thunderclaps of strife and discord. Now they have rolled away, leaving in their wake a halcyon pastoral scene: Sheila well on her way to becoming a professional violist. As she stands poised to draw the first note out of the instrument that now seems to be a part of her, she is ecstatic that she did not get her own way. The sweetest words I never expected to hear: "Thank you, Mummy, for not letting me give up the viola."

WHICH INSTRUMENT?

Lorna was sixteen when we moved to Ojai; equally proficient on piano and cello, she had to choose which instrument she should focus on for her last two years at home. A first-rate cello teacher lived but five minutes away, while the only piano teacher who was a member of Music Teachers National Association lived at least an hour away (and that only if the god

of traffic was in a benevolent mood). We both knew that the
piano was Lorna's first and greatest love, but the geographical
considerations overwhelmed me, and I allowed them to dictate
our choice. Looking back, I deeply regret it. At the end of two
years, Lorna was not a cellist, but a pianist who was good at the
cello. The difference lies in motivation: for a cellist, dragging a
cello out of its case, tuning it, and locating a place to ram the
spike home without causing bloodshed is all part of the fun.
To a pianist, it is a daunting proposition at best, and at worst,
a pain in the neck; Lorna would far rather sit at a piano and
unlock its beauties with a simple touch. Fiona and Sheila, too,
find themselves drawn to the piano when they're home; it's so
inviting, and offers itself most obligingly for duets, accompani-
ments, and improvisation.

The ability to play an instrument is never really lost.
Lorna's cello teacher received a call from a forty-seven-year-old
man who explained that he'd studied cello as a teen, hadn't
played in over thirty years, but now his daughter was getting
married and he wanted to play *Ave Maria* at the wedding.
Angie's heart sank. This sounded painful. But her interest
was piqued, and at her request, he arrived for his first lesson
not having practiced at all. Angie tuned the cello, handed it
to him—and he played! Intonation came back to him as she
listened, and within minutes he was playing in tune. Vibrato,
the bane of the adult beginner, was still right there; he remembered how to read the notes, and his tone quality, scratchy at
first, rapidly improved.

So even if Lorna has moved on and chosen to develop that infinitely portable instrument—her singing voice—piano and cello technique lie dormant in fingers and brain, awaiting a reawakening when she again has time to practice. Who knows, perhaps one day she'll be playing Bach unaccompanied to her unborn child.

12

SPORTS AND FITNESS

*O*verweight and bespectacled, I was always the last one chosen for any sports team. Whenever there was an odd number of players, I was the one left over. When the number was even, however, I got my chance to shine.

Rounders was a primitive form of baseball played in English girls' schools in the middle of the last century. For all I know, it is played to this day, though I rather hope not. It was a cool, damp day in late April when my bat connected with the ball and I dribbled a weak hit to left field. My glasses steamed with pride. *Now I'll show them*, I thought. *Now they'll see how fast I can run.* And run I did, all the way to third base. What I didn't realize until I stopped was that our team's star runner had been holding on second. As I zoomed triumphantly past her, I unwittingly relegated her to the benches. My ears burned under the castigation I received from my teammates. Team sports and shame became permanently linked in my brain.

Meanwhile, in North Dakota, Robin was finding his own reasons to give up baseball. It was the bottom of the ninth, his team was ahead by three runs. Bases loaded: two outs. The batter hit a routine fly ball into shallow left field. At shortstop, Robin moved back to catch it. He waited confidently as the ball began its descent, glove at the ready. This was his game-winning moment. But what's this? The ball bounced off his right shoulder, into left field. Two runs scored. Frantically, he chased down the ball, and threw it—straight into the bleachers. Two more runs scored. Robin had single-handedly lost the game. He took off his glove, stuffed it under his arm, and rode away on his bike without a word. Later that week he got glasses, and his whole world changed. Things looked sharp, and in focus! *Now* he understood what the coach meant when he said, "Watch the ball into your glove." But alas, it was too late for Robin.

Despite his parents' insufficiencies on the sports field, the first time Iain saw a ball it was love at first sight. Playing catch in the front yard soon became our favorite pastime; high fly balls were interspersed with hard line drives to keep him diving into the flowerbeds, or rolling on the lawn, as he made a brilliant succession of game-winning plays that brought the Mariners closer to their pennant ambitions. Some evenings we played so long and with such fervor that I awoke the next morning unable to move my right arm. Trips to the ocean spelled death to my shoulder—so inviting was the vast expanse of beach that we only stopped playing when the last light had drained from the western sky, and Iain was a sodden, sand-encrusted lump.

My enthusiasm was more muted, however, when it came to organized sports: baseball practices and games involved driving clear across town or even further. Andrew and Fiona made their disapproval very vocal and the hours spent watching practices in the boiling hot Washington sun (well, it felt like that to me) dragged on interminably. Having a Newfoundland for a backrest attracted pretty well every unattached sibling on the field, but as weeks turned into months, my enthusiasm for revealing that she weighed 135 pounds and ate only three cups of dry dog food per day began to dwindle. Had Iain been even a little bit happy or enthusiastic on the way home, I might have felt that my heroic efforts were sufficiently rewarded. As it was, he seemed to be perpetually frustrated: either he'd played well and his team members had let him down, or he had played poorly and let his team down. Either way, it was not pleasant. I soldiered on. *Sports are so popular*, I told myself. *I must be missing something...*

Many years later, watching Evan play baseball, I would revise some of my earlier opinions. More than just an exercise in futility, participating in organized sports helped Evan learn about teamwork and the importance of keeping his body in good shape, not only because Mum and Dad told him to, but because his coach did too and he did not want to let his teammates down.

However, I was still underwhelmed by the amount of actual exercise that the many hours of practice yielded, and deeply resented the way they cut into our family time. This had been true back when Andrew started playing special ed baseball, thus putting an end to family dinners and leisurely evenings for the foreseeable future; I rebelled. I said, "Time and finances allow for either music *or* sports. Only a tiny minority of athletes go on to play sports beyond high school, whereas music stays with a person their whole life." I pulled myself up to my full height, which was still, at the time, significantly taller than all my children. "In this family," I proclaimed, "we are going to do…MUSIC!"

So music it was. This left the question of how to instill and maintain habits necessary for good health: the Bernhofts were not going to become a family of couch potatoes—not even singing couch potatoes—if I could help it. I wanted to create a family culture that involved the expenditure of energy in a variety of everyday ways; sprinting, walking, and gardening all utilize muscles and burn calories, but appeal to rather different lifestyles.

I looked to my childhood for hints.

MY FAMILY BACKGROUND

I was fortunate enough to have been brought up in an active family which greatly valued physical fitness. My father was director of music at Clifton College, a private school for boys in Bristol, England. When not riding his bike to and from the school, he made year-round use of the squash and fives (handball) courts. Somehow, despite sending a small, hard, rubber ball hurtling at terrifying speed and ricocheting wildly off floor, walls, and ceiling, he and his playing partner (not infrequently, my brother Ian) avoided grievous bodily harm. Tennis was reserved for those fleeting summer months when the sun put in its tentative appearance; I would either coerce Ian or a friend into playing with me, or spend hours hitting a ball against an ever-obliging brick wall.

I learned, to my astonishment, that my father's mother — *my grandmother* — actually played at Wimbledon! Admittedly, this was back in the days when ladies' tennis was a rather polite affair that involved patting the ball back and forth over the net while taking care not to trip over voluminous white skirts. A time-warp contest between Margaret Prentice and Serena Williams would be like pitting a push lawnmower against an armored tank. Nevertheless, I looked with renewed respect at the shriveled, crotchety figure, gasping into her inhaler between Woodbine cigarettes. Perhaps all those years patting balls back and forth were what gave her the strength and willpower to outlive her doctor's prediction by twenty wheezing, chain-smoking years. Be that as it may, knowing I had such an illustrious forebear gave my virtually nonexistent athletic ambitions a decided boost.

Although my father was a star player in Clifton College's master's cricket team (self-deprecatingly dubbed "The Lobsters" on account of their somewhat unorthodox style of bowling and the color most of them turned in the course of an afternoon game), in my eyes, his *tours de force* happened off the playing field. He was fond of "going inverted," and could not only stand on his head for extended periods, but could drink a pint of beer while doing so. I have never met anyone else who can make this boast, and was beginning to doubt my memory, but YouTube provided a burly chap in an English pub doing the deed, albeit with considerably more profanity than I remember of my father. Sad to tell, though I became quite adept at standing on my head, and even found it surprisingly restful in the later months of pregnancy, I never managed to polish off so much as a small glass of dry sherry with my feet in the air. Perhaps this is one talent that will skip a generation.

He played the piano upside down, too. Not standing on his head (though if anyone could, it would have been him); instead he lay supine on the piano bench, head under the keyboard, forearms crossed, and improvised. Having perfect pitch and a phenomenal musical memory, he could play practically anything by ear; but playing it upside down was even more impressive, and locals at the pub showed their appreciation in pints of best bitter lined up on top of the piano. Not being of drinking age, the only part of this I was privy to was his morning-after headache. Many years later, inspired by Mozart's antics in the historically questionable but brilliantly entertaining movie *Amadeus*,, I found I could crank out a fairly reputable Bach minuet with my navel pointing at the ceiling: a pale shadow of my father's legendary abilities, maybe, but a shadow nonetheless.

When it came to acknowledging applause after a concert, he had another surprise up his sleeve. Doffing his jacket and removing keys and loose change from trouser pockets, he'd run a few steps and turn a complete handspring, landing on his feet to the tumultuous roars of several hundred young men and one blushing, adoring daughter.

My mother had been brought up in a golf club in eastern Scotland, so her greatest pleasure was to spend a warm Sunday afternoon hitting a golf ball—"bashing a ball about," she called it—in vacant fields near home. Arthritis set in early in neck and knees, but not before she firmly established the walking habit in me. She used to push me miles and miles—to the shops, to the library, to drop in on friends—first in a pram, then a pushchair. It was not long after I started to walk, however, that I became the proud owner of a bicycle, and left her behind while I enjoyed long evening rides with my father and brother. These rides augmented the more mundane joys of getting from point A to point B during the day, and even after the family purchased its first car when I was seven, foot- and pedal-power remained our primary form of locomotion.

CREATING AN ACTIVE FAMILY CULTURE

Shortly before leaving England, I was staggered to learn (in a documentary on Australia) that there exist in the world streets with no sidewalks, because *nowhere is within walking distance!* Shops, library, neighbors—you hop in the car. Unbelievable! I thought nothing of a five-mile stroll to the Bristol Art Centre and back to watch some obscure foreign film, and was never happier than when the skies opened to drench me. Not only did the rain give me a sense of solidarity with the sultry heroines in French movies, who seemed to hold their most meaningful conversations behind rain-swept car windscreens with the wipers going full blast, but it also dampened the ardor of amorous workmen perched on scaffolding, high above the street. Their wolf-whistles made me desperately self-conscious—*which* foot is it that comes after "left," again?—but not (quite) badly enough to make me abandon my trusty feet.

Even living in LA, my feet could take me to and from the bus stop a mile away, but in the interests of speed and economy I preferred to cycle everywhere surface streets could take me. Also in the interests of economy, the lights I chose were powered not by batteries but by the rotation of the wheels; thus when the pedals were not moving, the lights gave no clue as to my existence. I was invisible. I looked on my nightly passage through the gridlock on Wilshire Boulevard at the I-405 overpass as a contest with Fate. Every time I emerged successful, I mentally chalked up another notch on my tally. I had cheated death one more time.

So it was not until we moved to Everett that the Australian nightmare became reality: there were no sidewalks on our street! My London-inspired dream of living without a second car withered and died; my sole act of defiance against automobile culture lay in pushing one or more of the children six tenths of a mile up the hill to the gas station, and returning home with three gallons of milk strapped securely in while the ousted children walked. (Another small triumph: most weeks I bought significantly more gallons of milk than petrol. I'm not sure if there is an environmental award for this; there definitely should be.)

These enforced walks, however, were hardly enough to keep the family fit, so I looked for a Plan B. It helped that Robin set a good example as an ex-marathoner (the first marathon he ran was the original course in Greece!) who still pounded the pavement regularly, lifted weights, and practiced *Qigong*. It also helped when our low-energy Newfoundland passed on to that great dog-treat factory in the sky, and was replaced by Enkidu, the Portuguese water dog, who required at least two thirty-minute walks a day to keep his canine exuberance in check.

What an opportunity for some mother-child quality time, I thought. *Walking together—what wonderful, Hallmark-worthy memories we will make!* I could almost hear the fond reminiscences, many years in the future: "I remember on our daily walks, how Mum always used to say…"

Or not. The only audience for my rambling soliloquies on the Meaning of Life had four legs, and the high point of *his* walk came when we stopped at our regular lamppost so he could, as I liked to put it, "check his pee-mail." I imagined what Kidu "saw" as he sniffed the messages left by his doggy pals, and amused myself no end with images of a canine election campaign, scratch 'n sniff posters of the candidates' rear ends adorning every lamppost. "VOTE FOR ME, I SMELL DELICIOUS!" (This may help explain why the children were so eager to stay home…)

"PLAN B" UNFURLED

Shortly after Lorna was born, we rented a house by the beach. Two-year-old Fiona toddled determinedly towards the water, squealing at the top of her voice, "I'm going to swim in the BIG swimming pool!" Robin and I looked at each other in horror, made a frantic lunge, and successfully restrained our would-be mermaid, but it was agreed: learning to swim was nonnegotiable. We both wanted to be able to relax in or near water, knowing that nobody was likely to drown. I signed them all (apart from Baby Lorna) up for lessons.

Because of the layout of the public pool, each child spent only a few minutes of their thirty-minute lesson in the water, and a tiny fraction of that in direct instruction. My gremlin's alter ego (the encouraging one) chimed in: "That's pathetic," he said, witheringly. "Even *you* could do better than *that*." My ears pricked up. Could it be that, for once, he was talking sense?

If proficiency as a swimming teacher were measured in goose bumps, I'd be among the best qualified on the planet. As a girl, I swam regularly in the outdoor pool of Clifton College, which, heated only by the slanting rays of a feeble northern sun, I considered balmy at 62°F, a bit more of a challenge in the high 50s. The skin color associated with swimming was a rather fetching pale greyish blue, splotched delicately with vermillion. These subtle hues were nothing, however, compared to the deep navy blues and magentas occasioned by my Easter dips in the North Sea, that frigid, Arctic-fed body of water lying between the east coast of Scotland and Norway. That I did not instantly succumb to hypothermia was due in part to my determination ("giving up the will to live" is a prime cause of death in these waters), and in part to the pebbly beaches. The pounding waves stirred up a ceaseless barrage of small rocks which pummeled first my lower extremities then, as I braved body-surfing, my whole torso; without the challenge of providing blood to so many superficial lacerations, my circulation might well have shut down altogether.

Thus I felt admirably well equipped to introduce my wee bairns to the temperate waters of Forest Park Swimming Pool, and to thrill them with tales of my adventures in the North Sea when they complained about being a bit chilly. (I'm certain they found my stories inspiring, though they never actually said so.) Swimming lessons started at home; they blew bubbles in the bathtub, which accustomed them to the feel of water on their faces—and up their noses. Weekly swim sessions soon appeared on the schedule. To keep the gremlin firmly on my side (it was rather pleasant having an ally for a change), these were geared to providing maximum H_2O exposure all round. I swam laps with one child clutching each arm and Andrew clasped round my neck, destroying my right eardrum in a shrieking aquatic frenzy.

Once the vital skill of keeping water out of the nostrils without holding one's nose was mastered, each child was confident enough to figure out, largely by trial and error, how to stay afloat, and even attain forward momentum. A bit later, Iain and Fiona both enjoyed a good workout for a season with the YMCA swim team, in the course of which their form improved dramatically, but for recreational swimming, some variant on the doggy-paddle worked just fine. "Whatever floats your torso," one might say.

A baseball field just up the road was the site of many all-family games. (I particularly remember one a few days before Evan was born—my strike zone was unusually small, and my hustle to first base more of a waddle.) Usually, however, we played in the front yard, in the long, soft summer evenings of the Pacific Northwest. Wooden bats and softballs gave way to their whiffle counterparts as the children grew stronger and could routinely hit the ball "out of the park," but they emphatically drew the line at sponge balls and bats, judging them too big an insult to their prowess. We also played some fairly wild and woolly football games, with rules adapted to the children's ages, abilities, and tendencies to get hurt, but football never quite achieved baseball's mystique.

Basketball proved infinitely adaptable: the little children shot rolled-up socks into wastepaper baskets, while Iain was something of a fixture at the hoop above the garage door, practicing free throws and charging the net against a host of imaginary foes. As his siblings reached the required level of mastery, they joined him in games of H-O-R-S-E; Iain amused himself by making stupendously balletic moves which even he was hard-pressed to repeat, and his little siblings' efforts to do so almost always ended in sweat and tears, and not infrequently, blood.

SPORTS AND ACADEMICS

Although his athletic ambitions were thwarted by his mother's infuriating lack of vision, sports still played a vital part in Iain's education. He looked on reading as a curiosity to be dabbled in only enough to keep Mum's insistent prodding at a bearable level—until that magical day, somewhere in his seventh year, when he realized that the *Everett Herald* that plopped on our doorstep every afternoon was filled with everything he wanted to know about the Seattle Mariners baseball team. Now he had reason to read and there was no stopping him. True, it took a few years to widen his interest beyond the sports section, but since then the scope of his reading material has left me in the dust.

Also thanks to the Mariners, our whole family learned what a bar graph is. Iain stuck a sheet of graph paper on the wall and, starting from the middle line, filled in one space up for every game they won, and one space down for every game they lost. It wasn't long before he devised a color scheme to track the other teams as well: each team had its own colors, listed on a separate key. At a glance, we could tell how many games the Mariners had lost against New York, and estimate how far below 500 they were. (Except in the glorious 2001 season, when they won 116—count 'em!—games. That was the only year Iain was sufficiently motivated to finish out the season with the bar graph.)

During our customary morning sessions playing catch, I perfected a handy method for practicing fractions and percentages. I throw the ball, he catches it. "One out of one: a hundred percent." I throw it again; he drops it. "One out of two: fifty percent." The next one, he catches. "Two out of three: sixty-six and two-thirds percent." And the next one. "Three out of four: seventy-five percent." And so on. The game kept me on my toes—quick, what percentage is four out of seven? Five out of nine? I didn't use a calculator; guesstimates were good enough. Once he'd become a serious baseball fan, batting averages and on-base percentages became part of Iain's mental framework, and our games of catch reverted to "just for fun."

Washington State mandated drug education as part of the health curriculum: my theory was that if a child once experiences what it is to be fit, to have a body that willingly does what is asked of it and has energy left over for more, drugs would be a hard sell. Accordingly, my anti-drug warnings were cursory: "(child's name)—don't do drugs." Groans and major eye-rolling: "Right, Mom." Sheila knows more about drugs than the rest of us put together, having attended an anti-drug lecture aimed at high schoolers, which might as well, she claimed, have been called "Twenty Ways You Never Imagined to Get Stoned."

THE TRAMPOLINE

Robin used to work in emergency rooms, so his reaction when I suggested buying a trampoline was an outraged, "Are you crazy?" He capitulated in the end, but insisted on three rules: only two people bouncing at a time, they must be of roughly equivalent weights (or the lighter is likely to go pinging off into the stratosphere), and no flips. This latter brought the most protests, but I was adamant. "You are perfectly free to break your neck," I'd say, "but not on our trampoline." Nobody ever argued with that! One time, the "only two people" rule was broken, and our sole accident resulted: Fiona put her front tooth through her top lip. Thereafter I enforced the rule strictly, and was gratified to see how ingenious the children were in finding their way around it. Anywhere from two to ten children would sit on the trampoline while one hardy soul tried to bounce them all. It's like trampolining in treacle—I know, I tried. But the letter of the law was obeyed: only one person was actually bouncing.

On a warm summer's afternoon, the area underneath the trampoline became a shady nook for a tea party. And more than one hot summer's night found the children sleeping soundly on its cool, flexible mat. Though the trampoline made the trek to Ireland, it did not make it back; we left it with some friends who, even all these years later, still refer to us as "the trampoline family."

FAT...OR PERHAPS NOT

Organized sports in schools have, to a considerable extent, fallen victim to their own success. Costs involved, from uniforms and tournament travel to summer camp, can be prohibitive, especially for the less affluent. Then there is the ugly problem of foul language and bad sportsmanship (and I don't mean by the players). Fond dreams of a full-ride athletic scholarship to a prestigious university can be dashed by a coach who fails to allot sufficient playing time, or an umpire's questionable call. With tens, even hundreds of thousands of dollars on the line, it's small wonder parents get ugly: the old saying "It's not whether you win or lose, but how you played the game" has been superseded by "Winning isn't everything; it's the only thing." Meanwhile, underpaid and buried in paperwork, at least one coach was rumored to have been overheard swearing that the best place to coach would be an orphanage.

And yet…team sports are popular for a reason: they're great games from humble origins, and they're really fun to play! Summer get-togethers of homeschooling families frequently involved a pick-up game of some sport or other, and it didn't take long to figure out that these games were considerably more fun if those involved had some faint idea of rules and basic techniques. Ultimate Frisbee, for instance, got quite a boost when players were able to throw and catch a Frisbee. As I talked to mothers, I learned that establishing and maintaining fitness was a concern for many. The way was paved for Family Athletic Training, FAT for short.

While in high school, Iain helped me organize and run FAT, partly from altruistic motives and partly because it would look good on his college application (which had a daunting amount of space for "Volunteering in the Community"). Iain and I found a nearby school that was not being used, and obtained permission to use the playing fields in fine weather, the basement when it rained. We consulted a library book about teaching sports in a homeschool setting. Our close friends were quick to sign up and help spread the word; soon, we had enough players for two teams.

Each session began with stretches, some remembered from my yoga years, and some found in books or online. Every student brought a jump rope, and the next ten minutes were devoted to learning this basic skill. I had purchased two long ropes, and for five minutes the children jumped in and out to chanted playground rhymes: "Apples, peaches, pears and plums/ Tell me when your birthday comes!" We even tried some Double-Dutch. The remainder of the hour was taken up with the basics of the sport-of-the-month: soccer, football, basketball, Frisbee, volleyball. The goal: for each child to know enough to avoid humiliation on a pick-up team, and maybe even to have a little Family Universal (k)Now-how, aka FUN!

HOWARD'S END

To my English friend Howard, who described himself as "physically inept cannon-fodder, the stomped-upon rather than the stomper," the sports field was the very pit of hell. Shunning it, he pursued fitness through a wide variety of activities including hiking, cycling, sailing, mountain climbing, and white-water rafting. The universal reaction to news of his death from a silent heart attack when he was only sixty-two was an incredulous, "But he was the fittest person I know!"

And so he was. While the incentive that team sports provide can be a positive force for some people, for the Howards of this world, there are many other physically challenging adventures that can pave the way to a fit life and an interesting, happy one. I think Howard would have approved of FAT, and it is to his memory that this chapter is most fondly dedicated.

13

IN WHICH WE GAIN PERSPECTIVE:
FOREIGN LANGUAGES AND HISTORY

*T*he best place from which to gain a new perspective on our world and our day-to-day problems is, arguably, outer space. Floating there, watching the luminous beauty of the blue planet we call home as it revolves around the sun, astronauts assure us that worries about dental appointments and mismatched socks tend to lose their urgency.

It is also true, however, that recreational space travel is unlikely to be a feature of everyday life anytime soon. Recognizing this, I purchased a set of postcards of Planet Earth taken from outer space, another set of the other eight planets (this was in the glory days before Pluto was demoted), and sent one periodically to each of the children in turn with enthusiastic recollections of extraterrestrial "field trips" we had taken. I was considerably more edified by my efforts than the children, however—it took me infinitely longer to look up scientific details and set them to paper than they spent reading them. *Uh-oh*, I thought, *maximum maternal effort, minimal student learning; ratio probably 10:1; sounds like a sure-fire recipe for burnout.*

Happily, I found an easier way to observe the strengths and weaknesses of contemporary culture: teaching foreign languages and history. Nothing helps us understand our own language like studying somebody else's, and nothing makes us appreciate the familiar comforts of home like traveling to different lands and time periods. This lesson was vividly brought home when we took a literary trip to the isles west of Ireland in the year 850 AD, and experienced a monk's terror as he awaited his fate at the dreadful hands of the Vikings. We read his fervent prayer that his monastery would be saved by the impending storm which promised to foil the marauders, but were left uncertain as to his fate—the monastery eventually fell, that we discovered without too much digging, but whether on this particular occasion or another was not clear. History tells us that the monks countered violence by sending missionaries to preach the gospel of love to their attackers, and that Iceland converted in 1000 AD, Norway shortly thereafter. Two lessons emerged: in the long run, love wins more surely than violence (as missionaries around the world are proving to this day), and secondly, we should be very, very thankful for our police force.

TEACHING FOREIGN LANGUAGES

"Learning a foreign language can be easy, effortless, and fun!" The curriculum introduction went on to explain that children under ten, brains already wired to acquire their first language, are at a premium age to soak up a second, or even a third. Now, what homeschooling mother worth her salt would pass up an opportunity like that? I would, for one.

Not that the logic fails to impress me: on the contrary, it is entirely persuasive. I even know families who are virtually bilingual, and I applaud them enthusiastically. It's just that my children would have replaced the adjectives "easy, effortless, and fun" with "tedious, boring, and futile." They steadfastly resisted my efforts to acquaint them with the beauties of the French language, in which I am relatively fluent, wondering out loud why anyone would call it a *pomme* when everyone knows it's an apple. Only when their cultural horizons broadened in the teen years did learning a foreign language start to make sense to them. I could identify with that. I had studied French at school for eight years before my first trip to France when I was sixteen, but was still absolutely stunned to discover an entire country where *literally everybody spoke French*! Even the two-year-olds, who looked on me as some kind of moron as I struggled to answer a single question out of the barrage they threw at me. It was a time of enormous change and growth for me, and I returned home with a new enthusiasm for all things French — including, I am happy to say, my language studies.

But my efforts to stir up anything but the most fleeting interest in a foreign language fell on stony ground. Take, for instance, my musings on language and temperament: *Which came first, a country's language or its national characteristics?* Each seems to flow perfectly from the other. French is the language of poetry, of emotional half-certainties, of love; German deals in hair-splitting precision, the minutiae of philosophy, in scientific exactitude. It is a truism to say that the national temperament follows suit—or is it vice versa? Not a flicker of interest did the children betray. If they had been cats, they would have yawned and gone back to licking themselves.

Iain had a modicum of French battered into him by the time he left for college, where further studies fulfilled his language requirement. Thanks to a summer job in Spain after his junior year, he is reasonably proficient in Spanish, while a couple of courses in grad school have rendered him fully conversant in Old English. Trouble is, Old English is known as a dead language for a reason: there are no native speakers for him to converse with. Thus his fluency remains untested.

Lorna easily picked up French in high school using Rosetta Stone; she also studied Greek for a year. She learned Spanish during her gap year, honing her linguistic skills to razor sharpness during the two months she spent volunteering at two hospitals in Guadalajara. The organization that oversaw the logistics of her stay seemed reputable enough when we investigated them online in Ojai, and they provided good references. In practice, however, they had a bad case of the *mañanas* — details were worked out in a distinctly seat-of-the-pants style. They promised two weeks of "focused, intensive language study" in preparation for working at the hospitals; unfortunately, not one single day was forthcoming. No one, apart from Lorna and her frantic parents, was the least concerned, and it took us days to discover the root of the problem: there was, quite simply, no teacher. The Guadalajaran solution was straightforward, but somehow missed the point: they merely reversed her schedule, with language studies coming *after* hospital work. Thus she was pitched straight into the operating room. There she first observed, then assisted in operations, holding retractors and passing the surgeon instruments whose names she gathered by trial and error, all the time struggling to pick familiar words out of the torrent of Spanish that engulfed her. Her aspirations to become a surgeon took a direct hit during a particularly gory scalp laceration; she was chalk white and on the verge of passing out when a kindly nurse suggested she *sientate*. In her light-headed daze, she was horrified to see scalpels and suturing implements flying through the air. Something hurtled toward her; instinctively she ducked. Fortunately, it was the blunt end of a hypodermic syringe that bounced off her shoulder, not the contaminated needle. *How many days till I go home?* she wailed inwardly. *¿Cuántos dias?*

Lorna's trip preceded the current wave of kidnappings in Mexico, and she was street savvy enough to navigate the city safely on the buses, which proved a sanctuary of sanity from the chaos of her daily grind. The city's pollution level is high, however, and the toxicity badly affected her health. When I suggested she see a doctor at the hospital, her response was a horrified and emphatic *no!* She had seen too many health code violations, including a surgeon who went from case to case without so much as a drop of water anointing his hands; she wasn't about to entrust those doctors with anything as precious as her health.

Despite Lorna's less than enviable experience, my enthusiasm for travel abroad remains undimmed. At the very least, we can all learn a few phrases in a new language and try them out at an ethnic restaurant. Most *restaurateurs* are thrilled when a customer attempts a few words in their native tongue, with the notable exception of the French. Parisians are the worst, staring in undisguised horror at anyone who *dares* desecrate the most beautiful mother tongue with their horrible English *embouchure.* Fortunately, the owner of our neighborhood Vietnamese restaurant in Everett had no such scruples—he loved to converse with me in his lilting French, thus reminding us indelibly that Vietnam was once a colony of France. To this day I remember the deep sadness in his eyes, haunted by memories of the unspeakable hardships he had endured leaving Vietnam.

I also have my doubts about trying out our linguistic skills in a Korean restaurant. We may have the best of intentions, but considering that the only phrase Sheila ever gathered from Mint, her Korean roommate, was "Your mother smells like a duck," I have some doubts as to our reception.

LATIN

The language that has given the most bang for the bucks by far has been Latin. A student of Latin is halfway to learning any of the Romance languages (Spanish, Portuguese, French, Italian, and Romanian) as well as understanding English grammar, vocabulary, and spelling. I never could remember how many *d*'s, *t*'s and *r*'s *Mediterranean* had until I put the Latin together: *medi*—in the midst of, and *terra*—land; the Ancient Romans believed their sea was the center of the world, and named it accordingly. (Google "teach children Latin" to find a wealth of resources, many intended specifically for homeschoolers. Our family studied medieval, or church, Latin, which was the *Lingua Franca*, the common tongue, of the educated Christian world from roughly 500 AD to the Renaissance, and is still in use by the Catholic Church today; it differs from classical Latin mostly in pronunciation.)

An inflected language works very differently from our own: meaning is found in word endings, not in word order. *Boy bites dog* means something very different from *dog bites boy*, because meaning in English is determined by word order. *Puer canem mordat*, on the other hand, means exactly the same as *canem puer mordat* because the boy (*puer*) is in the nominative case, and thus is performing the action, no matter where in the sentence he is. Likewise *canem*, the unfortunate dog, is in the accusative case and thus is the victim of the rabid boy even if the sentence reads *canem mordat puer*. In order for the dog to assume his more normal role of aggressor, the case endings have to change: *canis puerum mordat, puerum canis mordat*, or *puerum mordat canis* all signify that the dog is biting the boy. It is difficult to explain subject, object, and genitive to an English speaker, because the words stay the same and are modified only by word order and prepositions. In an inflected language, on the other hand, grammar becomes crystal clear.

Thousands of English words are derived from Latin and Greek, and a student who is familiar with root words will have no trouble with the meaning of *auto* (self) *graph* (writing), or understanding that in an *automobile*, one can move oneself. The prefix *tele* signifies distance; thus, a *tele*-vision allows us to see things from afar, as does a *tele*-photo lens, while one versed in the mystery of *tele*-kinesis can move things at a distance. The science-fiction miracle of teleportation transports the heroine to her desired location instantly—no security lines, no delayed flights, no lost luggage, and no ticket fees. And it all happens just by combining the prefix *tele* with the root word *porto*, I carry. Would that real-life travel were so easy.

HISTORY

As Iain's education lurched through the middle school years, my thoughts turned to high school. Specifically, they turned to history. It did not seem to me that my somewhat haphazard approach was adequate preparation for the rigors of the high school history curricula that I had perused at homeschool conventions, and I determined to do better with the girls and

Evan. The words of George Santayana, "Those who do not learn from history are doomed to repeat it," pierced my very soul. But how to begin?

I thought back to my school days, and Miss Smith. Standing ramrod straight, hair scraped back into a severe bun from which no stray strand dared escape, she marched into our classroom twice a week, slammed her books down on the desk, and taught. She dictated, in forty-minute segments that we dutifully committed to paper, then (in theory at least) to memory, the history of Europe—its rulers, battles, and treaties—from the French Revolution to World War One. Except that we got bogged down in Bismarck, and never quite made it to 1914. Even so, she somehow avoided imparting to us the one thing about Bismarck I have since found memorable: he wittily observed that, "Those who like sausages and legislation should never watch either being made."

A school friend divulged the shocking news that she read the books of Rosemary Sutcliff—*for fun!* "Historical fiction" she called it: imaginary stories featuring made-up characters, set in accurately researched historical situations, possibly involving actual historical personages. I was scandalized. Such a betrayal! Imagine an author being so underhanded as to sneak *learning* into the hallowed halls of pleasure reading! Imagine my friend actually falling for it! *Not me*, I thought, *nobody's going to sneak spinach into my lemon meringue pie!*

But time will have its way, and years later, I found myself reading Sutcliff's *Warrior Scarlet*, a story about a young boy

with a handicap coming of age in Bronze Age Britain. I remember the moment vividly: we were staying at a beach house
in Southern California, where Robin was heading a coali-
tion of doctors to fight a euthanasia initiative. Sheila was four
months old and I was bathing her in the kitchen sink, when I
found myself agonizing over young Drem and his problems as
if he were a real person. *What's this?* I asked myself. *Drem is
a fictional character living in Bronze Age Britain, and here you
are worrying about him as if he were one of your own. Are you
crazy?* Far from it—I had just uncovered the key to teaching
history: historical fiction was to form the backbone of Entropy
History.

Incidentally, the Miss Smith story has a happy ending.
One day she wafted dreamily into class, hair softly waved, face
suffused with a luminous blush. Absentmindedly dropping her
books on the floor, she turned coyly to face the class and show
us the ring on her finger. *Yes! The indomitable Miss Smith was
in love!* She left our school soon after, and I was not invited to
the wedding. But I hope she served sausages at the reception.

FIELD TRIPS

Better even than historical fiction are field trips to the places
where it all actually happened. Some families have gone so far
as to spend an entire year touring the US in an RV, learning
history firsthand. For most of us that's not practical. What may

be more feasible is what our family did for Thanksgiving a few years ago.

We converged on Williamsburg, Virginia, and spent a week immersed in Colonial America. At the wigmaker's, we were scandalized that Lorna's waist-length blonde hair was worth precisely nothing, thanks to sun damage. The silversmith informed us that metal has to be beaten into shape rather than poured into a mold if it is to be strong enough for jewelry. "Who knew?" I said. "Stress makes you stronger! I should have beaten you more often." Not being fond of Metaphors for Life, the children looked the other way and hummed loudly. Evan listened intently as a costumed reenactor demonstrated how unpredictable firearms were before the invention of rifling. Facing an army of hostile Redcoats, the Patriot loaded his musket and fired. Nothing happened. He reloaded and fired again. There was a muffled click, a puff of smoke. Again he reloaded. Third time, as it happened, was a charm, but the bullet veered wide of its target—the Brit, who by then had grown weary of waiting, finished our hero off. Andrew, meanwhile, was more interested in the cannons. At least they fired reliably.

Williamsburg's Living History was supplemented with the more modern pursuits of shopping and bowling. Our lodgings were not a four-bedroom unit as advertised, but rather two adjacent two-bedroom units. That meant two living rooms, neither of which could accommodate us all comfortably, and two kitchens, both of which were fully used as the children prepared a full-blown Thanksgiving feast, complete with all the trimmings. We pushed the two round dining tables together and covered them with a festive, rectangular tablecloth brought from home. Andrew was deeply offended to find that there was no table beneath the cloth in the gaps. (He tends to take such things rather personally.) The kitchens divided largely along gender lines, with much frantic to-ing and fro-ing by Iain, the master chef. One sixteen-pound turkey, two types of potatoes, broccoli, asparagus, yams, bread sauce, onion sauce, gravy, and three types of pie. I'll wager those units never saw the like, before or since.

And we ate it all. Leftovers consisted of a nearly empty bottle of salad dressing and a solitary muffin. Minds numbed by an overdose of turkey, we sat around the unbelievably kitsch, synthetic fireplace in one of our cramped units and recalled our first trip to Pennsylvania, ten years earlier.

CANOE DÉJÁ-VU

Historical excursions around Everett were limited almost exclusively to Lewis & Clark exhibitions and Native American potlatches, and the children were adamant that, in each case, once was (more than) enough—even the creation of a dugout canoe failed to move them: "The crafting of a canoe/ Gives us terrible déjà-vu," they sang. Nor did my oft-repeated joke change their hearts: When I learned that a member of the famous expedition was named Patrick Gass, I quipped that every morning Lewis made sure he was behind Private Gass on the trail; that way he could always overtake him and write truthfully in his daily journal, "Today, I passed Gass." We were at an impasse: a mother determined to teach hands-on history, jokes included; children willing to go to any lengths to avoid further exposure to Lewis, Clark, or Private Gass. So when the opportunity arose for a temporary move to a more historic location we seized it, as Iain said, with both feet.

Robin had been disabled from surgery by an allergic reaction to soap. Not being able to wash his hands posed rather more of a problem in post-Semmelweis America than it apparently did in Lorna's Guadalajaran hospitals, and he was forced to hang up his surgical mask forever.

He was offered a job running a gubernatorial campaign in Pennsylvania—no worries about dirty hands in politics— and I jumped at the opportunity of spending three months near Philadelphia. As I scoured the AAA book, I was inspired by the plethora of field trips within driving distance of the eighteenth-century house we had rented just outside Pottstown—on Evans Road, funnily enough. Every Thursday was designated field trip day, with excursions into the mystical maze of the surrounding countryside whose roads, I swear, rearranged themselves every night while I slept.

Undeterred by my navigational shortcomings, I left one morning with the children on an extended trip to Plimoth Plantation and Boston. By four o'clock that afternoon (tea

time, hooray!) we were entering Massachusetts, the sixth
state of the day. West Coasters all, we were astounded—it
usually took us that long to traverse *one* state. Quite apart
from everything being so small-scale, it was mightily confus-
ing for the ocean to be in the east; as any Washingtonian,
Oregonian, or Californian will tell you, it belongs in the
west. This, coupled with the Boston Town Fathers' helpful
habit of placing freeway exit signs immediately *after* the exit,
made for some jolly times indeed.

Nevertheless, we paid our respects to Plymouth Rock,
where the "first" settlers arrived in 1620—that is, thirteen years after the founding of Jamestown, in 1607.
(Massachusetts was the first colony to institute public
schools; thus, Boston-based historians wrote the history
books, and so we have it: Plymouth Rock, 1620, was where
it all began.) At Plimoth Plantation, the living museum,
we tried relentlessly to get the actors to step out of character. One time, I succeeded. Commiserating with a young
woman about how sad it was to have left her family behind
in England, I sighed, "I know what it's like." My accent
told her that I spoke true; she sighed even more deeply in
response. "And the worst of it is," I went on earnestly, "*you*
can't even email them." Just for a moment she nodded her
head, and looked so sad it almost brought tears to my eyes.
Then she snapped back into character. "Is this your mother?" she asked Iain. "She is addlebrained." Iain concurred
wholeheartedly.

Robin joined us on our trip to Gettysburg. It was an extraordinary experience, solemn, almost holy. Two million visitors a year pause to reflect on the enormity of the sacrifice that was made, to wonder what these young men might have accomplished had their lives not been cut short by fellow countrymen, perhaps even by brothers. There is no neon, no touristy glitz at Gettysburg; locals we spoke to looked on living there as a privilege. It was profoundly memorable.

Historical fiction gave us a feel for the eras we would be visiting, but even so, surprises abounded. Hopewell Furnace, a nineteenth-century village that sprang up around an iron-smelting works, sounded about as inviting as the industrial north of England. In fact, it was so lovely that we went there three times, enjoying the idyllic village with its period craftspeople: lace-makers, woodturners, spinners, apple-pickers, and that pivotal figure in the production of iron, the charcoal-maker. We had read *The Clock* by the Collier brothers, and this, together with our on-site visits, equipped us to weigh the pros and cons of the Industrial Revolution: in the pro column, more stuff (pretty, floral prints replaced the drab homespun that was ubiquitous at Plimoth); in the cons, a loss of personal identity as people were reduced to units on a production line, or to mere consumers.

How does the Industrial Revolution continue to affect us? It takes a lot to keep an industrial economy running, and as consumers we must be conditioned to want more of what manufacturers produce, whether we need it or not. We watched TV ads to figure out the techniques advertisers use to "create a need," and recalled that, to big businesses, we are nothing more than statistics that have the potential to pad their profit margin. Advertisements imbue everyday items with an almost magical power to transform our lives. *Why settle for a fabric softener that will simply reduce static cling*, they imply, *when the right brand will make you young and lively, the envy of your friends and even strangers you pass in the street?* The right beer will not merely slake our thirst, it will banish all our social woes and make us younger, sexier, and more desirable. And men—if your testosterone level needs a boost, just get behind the wheel of a four-wheel drive truck and start ripping your way through a fragile wilderness ecosystem. Instant super-hero status! Advertisers study people's insecurities and capitalize on them ruthlessly, eyes fixed on the bottom line. *Never mind if the models in our clothing ads inspire teenage girls to become anorexic—our stock has never been higher.* Awareness is the first line of defense; once the children recognized how shamelessly advertisers were bent on parting them from their hard-earned cash, they weren't having it.

This made them significantly countercultural. Because they watched virtually no commercial children's programming, and were inured to any ads they did chance to see, they had no clue that they "ought" to want the season's hot toy that parents were lining up before dawn to purchase. We, meanwhile, sat around the fire in dressing gowns and slippers, drinking tea and cocoa, reading stories of the saints.

When Evan was eleven, a store clerk was surprised to hear his answer to her stock query, "What is Santa bringing you?"

"I don't know," he said, "maybe some knitting needles… and some yarn."

Take that, Wall Street!

COAT HOOKS

It hurts to admit this, but when I started homeschooling I would have been hard-pressed to place the four ancient western civilizations—Egypt, Greece, Rome, and Israel—in chronological order. I wanted better for my children, but was unsure how to go about it. Fortunately, I came across the ideas of Julia Fogassy: in her brilliant work *The ABC's of Christian Culture*, she suggests dividing up the grand sweep of human history into manageable chunks, or epochs, and covering the entire sweep every school year at the rate of one epoch per month. The student will thus cover the same ground every year, but approach it from a different perspective each time and begin to perceive the connections that make sense of human history. Connections that are lost in the traditional one-period (or civilization)-per-year approach. Connections that make putting the four ancient civilizations in order a breeze.

The key lay in establishing (non-surgical) "coat hooks" in the children's brains. Here's what I mean: most of us have a coat hook for 1492, thanks to a famous little rhyme that tells us what Columbus was doing that year. On the same hook goes Leonardo da Vinci, who died not thirty years later, in 1519; the artistic Renaissance thus meshes with the great Age of Discovery. It is then easy to see how discoveries of new lands fueled the philosophical, scientific, and artistic revolution sweeping Europe, and how recently acquired tastes of the newly formed middle classes for things that were beautiful (like silk), or fragrant (like spices), or sweet (like sugar) both motivated and financed many voyages of discovery. And all this information gets hung on that convenient 1492 hook.

The historical ages were divided into the four ancient western civilizations and the seven modern ages (the Dark Ages, the High Middle Ages, the Renaissance/Age of Discovery, the American Revolution, the Civil War, the Great Depression, and World War Two). I chose as a starting point the year 3100 BC and the unification of the two crowns of Upper and Lower Egypt, because many scholars believe this was when writing first appeared, turning prehistory into history. (There are, incidentally, "prehistoric" peoples alive today, who have never committed their history to writing. All we know about them comes from their tribal stories and archeology.) My emphasis was on European history, switching to American after the Renaissance, giving the children a firm mental framework of western civilization before moving on to explore world history. Accordingly we focused on the stories and events that reflected our cultural background, though we never went quite as far as cooking haggis.

The school year was eight months long, so I could not cover all eleven periods. Most years I selected two of the ancient civilizations—say, Egypt and Israel—and two of the first three from the Modern list. The four periods of American history were covered every year. I was dismayed at how much this left out, but consoled myself that students entering high school who are familiar with these periods and have become well-acquainted with some of the central historical figures of the times are most likely way ahead of the curve.

Throwing caution to the winds, I volunteered to teach young people from several additional families. Now thoroughly motivated, I embarked on my personalized crash course in history, starting with Usborne books and a couple of musty children's histories from second-hand bookstores. Moving on to information-packed entries in a children's encyclopedia, there was no stopping me—even though in those pre-Wikipedia days one actually had to take a book off a shelf to locate the date of the fall of the Roman Empire. Rarely did I venture into the impenetrably detailed thickets of high school textbooks, though I found the series Critical Thinking in United States History to be absolutely fascinating and thoroughly user-friendly.

Each period was brought to life by historical fiction, and rounded out with additional studies appropriate to age level and interest. Ancient Egypt became real to us thanks to the feistiness of *Mara, Daughter of the Nile*, and the dashing figure of Sheftu, hero of *The Golden Goblet*. We studied the crops that farmers were able to grow thanks to the annual inundation, and one most ingenious student, Dominic, helped us understand how irrigation worked with his impressive model *shaduf.*

The characters in our books stayed with us. When Fiona's freshman history course at Thomas Aquinas College touched on the Norman Conquest, 1066 AD, she was ecstatic to reencounter King Harold of Wessex; thanks to our reading of *The King's Shadow* seven years previously, it was like meeting an old friend.

The books served a double function: through them, students were introduced to various literary devices—mood, setting, character development, and conflict. Every story must have a conflict, and this will fall into one of four categories: person against self, person against society, person against nature, or person against person. The most engrossing stories involve more than one source of conflict, and some of the conflicts may be hard to categorize. There was heated disagreement, for example, concerning Johnny Tremain's burnt hand. Some students argued it was a case of person against self—it was, after all, Johnny's hand; some saw it as person against person—the incident was brought about by Dove's deliberate actions; and some, pointing out that burning is a natural force, opted for person against nature. No matter how off-the-wall their ideas might seem, I always tried to be respectful of my students. Provided, that is, their opinions were backed up with sound textual references.

THE FUZZY TIMELINE

There is a popular fad nowadays which claims that knowledge of dates is unimportant—that understanding is what
really matters. Even Albert Einstein appears to have joined
the ranks of educational revisionists with his famous dictum,
beloved of T-shirt companies and bumper sticker manufacturers: "Imagination is more important than knowledge." But this
poses something of a false dichotomy for, in the real world,
imagination presupposes knowledge. Scientists stand on the
shoulders of those who preceded them, as Newton observed;
the extraordinary imagination that enabled Einstein to formulate his theory of relativity would have been useless had he not
been thoroughly conversant with the scientific knowledge of
his time.

If knowledge of at least some dates is important, it was also
important to concretize the chronology of the books we read.
We needed a timeline, and I set about making one using adding machine tape in two-inch wide rolls, one green and one
pink.

Problems were legion. First, even using a conservative one
foot per hundred years, four thousand years still added up to
a whopping forty feet. Should the advancing years go in rows
on the same wall, which effectively negated any sense of visual
continuity, or stretch out of the kitchen and along the hallway? If the latter, what about the bathroom door: do we skip
it, or does Ancient Greece disappear into the bathroom every
time the door is opened? And frankly, the chances of anyone

spending much time perusing the coat closet door for details of the High Middle Ages seemed negligible at best. An additional drawback was that, once in place, the timeline rapidly lost its impact, becoming as visually arresting as wallpaper.

A successful timeline, then, needed to be interactive. Looking at the yards of adding machine tape, which had become so cluttered with important personages, discoveries, and inventions that the years AD were a hopeless hodgepodge, I deduced that it also needed to be simple. Like a terrier with a bone, I worried at the problem while weeding the garden, pushing the grocery cart down the cereal aisle, scrubbing the high-tide mark after their evening bath. Inspiration, when it struck, brought the "fuzzy timeline."

Consisting of three strips of felt (hence the "fuzzy"), eighteen inches long and cut from six-foot-wide bolts, the timeline unrolls to eighteen feet in length. Four thousand years BC take up twelve feet, and the felt is dark blue to represent the world's darkness before Christ; the six feet of AD are dark red to represent Christ's sacrifice for us. Down the middle runs a somewhat erratic line of chain stitch. (I could probably have done this in ten minutes on the sewing machine, but being English, preferred to do it the inefficient, wiggly way—by hand. It took months.) I embroidered the date every hundred years—six feet per two thousand years translates into just under three and three-quarter inches per hundred years—and set about collecting or making "artifacts" to represent each book and its time period.

A Sculpey model of the two crowns of Upper and Lower Egypt marked 3100 BC and the invention of writing. Stonehenge and the wheel predate that, but since nobody wrote about either, we don't know when to date them. (Imagine the prehistoric journal entry: *Today, my brother Ug invented the wheel, and you would scarce believe how much more smoothly our ox cart runs!*) We reflected that, even five or six thousand years BC, every day was the same length as ours, and people were every bit as individual as they are today—they woke up with the sunrise, worked, ate, argued, cracked jokes, fell in love, told stories, and went to bed when darkness fell. The only reason we don't know about their exploits is that they were never written down.

In the days before online shopping, our timeline "artifacts" had to be procured by hand. Museum gift shops yielded several—a pyramid at the Smithsonian, for instance, from roughly 2500 BC—while the streets of Florence positively bristled with diminutive replicas of Michelangelo's *David* to represent the Renaissance, circa 1500. Some were made by students: I am particularly fond of an arrow piercing a bloodshot human eye—King Harold's untimely end at the Battle of Hastings, 1066. Each item acts as a coat hook. The toy train placed in the early 1860s serves as a reminder of several things: Lawrence Yep's *Dragon's Gate*; the building of the Transcontinental Railroad with its attendant brutal working conditions; Asian immigration; and the Civil War. The children take turns finding the date and placing the items on the timeline, and retrieving them in order when the lesson is over. I'll never forget the first time we laid out the fuzzy timeline. It was staggering to see the grand sweep of history reduced to eighteen feet—*so much of it was BC!* How very small were the eight-and-a-half inches from the Liberty Bell, 1776, to the present day. It is altogether remarkable how much history America has packed into 240 years.

More people died violent deaths in the twentieth century than in all previous centuries combined. If the same is not going to be said of the twenty-first, we desperately need a generation of history-savvy young people who will transform the world by kindness rather than military might. I fully intend that my children will be among their number—morbid fascination with historical eye-piercing notwithstanding.

14

BUILDING FAMILY UNITY, PART I:
DOMESTIC TRADITIONS

*R*obin and I hail from European stock. He is half Icelandic, half Scots-Irish; I'm half English (with possible Welsh undertones) and half Scottish. Despite this unusual degree of cultural homogeneity, problems in communication have been legion.

In the early days of our marriage, Robin asked if I'd like to go to a movie. "Hmm," I responded, my vocal inflection outlining a descending minor third. Nothing happened.

A few minutes later I inquired rather petulantly, "I thought we were going to a movie?"

"But you said you didn't want to go," Robin countered.

"No, I didn't."

"Yes, you did."

"No, I didn't."

"Yes, you did."

After several minutes of this witty banter, the truth dawned: to me, a descending "hmm" meant, "Gosh, yes, that would be wizard brilliant," while to Robin it signified, "Thanks, but no thanks." We were living out Churchill's observation that Britain and America are "two countries separated by a common language." Given that we adoring newlyweds all but came to blows over a misinterpreted "hmm," I take my hat off to marriages that share neither culture nor language, yet manage to survive the decades. As for creating "mixed heritage" family traditions…bring in the heavy artillery, and let battle commence!

Take Christmas. Our first was in San Francisco, where Robin was working between 100 and 168 hours a week (yes, I know, that's all of them) as Senior Resident in surgery; thus we were pathetically grateful for any time together. Since we were in England the following year, Christmas was distinctly and unarguably British. So it was not until the third Christmas, our first in Everett, that the storm clouds came to a head: Robin was for going to church and opening presents on Christmas Eve, following his family's Lutheran tradition, while I, raised in the Church of England, was every bit as determined to hold out till Christmas Morning.

What would we do? Either way, one of us would emerge victorious while the other tasted the bitter ignominy of defeat. Should we alternate? Sentiments of "This year I get to choose, yay me!" hardly seemed conducive to peace and brotherly love. But then, neither did divorce or murder, which occurred to both of us more than once.

Creative thinking, born of desperation, led to some big changes. First to go was the primary focus on the Two Big Days; instead, I looked to Advent for inspiration. The Church has carved out the four weeks preceding Christmas as a time of eager anticipation, and we joined in the expectancy every Sunday evening as we gathered around the dining-room table. The children lit candles on the Advent wreath and took turns reading Bible verses by candlelight.

The first Sunday concerned prophets, with Old Testament Bible verses found in a biblical concordance foretelling the coming of the Messiah (selected from Genesis 3:15, Isaiah 9:2, Isaiah 11:1–3, Isaiah 40:3–5, and Isaiah 52:13 to 53:12). The manger scene was set up on the hutch, while the Magi began their long journey from distant lands/another room; each day they moved closer to the stable—unless Andrew had other ideas, that is, in which case a game of "Hunt the Magi" was in order. The second week, we reflected on Bethlehem—literally "House of Bread"—where God became Man, born in a manger (from the French verb "to eat"), to be our Bread of Life (Micah 5:2–4, Isaiah 7:14, and Jeremiah 31:15). On Gaudete (Latin "rejoice") Sunday, the Church celebrates that we are now more than halfway to Christmas, and the theme is shepherds. We read Luke 2:1–20, and pondered the significance of Christ revealing Himself first to shepherds who, because of their itinerant way of life, were ritually unclean and not permitted to testify in a court of law. Truly, "the last shall be first"; God indeed uses the foolish things of this world to confound the wise. The last Sunday was all about angels. We read Luke 1:26–38, Colossians 1:16, John 1:1–3, as well as various Old Testament passages, and marveled at the numerous episodes of angelic intervention woven through the Gospel narratives. When Iain was in kindergarten, he drew a picture on an index card of each angelic visitation; such as survived have attained an almost iconic significance for the younger siblings.

Platefuls of Christmas cookies, baked each Sunday afternoon, made their appearance along with mugs of hot, spiced apple cider, while I unveiled the craft of the day. This might be paper snowflakes to snip, or a tree ornament to cut, sew, stitch, or glue (many came from the HearthSong catalog, others from the fabric store). The second Sunday was set aside for decorating spherical candles with designs cut from sheets of colored wax, on the theme "What meant most to me this year." The serenity of the evening was usually marred by any number of misadventures, from spilling things—cider, glue, glitter, paint—to squabbling about who had taken the most cookies. Imperfect as they were, those Sunday evenings marked the progression towards Christmas Eve, and kept our focus on the true meaning of the season. They also provided us with a tree full of ornaments, which will in time decorate the children's own trees. Each year, I bought everyone an ornament of some personal significance, preferably from a historical site we had

visited. Fiona's is, as often as not, a frog; the year Iain studied
in Florence, I tracked down a glass Leaning Tower of Pisa.
Sadly, I was unable to find a festive hypodermic syringe to me-
morialize Lorna's time in Guadalajara. On reflection, perhaps
it's just as well.

THE GRUESOME QUESTION REMAINS...

Celebrating Advent, however, did nothing to resolve the
thorny problem of when to open presents. It was an impossible question, so I changed it: How about both? Spreading the
opening over two days should defuse the usual explosion of
acquisitive hysteria, and avoid its aftermath—that anticlimactic
feeling that lay like a pall of doom over Christmas afternoon.
Anything that would reduce the frenzy and give the children
space to be interested in what others were getting, struck me as
a Very Good Thing.

Accordingly, Christmas Eve celebrations began with a family present around four in the afternoon. This was something
for everyone to enjoy: a dartboard, a cappuccino machine, a
foosball table. Then came the traditional dinner of Christmas
bread (recipe from *The Tassajara Bread Book*), cold meat, dev-
iled eggs, chips, and vegetable dips—finger food that overexcit-
ed little ones could eat on the run—before opening gifts from
the immediate family.

The year of the trampoline, I added something novel to the
menu. Although the family had a deep and abiding mistrust of

anything calling itself a salad that also contained a member of the marshmallow family, I had been cajoled by a highly persuasive bank teller into trying a questionable recipe from their fundraising cookbook. It featured tiny acini pasta and a disturbing quantity of miniature marshmallows, but she assured me it was a feast fit for a king, an unforgettable treat. I should mention that in its cooked state, acini bears a disturbing resemblance to frogspawn; add miniature marshmallows, and it looks barely fit for human consumption.

It came as small surprise, then, when nobody was willing to give it the taste test; but what I couldn't understand was why no one was even looking at the trampoline. The first bite of frogspawn ("Please, just for me, everybody try just *one* bite...") told me why—stomach flu had us in its clutches. Results were as predictable as they were lacking in festive charm. There were no Yuletide photographs that year; everyone felt too ghastly. How I wish I had mustered the strength to line them up on the sofa and click the shutter—it would have been our most vivid Christmas picture ever! (The bank teller was right about one thing: the "unforgettable" bit. Our memories of Frogspawn Salad have long survived its final voyage down the garbage disposal.) After what would have been dinner, the children barely had enough energy to open presents and their reactions were muted, to say the least. There remained only one more tradition before bedtime.

My friend Sharon once surprised me by revealing that she made Christmas nighties and pajamas, and hid them under her children's pillows at bedtime on Christmas Eve. At first, this struck me as a colossal waste of effort—*sewing matching clothes, which no one but family sees?* If I went to that much trouble, I'd want EVERYONE to know! But over time, I changed my mind. There was something rather touching about *not* parading the fruits of my labors at church, *not* basking in ego-stroking cries of "However do you find the time?" that made it all the more intimate, more personal.

I made the first nighties when Lorna was one, Fiona three, and our fifth child still four months from Grand Entrance, due April 1st. No tests were needed to convince me that this was a boy; my mother's instinct told me he had a Y chromosome in every cell of his body. I was relieved that next year there would again be only two nighties to make—boys' patterns are so much less demanding. (You may recall that my "April Fools' boy" turned out to be Sheila, born on April second. And she's been surprising us ever since.)

As I sat at the sewing machine, Fiona crawled into my lap. "What are you making?" she asked.

"Christmas nighties."

"Oh, I see. Who are they for?"

"They're for two little girls who are just about the same size as you and Lorna." (This was, strictly speaking, true.)

She breathed a sigh. "They are lucky. When you've finished, please will you make one for me?"

"I won't have time before Christmas," I said, "but I'll make you one after Christmas, if you still want one."

Fiona didn't still want one after Christmas, of course, and that particular trick only worked once. In subsequent years, I got up early to put in an hour's sewing while the house was still quiet. (Having the whole house to myself was such a luxury that it invariably gave me aspirations of rising early every morning, but these never survived the New Year.) Nightie production became infinitely more streamlined the year I stored the pieces for each child in a labeled, two-gallon Ziploc bag. To keep things interesting, sleepwear might follow some special theme. In 2001, the girls' nighties featured a lacey baseball with "116" embroidered on it—the number of games the Seattle Mariners won that year. In 1998, the year we went to Philadelphia, I was inspired to make up my own pattern according to the rules of Colonial dressmakers, which was an education in its own right: curved lines were out (they waste too much fabric), gathers and gussets were in. I stretched the rules somewhat, sewing the seams with a machine, not by hand, and allowing elastic instead of fabric ties at wrists and the boys' waists.

Christmas morning began with stocking presents. Wrapping these the previous night became ridiculously easy the year I assigned a specific wrapping paper to each child. Orange juice and toasted Christmas bread fortified us till breakfast proper, which consisted of eggnog oven pancake, served with fruit from the garden frozen for the occasion the previous summer. (It was deeply satisfying to think ahead to Christmas as I picked and froze the garden's late-summer bounty.) Kidu magnanimously shared his annual mega-bone with the newest kitten.

Slowing steadily under the brutal assault of caloric intake, we rallied to prepare Christmas dinner, eaten around four o'clock. Turkey is the meat of choice in England, but since Andrew alone had an appetite for the bird so soon after Thanksgiving, we generally veered to the beef side of the market. One year, my mother cooked Beef Wellington; it was a labor of love, unforgettable, unrepeatable—tender beef baked in a flaky pastry crust. After dinner, it was time to open presents from extended family and friends; these were appreciated quietly, in a postprandial stupor. Spreading the presents over such a long time kept the hysteria at manageable levels and was, says Sheila today, "totally awesome."

BOXING DAY

"Boxing Day do's and don'ts" were etched into my psyche at an early age. The date was December 26, and there came a ring at the door. There, to my surprise, stood the garbage collector (euphemistically known as "the dustman").

"Merry Christmas," he smiled, doffing his cap. I was deeply touched by this spontaneous outpouring of good cheer.

"Merry Christmas to you, too!" I echoed, and with a warm glow in my heart, closed the door.

"Who was that?" asked my mother.

"The dustman. What a nice man! He wished us Merry Christmas."

A note of panic crept into my mother's voice. "And what did you do?"

"I wished him Merry Christmas back."

"You did WHAT??!!!"

"I wished him Mer..." But I was talking to myself.

I heard her anguished bellow, "Ali wished the dustman a Merry Christmas!" and my father's laconic "Hmm" in response. (He never was the excitable sort.) Then she was gone, running full tilt down the street, frantically waving a five-pound note at the retreating dustman's back.

Talk about flummoxed...what had I done wrong? And *why* must England have all these unwritten rules that were so easily broken, and bore such dire consequences? It turned out that dustmen were chronically underpaid and traditionally took their boxes (hence *Boxing Day*) to greet customers on 26 December. Those that knew what was good for them would slip "a little something" into the proffered box; those that didn't, like me, might come home next Monday to find their garbage "accidentally" strewn all over the driveway. Happy to relate, my mother reached the dustman in time...but it was a long while before I wished anyone a Merry Christmas without a twisting feeling in the pit of my stomach.

The day after Christmas was invariably a colossal letdown, so I livened it up with a Boxing Day party. No hidden financial agendas here—just friends getting together to enjoy buffet-style finger food, good company, and above all, music. Anyone who played an instrument brought it, and I accompanied a wide selection of Christmas carols on the piano. For centuries, England has been famous for music-making in the home, and this was one tradition I was only too happy to continue. Our friends included two members of the Seattle Symphony Orchestra; they came when their schedules permitted, and when they did, the standard of music-making was phenomenal.

HOGMANAY

A dark, handsome stranger rings at the door. "Lang may yer lum reek!" he booms in a broad Scots dialect, as he presents the happy homeowner with a lump of coal and is invited in for a "wee dram." It is just past midnight on New Year's Day, Hogmanay, and this "first-footing" ritual ensures that the domestic chimney (lum) will keep smoking (reeking) for the coming year.

In Calvinist Scotland, alcohol consumption at Christmas was severely frowned upon. But no such scruples applied to the secular festivities surrounding Hogmanay. When I was too young to indulge in a wee tipple, my Scottish mother made sure I celebrated the New Year in style with all the Coca Cola I could drink. The whole family fairly raised the roof with wild Highland dancing to the music of Jimmy Shand and his Band, till the "wee sma' oors" somewhere between midnight and the first glimmer of dawn saw us stumbling off to bed.

Robin's family, on the other hand, did not celebrate New Year, and his years of working in ERs had taught him to expect nothing but trouble as the old year drew to its close. If he was lucky, he might snatch a couple of hours sleep before the sirens' wail summoned him to the bedside of an intoxicated driver whose first engagement of the new year had been with a lamppost. I had to be content to see the New Year in alone, remembering the glory days of my youth and listening to Jimmy Shand with the volume turned down.

Everything changed once the girls were old enough to stay up. I had company! At the stroke of midnight, we ran barefoot along our frost-rimed street, wishing the world a resounding Happy New Year! and answering the blaze of the neighbors' illegal fireworks with fortissimo toots on our noisemakers. When the protestations of our numb feet grew too loud to bear, we retreated inside; I made cocoa all round, and treated each girl to a New Year's foot massage before we wended our bleary way to bed. It was only a couple of years before Fiona wanted to welcome in the New Year with her friends instead, and the other girls soon followed suit; but those Hogmanays we shared were, to me, absolutely, unforgettably marvelous.

THE BOAR'S HEAD

The Twelve Days of Christmas begin with Christmas Day and end on Epiphany, January 6. It is traditionally a time for parties and social visits, but in this culture, where Christmas begins

just after Halloween and ends with the dismemberment of
the tree on December 26, extending the season into January
proved impossible. Nevertheless, I was always on the lookout
for things to celebrate during the Twelve Days: one of our two
annual dances was scheduled around Epiphany, and the Boar's
Head Feast gave us further excuse for revelry. (We normally
celebrated it at the Boxing Day party.)

New College, Oxford, was founded in 1379. ("New,"
in this case, is relative.) Legend has it that a student was
wandering the hills outside Oxford one Christmas Day,
with nothing but his trusty copy of Aristotle for company.
Suddenly, he was surprised by a charging wild boar, tusks
lowered, mouth agape. Swiftly, our intrepid hero seized the
only weapon at his disposal, ramming his Aristotle into the
gaping maw and killing the beast on the spot. (One might
deduce that the boar had no appetite for the classics.) The
student's peers eagerly retrieved the carcass. That very night
a succulent feast of wild boar was borne into the dining hall,
preceded by the head held aloft upon a platter, while the
students sang:

> *The boar's head in hand bear I*
> *Bedeck'd with bays and rosemary;*
> *And I pray you, my masters, make merry—*
> *Quot estis in principio (as many as are in the feast)*
> *Caput apri defero (the boar's head I offer)*
> *Reddens laudes domino (giving praises to God).*

Having decided to piggyback the Boar's Head Feast onto the Boxing Day party, my quest for the necessary part of porcine anatomy began among the butchers' shops of Greater Seattle, and I found it most discouraging; the only source within driving distance offered a pitifully small beast, whose head was about the size of a Cornish game hen. Time to improvise! Our "head" was a whole leg of pork, roasted to golden perfection. Under the expert direction of our artistic friends, Jon and Marilyn, the sizzling head was transformed: marshmallows and prunes on toothpicks became eyes, bananas turned into tusks, while a cardboard replica of the fatal Aristotle was stuffed into the carved crack that served as a mouth. Rosemary abounded in the garden, and rhododendron leaves would pass for bay. Arrayed on a platter, the Boar's Head looked very much like the real thing as it was carried on high from the kitchen to its final candlelit resting place on the dining-room table. The Boar's Head Carol rang out as it had done for hundreds of years, with its chorus of four parts; in our version, a bodhrán drum contributed an insistent pulse. I wondered fleetingly how Robin's Irish ancestors would feel about a treasured national instrument being co-opted for such heathenish Sassenach rituals; fearing the answer would be enough to make my hair curl, but not wanting to pass up on the mediaeval flavor the drum imparted, I went ahead anyway.

EPIPHANY

By the time Epiphany came around, my present-wrapping wad was pretty well shot, and the children were lucky if their "last hurrah of Christmas" books came in anything as festive as a grocery sack. Homeschool was underway by January 6, so we took the morning off to sample classics, picture books, puzzle books, and anything else that had tickled my fancy.

Theoretically at least, Epiphany spelled the demise of the Christmas tree that had graced our living room since the day after Thanksgiving. Yielding to the children's entreaties, I once left it up until Valentine's Day; but witnessing the instantaneous *whoosh!* of its conflagration outside that night scotched any future appeals to keep a bone dry tinderbox in our living room. I never wanted to hear that roaring sound indoors. Besides, as the days lengthened, those twinkling lights started to look distinctly out of place.

TRADITION AND THE CAT PEE BEADS

The children were still small when I purchased, during the post-Christmas sales, a string of pearlized beads to wrap around the trunk of next year's tree. Back home, an odor assailed my nostrils as I took it out of the bag: a faint but distinctive smell, as if the feline contingent of the family had done their worst (or perhaps, strictly speaking, their second-worst). *Never mind*, I thought, *the smell will have worn off by next year*. But it hadn't. It had grown stronger. Undaunted, I wrapped the strand around the trunk, where it was all but invisible apart from an ungainly knot at the top of the tree. Come January, it was summarily returned to its box. Every year the ritual was repeated; every year the smell grew worse.

Finally, it dawned on me that the beads were not adding much, if anything, to our aesthetic appreciation of Christmas. Might this be a good time to relegate them to the garbage bin? The ensuing howls of protest could be heard across five counties. "You can't get rid of the cat pee beads—they're a TRADITION!" Apparently, tradition is quality blind: simply by repetition, a thing becomes sacrosanct. The cat pee beads were a treasured part of six children's Christmas memories, and woe betide anyone who tried to mess with them. I sometimes wonder how this particular tradition will endure. If, in years to come, you see parents with young children marching the aisles of Christmas decorations, carefully sniffing garlands of beads, you will recognize a Bernhoft family tradition stretching into perpetuity.

EVERYDAY TRADITIONS

As well as adding pizzazz to extraordinary days, like holidays, traditions made ordinary days run a whole lot more smoothly; indeed, I don't know how I would have survived mealtimes, the pre-dinner "arsenic hour," and bedtime without them. These are times of maximum stress—after all, everyone is either hungry (mealtimes) or tired (bedtime); additionally, professional voices intone dire pronouncements about the importance of regular sleep patterns and a well-balanced diet if your child is to avoid a diagnosis of ADHD...But what about a child who consistently refuses to go to bed, and whose diet consists of spaghetti (no meat, cheese, or sauce, thank you) and peanut butter?

Enough books to fill a library have been written on the subject, but I found some basic ideas helpful. Regular, predictable patterns meant that, at the very least, we all knew what *ought* to happen. Even something as simple as assigned places at the table got rid of one possible source of contention (in particular it kept Andrew happy—he tended to regard change in his personal routine as a vindictive personal assault). In the interests of dishwasher space, the youngest children used small plates. It never occurred to me that this was a tradition until Lorna pointed out that Evan, now a hulking teenager, still insists on cramming his man-sized portions onto a small plate and shoveling the food into his gaping maw with a small fork.

As regards mealtime decorum, the rules were simple: no singing at the table (I suspect that this may not be a problem in most families), indoor voices only, and no chewing with open mouths. I learned to eat fast and to develop an appetite for cold food, so as to be free to whip out a book at breakfast or lunch when the noise level got completely out of hand. Even the most raucous behavior would simmer down for a chapter of the latest read-aloud. Everything had to be at least tasted; if a proffered dish was so vile that even a tiny taste would induce nausea, a peanut butter and jelly sandwich could be substituted. When a child refused something she liked perfectly well, I threatened, "If you don't eat this, there's nothing for you till the next meal," and meant it. I rather envied mothers whose children were on sports teams, for theirs was the handy threat, "If you don't finish your dinner, you can't go to soccer practice." If Mom was true to her word, and had the courage to call the coach and explain, "Samantha won't be at practice today because she wouldn't eat her spinach," it made a huge impression. "Wow! Mom really means it!"

I had great ambitions for dinnertime: laughter, camaraderie, interesting discussions of what had been learned that day. Unfortunately for me, our family has a great propensity for arguing. About baseball, white buffalo, or pretty much anything else you care to mention. If our children were asked to finish the sentence, "When our family gets together to eat dinner, we always…" they would say with one accord, "argue." And then, after a moment's hesitation, they might add, "about baseball."

Several family members are highly interactive conversationalists: they think with their mouths in top gear. As soon as they hear a topic, they know everything they have to say about it. Others of us don't have quite that degree of mental alacrity, and like to think awhile before we speak. It is an ongoing challenge to make sure that the quieter family members have a chance to be heard, especially when the noisier ones can be so entertaining.

TIME FOR BED

Bedtime was ever the same: bath, book, bed. I adored bath time when the children were little enough that any number of them could fit into the tub, when songs, toys, and games were the order of the day. Then, clean and sweet-smelling, the youngest would snuggle up for a story, either a new one from the library or an old faithful from our collection. An older child might curl up in front of the fire to listen, sighing, "I love this book!"

It was hard to find a read-aloud which would captivate the oldest children while entertaining the young ones, but ideally a chapter of Tolkien, or one of Brian Jacques's Redwall books would precede bed. No kind of electronic screen played a part in our nightly rituals. We set a specific bedtime, giving Robin and me some treasured grownup time to enjoy one another and discuss the day's events. If the children weren't sleepy, they looked at books till they were ready to "fall into the arms of Morpheus." (For Lorna in particular, this allusion was more inviting than a perfunctory "go to sleep.")

These regular, daily patterns were the primary foundation for our family identity: they gave us a sense of security, and a framework on which the many activities of the day were hung. Some variation was permissible—I didn't want the framework to become a prison—but when outside activities threatened to overwhelm the pattern of our days, it was time to evaluate, prioritize, and return to the familiarity of everyday traditions.

15

BUILDING FAMILY UNITY, PART II:
IN WHICH WE VENTURE
AWAY FROM HOME

*W*ith a view to facilitating those "get up and go" moments when routine is thrown to the winds of adventure, we purchased a tent trailer—a type of diminutive motel room on wheels, combining all the disadvantages of a tent and an RV. Its maiden voyage was very nearly its last, as far as I was concerned. Sheila was three months old, Lorna not quite two and still in diapers. We left a roasting hot Everett and drove four interesting hours (I should mention I don't travel well with small children) to the Pacific Ocean, where we found a campsite shrouded in freezing cold fog. Everybody was hungry, Sheila bellowing her outrage to the entire campsite, and both she and Lorna needed tending to at the "other end."

This was when we came to appreciate the wisdom of trying out new camping equipment before hitting the road: the hose connecting our inside sink to the outside faucet was faulty and sprayed the inside of the tent trailer liberally with water before Robin could pinpoint the problem. What had seemed a thin patina of dust turned into a veritable slurry of mud. The howls redoubled, almost drowning out Robin's dire imprecations muttered between clenched teeth, threatening grievous bodily harm both to the makers of the tent trailer and the hapless folk who sold it to us. Things did not look good. We considered beating a retreat—home suddenly seemed awfully inviting— but the prospect of four more hours in the car was intolerable. We stayed.

I learned a valuable life lesson over the next three days: seek out the good and magnify it. For every hour of sheer grunt work exerted in keeping two babies cleanish, fed, and warm, and ensuring they got at least *some* sleep (they took turns checking out Mr. Morpheus, thus maximizing my time spent hovering around the trailer) there were perhaps three minutes of joy. Two such moments I recall vividly: an early morning cup of coffee, courtesy of Robin, whose culinary skills rose magnificently to the challenge of campfire cooking; and an afternoon bonfire on the beach, when the fog thinned just enough to make it fleetingly possible to tell where the sun was. The moment was made complete with s'mores; I nursed Sheila and basked in the idyllic sight of Iain, Andrew, Fiona, and Lorna playing peaceful- ly in the sand. Then Lorna discovered a small stream running, strangely enough, parallel to the sea, and promptly fell into it. She emerged looking very much like a water nymph, hair and clothes streaming; but before I could impress her with the classical allusion, her long-held breath burst from her lips in a wail as deafening as it was piteous. End of joy time for *that* day!

WE'VE MADE THE MEMORIES—NOW WHAT DO WE DO WITH THEM?

There was time a-plenty for deep cogitation on that trip, and my thoughts frequently turned towards memories: specifically making, recording, and storing them. Memories are big business; it's as if we're frightened to live our lives but once, and must record them, whether on DVD or still photos, on Instagram or YouTube, to relive later. And if we lack the time or inclination to watch our visual history ourselves, we post it on Facebook and hope someone else will watch it: *I share, therefore I am.* More than one parent has bewailed missing their child's triumph—a recital, perhaps, or a race—so busy were they recording it for posterity. It struck me that the best Memory Retrieval System may well be the family: more heads are definitely better than one for recalling details. Preferably desperate ones—maybe it's just us, but happy memories where everything goes right and Mum is in a sunny mood are *very* few and far between.

Indeed, the truly ineradicable Bernhoft memories are light years from any Kodak moment: *Remember our second tent trailer jaunt—remember the wasps?* Everyone shudders. Ah yes, we remember the wasps—how they swarmed over the trailer while we ate dinner. How they found a dozen points of entry and one of them stung Fiona. How we all leaped into the van and roared off to purchase duct tape and cotton balls in an attempt to wasp proof our home. How Robin and Iain squashed the enemy invaders, and papa lion Robin put the broom handle through the netting of the door in an attempt to eradicate the villain that he swore had stung his treasured cub. All in all, hardly the images we had entertained in the tent trailer showroom. Those came later, as we sat around the campfire reading "just one more chapter—*please!*" while the light seeped slowly from the purple sunset sky; when we explored tide pools, threw sticks along the beach and raced the dog to fetch them, and discovered by trial and error which foods can be cooked on a campfire and which cannot. Fearing boredom, at first I took along a superabundance of things to do—books, bubble mixture, balls, and Frisbees. But it soon became apparent that the great outdoors, whether beach, mountain, or anywhere in between, comes complete with its own entertainment; my job was simply to play with the littlest ones, and keep at least half a watchful eye on the older siblings.

As for memories, I took the easy way out, trusting the manufacture of recollections to our fallible human memories. To me it seems preferable to experience life once, directly on the retina, rather than a half dozen times through the lens of a camera, whether still or video.

WE SPLIT UP

As far as I was concerned, building family unity meant only one thing: doing activities together, as a family. It gradually dawned on me, however, that fortifying individual relationships also helps strengthen the whole. Accordingly, Robin and I alternated weeks taking each child out in rotation, usually for breakfast. At least, that was the idea; in practice, things were far more haphazard—life had a habit of intervening in the form of illnesses, late nights, or just, well, stuff. Even when the breakfast dates happened, I was frequently discouraged by my inability to converse with my children. I've never been a great one for small talk, and true to form, frequently paralyzed my breakfast partner with a barrage of questions which, intended as conversation openers, had exactly the opposite effect. I could understand it with the boys—after all, why go out for breakfast except to mop up enormous quantities of food?—but I thought girls were supposed to be more relational.

Seeking safety in numbers, I instituted "Girls' Night Out." Once a week, we girls had a date. Depending on our budget, this could be as simple as a walk and a picnic, or it might run to ice-skating and dinner at a restaurant. At first, movies were out—after all, theaters are for watching movies, not chatting with your neighbors—but two things changed my mind. First, movies can provide terrific discussion fodder on the way home and beyond, and second, enjoying something for its sheer entertainment value can be a tremendously bonding experience. Carl Laemmle, who founded Universal Studios in 1912, said he wanted to make America "laugh, cry, and sit on the edge of their seats," and he has definitely succeeded with the Bernhoft girls. At the same time, we had fun developing our "scumbag index," discussing at what point in the movie we realized that the villain was a blackguard, and how the writer or cinematographer had led us to suspect him.

Not knowing what it was, I found "shopping" most intriguing. Growing up in England, I had never regarded buying clothes as a pleasant diversion, much less a way of life; it was a functional, need-based activity. Let's say a clothes moth had a field day with my best wool sweater. I'd wait for the January sales, force my way into the milling throng overflowing the shops, seize my cherished bargain, and retire to lick my wounds over a nice hot cup of tea. (Either that, or knit a sweater myself.) Shopping as leisure activity was a total mystery, but there lurked the unpleasant suspicion that I was missing out— or worse, depriving my daughters of their cultural heritage. I looked for help to six-year-old Fiona: lured by the sartorial carrot of a new dress, she followed me through the hyper-scented portals of Macy's department store. We were shopping!

It was an epic failure. Fiona showed no interest whatsoever in my selection of garments and answered my hopeful, "Would you like to try them on?" with a listless "No," followed by a heartfelt, "Can we go home now—*please*?" It was with a profound sense of relief that I obliged.

But helping the children find quality clothing at bargain prices—that was something I could relate to. It forced me to

curb some of my baser instincts: in England, almost any sartorial disaster will meet with effusive praise as long as it's accompanied by the panacea, "It was a *bargain!*" Now I know better.
If it's the wrong size, the wrong color, or just flat out wrong,
I leave it on the hanger—even if it's $129.99 marked down
to $3.00. After all, nobody wears the price tag. As my bargain
obsession dwindled, the girls sought my fashion advice more
frequently, confident that I would seek out quality fabrics that
would still look good after several washes. Left to their own
devices, they will still never pay full price. Their Scots Granny
would be so proud.

Teenagers, with their distinctive dress, habits, and culture,
were a product of the 1950s. Clothing manufacturers and
advertisers were swift to welcome this brand new market of
impressionable young people, playing equally on the adolescent's desire to be different and their conflicting fear of being
the outsider. "Prove your individuality! Dress like everybody
else!" Unfortunately for girls, "everybody else" is looking more
and more like ladies of the streets, and young men are behav-
ing accordingly. "Date rape" is shockingly common—one out
of eight high school girls report having been raped by someone
they knew, or a family member. "She was asking for it," the
perpetrator argues. "Just look at the way she was dressed!"

So, by way of analogy, let us suppose a healthy young man
is walking past a restaurant. His name is Ronald and he is hungry. Inside, Ronald sees a table laden with food, under a neon

sign proclaiming "ALL YOU CAN EAT!" Picking up a handy brick, he smashes the window and is busy stuffing food into his mouth and baguettes into his pockets when the irate owner rushes up, policeman in tow.

"What do you mean, I had no right?" Ronald remonstrates. "The sign says, *All You Can Eat!* I was only doing what it told me—you were asking for it! If you didn't mean it, you shouldn't advertise it."

Rape is an extreme form of human vandalism, that destroys another human being and can never be justified. The way a girl dresses *never* gives a man the right to treat her like an object, any more than a display of food gives a hungry man the right to loot. Shame on clothing manufacturers for putting adult signifiers of sexuality into children's clothing, even for babies, and shame on adult purchasers who see the sexual innuendo, recognize it for what it is, laugh, and call it "cute."

Any victim will tell you, there's nothing cute about rape.

THE INCIDENT OF THE MUMMIFIED CORNISH GAME HEN

While I love spending time with all my children, I have always particularly treasured time with my girls. When Fiona was nine, I initiated the practice of driving each girl in turn to a hotel an hour away, which boasted a diminutive swimming pool. (We were amused by the notice on the wall: "MAXIMUM OCCUPANCY 64." *They'd have to be wedged in pretty tight*, we giggled, *but perhaps it'll do for two.*)

The evening's format was simple: exploratory walks, hours in the pool sufficient to turn us into wrinkled prunes, dinner, then back to our room to play board games, read, and chitchat before bed. After a leisurely breakfast the next morning, we returned to relieve Robin, who took time off working at home to hold down the fort. On one occasion his good nature was put to a serious test. We called it "The Incident of the Cornish Game Hen."

Shortly before our Irish exodus, we studied Ancient Egypt; eager to demonstrate the mummification process, I applied it to a Cornish game hen. We fashioned papier-mâché canopic jars to hold the inner organs, dried out the hen in bags of salt, wrapped it in torn strips of cotton sheet, rubbed it with oil and herbs, and decorated it with hieroglyphs. Not having a pyramid handy, we left it in the Henrys' garage when we departed for the Emerald Isle. They promised to keep us apprized of any decomposition.

It was more than a year later when we retrieved our mummified treasure and found that, though it smelled distinctly unappetizing, it had certainly not putrefied. It was sitting in our breezeway, partially unwrapped, when Lorna and I went on our first overnight. We enjoyed a long walk, a brief swim, and dinner, and were just settling in for an evening of leisurely chitchat and a game of Rummikub when I got an agonized phone call from Robin. Kidu, still only a puppy, had somehow managed to drag the hen down from the shelf where it sat in state, awaiting its inevitable passage to the garbage can. Not being any too fastidious in his tastes, Kidu had chewed off and partially eaten one of our year-old mummy's legs. He was now wandering around the house in a delirium, bumping into furniture and peeing uncontrollably (truth to tell, peeing wasn't the worst of it). All I could do from thirty miles away was to suggest that Robin call the vet. She gave him the glad news that it was "just" saline-induced dementia; "Give him plenty of water and he'll be fine." Robin was definitely happy about the "he'll be fine" part: it was the "give him plenty of water" that gave him pause. Chasing a demented puppy around the house, brandishing mop and towels, attempting to force water down one end while simultaneously clearing up the not inconsiderable output from the other, was emphatically not his idea of an evening well spent. Kidu's recovery was swift, Robin's less so. It was some time before I dared suggest another overnight.

In fact, individual overnights with the girls never fully recovered; not only was there Robin's unmistakable lack of enthusiasm to contend with, but the trips also put a big hole in our academic week at a time when we were struggling to get anything scholarly done at all. I began to think about taking the three girls (and if possible, the dog) away for a weekend. The older the children grew, the harder it was to clear the calendar, but late one September we managed it. After a ferry ride and a couple of hours of driving we found ourselves in a tiny cottage near Dungeness Spit, at the northeast corner of Washington's Olympic Peninsula.

We had, as the saying goes, a blast. We shopped at an outdoor market, admired hanging baskets of geraniums outside the most picturesque police station ever, had milkshakes at a '50s diner, and walked partway along the spit. Plans to walk the entire five-mile length and back were shelved when we found that the firmest walking surface was a loose shale which absorbed our feet to the ankle at every step. To be perfectly honest, the mere suggestion of a ten-mile hike had been greeted with cries of studied horror from the girls, who swore they'd be perfectly content awaiting my return by doing something more productive, like throwing rocks.

As it happened, we all threw rocks for a while (actually, some of us were trying to skip them, though the casual onlooker might not have known it) before repairing to the cottage to prepare dinner. And drinks. After some devious machinations, the older two girls came up with a vile concoction prominently featuring chocolate milk, Tabasco sauce, and black pepper. Sheila was dared to drink it. Somehow, she managed to choke down half of it, thus not only proving the fortitude of her intestinal tract, but also making a cool five dollars. The rest of the dinner lies obscured by the mists of time, but chocolate milk, Dungeness-style, will never be forgotten.

If I had those years to do over again, I would clear the calendar more often; we came perilously close to a weekend at Harrison Hot Springs in Canada, but the tyranny of the immediate won out—there was always something semi-pressing to do at home, and besides, isn't there always next month? Now there can be no "next month," and I deeply regret the memories we don't have, of the trip we never took. *Carpe diem*, seize the day. All too soon, tomorrow will be here—and we never know what it may bring.

TEN-YEAR-OLD TRIP TO EUROPE

Sitting on a plane at Sea-Tac International Airport as it prepared to take off for our new life in Eire, I listened to eight-year-old Fiona snuffling quietly into her hankie. She was already missing her best friend, Jasmine, and with no prospect of reunion, the future looked bleak. In a moment of compassion, I promised her that on her tenth birthday I would take her anywhere in the world she wanted to go, knowing full well that she would choose Everett.

Two years later we were all back in Everett anyway, and for a happy Fiona, seeing Jasmine was almost an everyday occurrence. But the offer of a trip still held good, and with a little maternal manipulation, Fiona chose Italy as her destination.

Italy offers three levels of historical interest. There's the Roman Empire, traces of which may be seen all over Europe but nowhere more so, predictably enough, than Rome. Then there's the Italy of the Renaissance, which had its first flowering in that country. Last but by no means least is modern Italy, a country of extraordinary contradictions, combining the legendary Italian passion with an altogether unfathomable fondness for multi-level bureaucratic petty-mindedness. No other

European country offers this three-tier richness; for the history buff, art aficionado, and gelato enthusiast alike, all roads do indeed lead to Rome.

Scared half witless at the prospect of bearing sole responsibility for my daughter (not to mention myself) in a foreign country whose language was familiar to me only through musical terms and Grand Opera, I opted for a coach tour, with lodging, meals, and sight-seeing included. This turned out to be the equivalent of satisfying one's appetite at McDonald's — it gets the job done, but does little to titillate the senses. I subsequently discovered Rick Steves's *Europe Through the Back Door*, and was far more adventurous with Lorna; her trip included Italy, Salzburg, and an overnight train to Prague, complete with border officials who had obviously been watching far too many World War Two movies. All night long they crashed the doors open, blinded us with flashlights, and barked, "Achtung! Passports!" The compartment, which we shared with a family of approximately fifteen, was insufferably hot, but preferable to taking our chances with two rather scruffy, middle-aged men of indeterminate origin. Unburdened by worries about safety, Lorna adored every moment; her memories are considerably fonder than her mother's.

Things grew still more adventurous with Sheila, who beyond all else wanted to visit the musical metropolis, Vienna. After three incomparably atmospheric days of Mozart, Beethoven, Brahms, and Schoenberg, we took the by-now-obligatory

overnight train (thanks to the EU, without border guards) to
Venice. From there it was but a short hop to Florence, and
thence to Rome. To keep costs within reach, we traveled
during the off-season when airfares and hotel rates are lower,
and picked up most of our food at sidewalk cafés, bakeries, and
outdoor markets. We avoided expensive tourist traps: when
each girl begged for a fifty-dollar ride on a gondola, I insisted
on leaving that romantic experience for their future husbands;
instead we stood on the *traghetto*, the public bus gondola that
ferries passengers from one side of the Grand Canal to the other. This was technically a gondola ride, I pointed out, and all
for the low, low price of fifty cents. They were not impressed.
One exception to the tourist-trap veto was the bus trip Lorna
and I took in Salzburg, visiting places where *The Sound of
Music* had been filmed. It was a lovely outing, well worth the
money, and spoiled only by my discovery as the bus slid into
gear to depart, that the battery on my camera had just given up
the ghost. Murphy's Law strikes again!

There were innumerable advantages to planning our own
trip. When you go with an organized tour, your hotel will
be probably thirty miles outside Venice, or whichever city is
billed. Promptly at 10:00 a.m. your tour bus will disgorge its
contents (yourself included) at a drop-off point near the center
of town, at the exact same moment as a hundred other buses
are doing precisely the same thing. You will join a solid pha-
lanx of tourists, storming the crowded streets until the buses
descend at 3:00 p.m. to reclaim their willing victims for the

long drive home to a bland, American-style hotel and its bland, American-style food.

Meanwhile the adventurous travelers, with the help of Rick Steves or the always-informative Lonely Planet guides, have selected an atmospheric and surprisingly cheap hotel overlooking the Grand Canal. They rise early, not to sit on a crowded bus for two hours, but to explore the astonishingly colorful riches of the Venetian fish market; they linger over a cappuccino in a St. Mark's Square peopled almost exclusively by pigeons, and by the time the hordes of tourists descend to trample the passage between St. Mark's and the Ponte Vecchio, are back in their hotel room watching boat traffic on the Grand Canal, or exploring the multitude of back-streets and bridges. They play "Find the Bridge": standing on the Grand Canal, they look up a side canal, pinpoint one of the many bridges, and go find it. Sounds simple enough, but when we tried, we were glad we had brought a compass. Whoever designed the maze of streets must have used a plateful of spaghetti for a blueprint. One particular bridge proved infuriatingly elusive, but when we discovered an appliance shop, as well as a rather scruffy café full of extremely crumpled, middle-aged Venetian men, I was triumphant— *this* was the non-tourist Venice that the visitor seldom sees! Come four o'clock, the tide of tourists recedes and it is safe to venture out to the major attractions once more, or to wander the streets and savor the evening in the company of the locals.

Lest I make traveling à la carte sound too idyllic, let me concede that Fiona's is the only trip that inspired no "Misadventures with…" section for this chapter. Lorna's and Sheila's trips were fraught with near-disasters which would command a book in their own right. Puddleglum's exhortation to "expect the worst, and put the best possible face on it" ran through my head more than once; misfortunes, when they arrived, came in droves, and made me question Rick Steves's claim that he got by without even basic foreign language skills. Personally, I used every word I knew of Italian, French, and German, even in desperation throwing in my meager smattering of Russian (it didn't help).

MISADVENTURES WITH LORNA

Lorna and I enjoyed a marvelous last morning in Venice and confidently arrived at the *vaporetto* stop to catch the waterbus to the railway station. Never had I seen the Grand Canal look so deserted. Ignoring the ominous tug in the pit of my stomach, we settled in to wait. And wait. And wait…*We could have walked to the station by now…*

Finally, a Spanish woman descended on the stop. With my background in Latin, I could decipher her Spanish if she spoke slowly enough, while she was able to understand my French, at a snail's pace. To my horror I learned that the *vaporetti* had gone on strike (*sciopero*) at 11:00 a.m. It was now 12:30, and our train left at 1:00. I waved down a passing water taxi and brandished a $20 bill at him—we had used our last Italian money to buy two small rolls and two satsumas to see us into Austria. But no, he wanted $40 to go a distance of about three hundred yards (by water, it was a straight shot). What could I do but pay up?

We arrived at the station with seconds to spare, but the train, predictably enough, was two hours late. *That's $40 down the tubes—we could have sauntered and still been in time.* I was told that the train split in two at Villach, on the Austrian side of the border: half went on to Salzburg and half to Vienna. Our hotel, with its highly recommended dining room, was in Salzburg.

We entered a compartment. In my extremely rusty German, I inquired, *"Diese zug geht nach Salzburg?"* This train goes to Salzburg?

A strapping lass with long, blonde braids and a round, smiling face nodded, *"Ja, ja!"*

"Wirklich?" I queried, to be doubly sure. Really?

The bright pink cheeks beamed even more broadly. *"Ja, ja!"*

Just to be on the safe side, I asked again at Villach and met with the same assurance. It was not until the ruddy-cheeked ticket collector inspected our tickets as we left Villach that I learned the ghastly truth: we were on a carriage bound for Vienna. He bundled us off the train at the very next station. There, on the other side of the platform, stood a train. Good news! It was bound for Salzburg. Bad news! It stopped at each and every hamlet, however microscopic, on the way. More bad news—the conductor wanted us to pay for the extra, unintentional leg of our trip, and in Austrian money.

Urgently, I explained our predicament. I had no Austrian money. If I left the train to find some, my daughter would go on to Salzburg without me. He was unmoved. In desperation, I ransacked my brain for any remnants of German I could muster, and came up with a few lines of Goethe from my college days. I intoned them in my darkest, most sepulchral tones: *"Tiefe Stille herrscht im Wasser…Todesstille fürchterlich"* (A deep silence reigns in the water/ A terrible, deathly hush). He exited abruptly—*Oh dear, did my accent offend him?*—and reappeared a moment later with a second conductor. *"Noch einmal!"* he exhorted. Do it again! He demanded the saga of the wrong train in its entirety and made me stumble through it repeatedly to several different audiences, always insisting on the Goethe as a closing flourish.

Finally, his face creased into a smile and he waved his arms around to indicate we could stay on the train. *"Verklarte Nacht!"* I exclaimed ("Transfigured Night" was, happily enough, the title of the work by Arnold Schoenberg that was the subject of my undergraduate thesis). Deeply delighted, he left again; when he returned, still beaming, he bore an American newspaper, full of details of the Bush/Gore election stalemate—a peace offering, I suppose. Heads swimming with the traumatic events of our day's travel, it was strange indeed to read about the political passions gripping our homeland. The outcome of the presidential race seemed to us infinitely less pressing than finding something to eat.

By the time we arrived in Salzburg, it was 9:00 p.m. and we had eaten only the two rolls and satsumas in over twelve hours. I decided to splurge on a taxi and went to get some Austrian money from a cash machine. The ATM chewed my card pensively, hesitated, chewed it some more, and spat it out. A smiley face symbol appeared on the screen. *Our bank cannot communicate with your bank. Try again later. Have a nice day!*

Staggering under the weight of our backpacks, practically fainting with hunger, we sought out a taxi. Not only did the driver take American money, he even gave us a fair exchange rate; a generous tip rewarded him for restoring my faith in human nature. He delivered us to our hotel—just in time to learn that the famous restaurant had closed its doors five minutes earlier. No amount of entreaties would persuade them to offer hospitality to two starving travelers. Turfed out into the deserted streets, we searched for any establishment offering food, and had to make do with an American style, all-night eatery that charged an arm and a leg for—well, I'm not exactly sure what it was, but there definitely wasn't very much of it.

So traumatized was Lorna by the trials of the day that she steadfastly refused to leave our room the following morning. I had to coax her down the stairs cut deep into the stone walls of the hotel, step by fourteenth-century step, to the room where breakfast awaited. Twelve rashers of bacon, two fried eggs, and five pots of Nutella later, she was ready to face the day.

MISADVENTURES WITH SHEILA

Besides Vienna, Sheila was most eager to visit Venice; she had read and re-read the copy of *Vendela in Venice* that had been her tenth birthday present, and was more than ready to see *Venezia* through the young Swedish girl's eyes.

I had economized on our hotel so we'd have more money to spare for exploring Venice itself, but two hours into our visit, I was deeply regretting it. The bathroom was so tiny that I had to slide the sink over the toilet to get at the shower—and it turned out that the showerhead sprayed into every corner of the room, which was bad luck for the clean clothes I had put out in readiness. The towel was, incredibly enough, dirty, and when I retrieved my backpack from the "safe place" I had been instructed to leave it, the paper bag of Christmas presents from Vienna was gone.

Sheila and I left our Hotel of Horrors, our steps soon straying toward the Ponte dell'Accademia, the bridge near which Vendela and her father had stayed. Just for fun, we figured out which hotel was hers; just for fun, we went inside; just for fun, we asked if they had a vacancy…*and they did!* They had just had a one-night cancellation and when they showed us the room…*it was Vendela's room!* It was like a fairytale: we sat in the same chairs, in the same window, looking out at the same view, as Vendela. The plumbing was ancient and had its eccentricities, but that night was pure magic. I even got our deposit back from the Dirty Towel Hotel.

The management found us a room for the second night at their other beautifully restored hotel, in which each room was named after an Italian composer. Ours was *Cimarosa*, and it did not have a telephone. As we checked in, I had no idea how important this apparently trivial detail was to prove.

Throwing economy to the winds, we walked right past the stand-up pizza counters and into a small restaurant that boasted a menu of freshly caught fish (if anything living in the overgrown sewage lagoon that the Mediterranean has become can be described as "fresh," that is). Now here we were, back in *Cimarosa*; time for an early bed so we could get to the station in plenty of time for our 7:45 a.m. train to Florence.

Sheila, however, was very far from sleepy. Burning with fever, she was vomiting profusely and clutching at her stomach, which was unbearably painful. *Appendicitis? Or simply the fish?*

Grabbing my credit card, I tore down to the vestibule to call Robin from the public phone. It was in use. Seeing a demented woman hopping frantically from one foot to the other, the young man cut short his call—judging by his arm movements he had been planning a mass murder—and courteously moved aside. I rushed to call home. The connection clicked maddeningly; would it never go through? Hooray! Robin answered. His familiar voice seemed to enfold me; surely now everything would be all right. As I described Sheila's symptoms, he clicked into doctor mode. *Is the pain localized to the left lower quadrant?* I ran upstairs to check: yes, it was.

I hurtled back downstairs, where the young man was just picking up the phone. Taking one look at me, he relinquished it hastily. There was a distinct edge to Robin's voice: his little girl was ill, five thousand miles away. *Is it painful to the touch?* Back up the marble staircase. Sheila had thrown up again and was lying in the fetal position, weeping from pain and exhaustion. I pried her knees from her chest. *Yes, it is painful to the touch.*

Up and down that marble staircase I ran. Every time I looked at her, she seemed in worse condition. *Should I take her to an emergency room?* Robin ordered one last test: I positively bullied Sheila into getting out of bed and standing on the balls of her feet. She bounced down hard on her heels. *It didn't hurt!* Relief flooded over me. There would be no medical field trip after all.

We left the hotel not many hours later, me carrying both backpacks and trying to support my virtually comatose daughter as we stumbled through the early morning streets of Venice to catch the *vaporetto* (no strikes this time) and thus to the station. The train to Florence was punctual, Sheila's fever had abated, and a kindly onlooker came up with a strategic plastic bag in the nick of time. She slept all day, ate a little dinner in our room, and rallied the next morning for an extensive walking tour of Florence, including an interior tour of Brunelleschi's Dome which involved an impressive number of stairs. Truly, a recovery of epic proportions!

With hindsight, we see that her mock appendicitis was a dry run for the real thing three years later. At the time, it scared me witless. Back home, when friends gushed, "You went to *Venice*? How *fun!*" and time did not permit a full rendition of the *Cimarosa* nightmare, I simply rolled my eyes and muttered inwardly, "If you did but know…"

FURTHER MISADVENTURES WITH LORNA: PRAGUE

The German language is positively overflowing with useful words, and not just for Germans. Take *Schadenfreude*, for instance: literally "harm-joy," or pleasure derived from witnessing the misfortunes of others, it has its American counterpart in "rubbernecking." Both give rise to enormous traffic jams as drivers crane their necks to view possible carnage in a police incident on the freeway—only to discover that it is nothing more than a fender bender, or even a speeding ticket.

Nevertheless, this is a very real characteristic of *homo sapiens*, and the story of Lorna's and my two (make that three) taxi rides in Prague should go some way towards indulging it.

Bleary-eyed and feeling distinctly the worse for wear, Lorna and I emerged from the Prague railway station at 6:30 a.m. and swiftly decided to indulge in a taxi, which I had read were cheap and reliable.

Cheap, maybe; reliable—judge for yourself. After a disturbingly long drive, during which certain landmarks became rather too familiar for comfort, our driver (I'll call him Pavel) grew distinctly agitated. He assured me in his fractured English accompanied by wild gesticulations (which, to my horror, involved both hands leaving the steering wheel simultaneously) that our hotel was very close—so close, indeed, that it would be the easiest thing in the world for us to walk the rest of the way.

In vain did I search my Czech phrasebook for the Slavic equivalent of "not bloody likely, mate," but Pavel got the message; he decided to ditch us in short order and search for a more gullible fare. Assuring me that our hotel was not, in fact, accessible by road, he screeched to a halt just before a left turn onto a one-way street going the wrong way. He had just remembered—the hotel was but a hundred yards around this very corner!

Tired, disgruntled, distressingly in need of a shower—by now my ire was thoroughly up; I exited the taxi, marched the few yards to the corner, rounded it and there, just as I had expected—no hotel!

It was then that I experienced (literally) the expressions "her blood ran cold" and "her knees turned to jelly" as I realized the enormity of what I had just done: there I was standing all alone on one street, while the taxi driver and his vehicle containing all my worldly belongings *and my one and only ten-year-old daughter* were on another! Aware of no sound but a thunderous rushing in my ears, scarcely daring to breathe, I regained the taxi, counted out the preposterous amount of money Pavel requested, and retrieved both backpacks and daughter. (So great was my terror and subsequent relief that it was many years before I summoned up the courage to recount this particular story. Indeed it is still not lightly told.) A second taxi deposited us at the door of the elusive hotel which, unsurprisingly, wasn't even close to Pavel's corner. I had no qualms about requesting a room on a higher floor than the dingy excuse for a coat closet initially offered us, and we were rewarded with a small room hardly bigger than a garret, but with dormer windows that afforded a magical view of Prague's bewitching skyline.

Note to would-be travelers: five days in Prague in November will seem an eternity and give you the keenest appreciation for the beneficial effects of tourism. And of capitalism: the shadow of communism still lay over the city, whose filthy streets were lined with overflowing garbage cans, and people's faces looked tired and listless. We met a homeschooling family and the father's eyes grew wide with wonder when I showed him a family photo taken in our backyard. His family of seven lived in a three-room apartment surrounded by concrete and he could not imagine the luxury of children running outside to play *on grass*.

For my part, I couldn't imagine allowing my children outside to play in this foul, murky air that choked our lungs. Not since my days in the industrial north of England had I blackened my hankie when I blew my nose, and this was one memory I would have happily left undisturbed.

The powers-that-be were evidently trying to appeal to tourists; various public buildings, including the famous Charles Bridge (which, we were enlightened to read, was a hub of colorful activity—in the summer months) were identified by meticulously executed, clear Perspex signs, whose careful black lettering spelled out…total gibberish! It seemed that funds had not run to a competent translator, and sign-makers had relied on a Czech–Spanish, then Spanish–English dictionary for their vocabulary. It was rather quaint, endearing even, as long as one had no desire to discover anything factual about, say, St. Vitus Cathedral's artistic masterpieces.

Our last night in Prague was exquisite, a jewel among our string of memories. No more restaurant pork and overcooked potatoes for us; we purchased a picnic from a corner grocer. "*Dobry den* (good day)," we said as we entered. The shopkeeper's face all but split in two, so grateful was she for our feeble attempt at her native tongue. I'm pretty sure the torrent of Czech that followed included an invitation to their imminent family reunion, and I may unwittingly have married Lorna off to their eldest son when I smiled and nodded "*ano*," yes.

Back at the hotel we ate our cheese, bread, grapes, and crackers, and watched the sun go down behind the skyline that has earned Prague the nickname "City of a Hundred Spires." Together we worked on the little Mensa book, *Word*

Puzzles for Kids. I was loath for the evening to end; I loved being in my daughter's company and had a sneaking suspicion that, once back in the noisy chaos of our eight-person home, I could say *na shledanou* (goodbye) to time alone with her. Nevertheless, the sad fact was that we had to arise early next morning to get to the airport.

Ah yes, the third taxi…

Lurking in the back of my mind all through our five interminable, soot-caked days was the specter of how to get to the airport for our 10:00 a.m. flight. The hotel clerk strongly advised against the "unreliable" public transport *(what, worse than a taxi?!)*, instead recommending a taxi with an 8:30 pick-up time. Yes, the airport is *very* close, hardly any time at all… Get there thirty minutes to spare, will be plenty early…What? You want pick up at 6:00? *SIX O'CLOCK???* Crazy Engleesh lady, we don't even be up then! Very well, 6:30 it is.

The first thing to say about our taxi driver is that he was very, very late. The second is that the reason for his lateness was apparent in his red-rimmed eyes and unsteady gait.

Perhaps it was Pavel's brother; whoever it was, he was definitely, indisputably drunk.

By now, my desire to be safe at home was like a raging thirst and my metaphorical tongue was cleaving to the roof of my mouth. The drunken driver represented the only link between us and home, so with my heart in my mouth (another vivid expression comes to life) I steered Lorna and our backpacks into the cab.

As the dismal sun rose on the dreary landscape, I was appalled to see the roads become narrower, more rutted, and less…well, less like roads leading to a major international airport *should* look. In particular, signposts with airplanes on them first became scarce, then disappeared altogether. Time ticked by and with it apparently went all hope of ever reaching home. Frantically I scanned the phrasebook and asked, as we hung a sudden U-turn onto a one-lane dirt road, if he was quite sure this really was the best way to the airport.

Assuring me it was, his bloodshot eyes met and locked on mine in the rear-view mirror. Terror engulfed me (there we go again…) as I realized that the only way to keep his eyes even remotely focused on the road ahead was to avoid drawing any attention to myself whatsoever.

I put the phrase book away, closed my eyes, and prayed… AND WE GOT THERE!

Twenty-seven straight hours of air travel never looked so sweet as it did to us that morning—it led home.

While none of my female friends have emulated my European jaunts, the idea of a tenth birthday trip closer to home has won a few fans. What a powerful message it sends to a girl that her mother wants to spend all that time just with her. And how significant is the age of ten—she is poised on the brink of the monumental changes of puberty, ready, perhaps, to begin to relate to her mother in a different way. And ready to start exploring and appreciating different cultures, embracing new experiences with the passionate enthusiasm of one newly awakened. What a privilege it is to share in that adventure!

16

THOSE TREMENDOUS
TEEN YEARS

He may be cute now, the doomsayers cackled over Iain's crib, *but just you wait till he's a teenager!* I was struck with dread, imagining him sprouting horns and facial warts at the onset of puberty and going rapidly downhill from there. When Iain did become a teen, however, I found I liked him, if anything, even more. We had had the "little talk" about the glorious mysteries of hormones. I had warned him that his father and I might soon seem to him the most benighted souls on the face of the earth, but that he would probably find, as did Mark Twain before him, that this lamentable state of affairs would pass: "When I was a boy of 14, my father was so ignorant I could hardly stand to have the old man around. But when I got to be 21, I was astonished at how much the old man had learned in seven years." I assured Iain that, although he would no doubt extend the fourteen-year-old Twain's opinion to both his parents, nevertheless the three of us had some rather important things in common: we all wanted Iain to get the best education possible, to be happy, and to emerge into his twenties loving God, his family, and his neighbor. In this particular battle, we were on the same side.

Not that the teenage years are easy—far from it. There is a central tension in the teen/parent relationship: as the teen moves away from childhood towards independence, she needs the emotional security of childhood more than ever. Seeing that need, she despises herself for her weakness, for wanting, at some level, the familiar comfort of her mother's arms. She pushes her mother away, deliberately hurts her, even. The rejected mother retreats and promptly constructs a safety barrier—anything to avoid more pain. Thus is born a vicious cycle, which is not infrequently perpetuated to the grave. The reason I use the pronoun "she" is that the worst conflict tends to be with the same sex parent and the maternal relationship is the more primordial. Thus the mother/daughter conflict has the greatest potential for toxicity.

This poem, written by the Frenchman Jean Richepin, who died in 1926, may seem ghoulish to some, but will speak to any parent whose heart has been broken by a child of either sex. The original work is untitled, thus this title is only my suggestion:

For Those Whose Children Are Breaking Their Heart

A young man once did love a maid
Who taunted him. "Are you afraid,"
She asked, "to bring to me today
Your mother's heart upon a tray?"

He went and slew his mother dead
Tore from her breast her heart so red
Then towards his lady-love he raced
But tripped and fell in all his haste.

As the heart rolled on the ground
It gave forth a plaintive sound
And it spoke, in accents mild:
"Did you hurt yourself, my child?"

So how is a mother to gird herself for this potential emotional maelstrom? First, by refusing the role of victim. Her children's actions and opinions have no bearing on her intrinsic worth, nor is she defined by her offspring's perceptions. She clutches at her mantra: "This too shall pass." Those four little words worked wonders with morning sickness, with teething, with toilet training—they will work with teenage troubles too (given time and a mutual desire for reconciliation). It also helps to have the firm basis of a strong family life to fall back on and I was always eager for ideas to help us create a healthy family.

THE FAMILY MOTTO

Having once been a child myself, it shouldn't have come as a surprise to me that children are not naturally considerate, polite, and soft-spoken with one another. They shout, they squabble, they even (oh, horror!) indulge in physical violence. In vain did I drum into them that friends would come and go but siblings are forever. After one particularly harrowing argument, during which four-year-old Sheila had tried her sister's patience beyond endurance, Lorna wailed, "If Sheila is forever, let me die now!" Sheila flung herself to the floor, howling as though her heart would break. Something had to be done.

In mediaeval times, a motto emblazoned on the family crest called forth the virtue most lacking in a family; while I greatly envied my school friend's daring "Be Bloody, Bold and Resolute!" it didn't take me long to recognize that Love and Respect topped the Bernhoft list. Translated to the Latin *amor et observantia* and emblazoned on our family crest (the product of an impromptu unit study on heraldry and mediaeval history), Love and Respect were ready for battle.

Thereafter, I interrupted the bitterest arguments with "In this family we treat each other with…" and the children rolled their eyes, feigned a swoon, and growled between clenched teeth, "I know, I know, love and respect." Sheila squealed in agony as Lorna dug her fingernails into her forearm to emphasize "respect." Whether they meant it or not, they had to say it, and perhaps it had some effect: Sheila and Lorna are now the best of friends (and the fingernail marks no longer show).

That was not the only time the children had to say things they might not mean. I once asked them what they thought "I'm sorry" meant; surprisingly enough, they didn't know. My answer: "I wish I hadn't done it and I won't do it again." They hated it, but they repeated it. That was enough for me.

RITES OF PASSAGE

Many cultures celebrate a child's transition to adulthood with some ceremony in the early teenage years. Neither Britain, Ireland, nor Iceland offered anything to fit the bill, so Iain had to make do with camping trips to ease him into manhood, as well as skiing expeditions and Mariners baseball games with Dad. When Iain was away at college and Robin was on the road, I impressed Evan with his status as Man of the House. This was a role he filled admirably one particularly windy day, when our old magnolia tree blew down and Evan saved both the power lines and the day by chopping up the fallen limbs with his trusty machete.

The girls needed something with a little more TLC. When Fiona came of age, I was ready with a plan. Robin was to take her out for dinner and give her two roses—one red, symbolizing her becoming a woman, and one white for purity. Waiting at home, I fondly imagined the tender father-daughter scene unfolding in the candlelit ambience of Gianni's Italian restaurant, and anticipated Robin's report of this momentous occasion.

When they walked in, Robin seemed more than a little sheepish; he answered my eager "How did it go?" with a non-committal "Fine." There ensued an awkward silence. "They didn't have roses at Safeway," he volunteered at length, "so I got her this instead." From behind his back he drew—a yellow cactus. Nonplussed at my howls of laughter, he protested indignantly, "Well, it'll last a lot longer than a couple of cut roses, won't it?"

Yes, it did indeed. It's just the symbolism, you see—oh, never mind. A yellow purity cactus: just what every girl dreams of.

SELF-CONTROL

All my life, I've struggled with self-control. I have had to deal with events that included crushing disappointments and worse; it made me angry and frustrated to have no control over the bad things that happened.

Stephen Covey's *The 7 Habits of Highly Successful Families* came as a revelation to me. According to Covey, between any negative stimulus and one's reaction there is a pause, and in that pause lies the freedom to choose: will I react in an unthinking, automatic way, or filter my response through what I have learned of the redemptive power of suffering and my concern for others? Suppose I pick up a plate and it burns my fingers; my natural response is to drop it. Now suppose that plate is a piece of Josiah Wedgwood's first set, dating from

1759; I overcome the initial urge to let go and, even though it burns my fingers, put it down carefully. There is a higher order at work than animal instinct.

For some types of temperament, and when hormones are raging, instinct is very close to the surface and reaction is all but instantaneous; but the pause, however small, is always there. My gift to the two younger girls when they became women (one purity cactus was enough) was a distinctive brace-let they could wear at their time of the month. It was a signal for me to treat them with a little extra love and respect, on the understanding that this would be the only indication they'd give: no histrionics, no temper tantrums. The choice to control our behavior, to respond like a rational being rather than react like an animal, is a freedom that is ours for the claiming.

ILLNESS

The girls insist that they were unfailingly dragged out of their bed of sickness by a tyrannical mother screaming at them to clean the house, or else. That a 103° fever was not sufficient to relieve them of vacuuming duties. That while other mothers solicitously tucked their flu-stricken offspring in front of the TV with tempting drinks and a cool, lavender-scented wash-cloth, all they got was *Winnie the Pooh* on tape and a glass of tap water if they fetched it themselves. That's not quite the way I remember it, but it's three against one…

Whatever injustices they may have suffered, the girls are

grateful now; in the real world, neither college finals nor a senior recital are put on hold for the flu, and the girls have muscled through both. Lorna was aghast when a friend of hers at university didn't go to Germany for spring break because *she thought she might be getting a cold.* Lorna knows that life goes on in the face of illness. To help her cope with friends who have not yet learned this, I penned the following poem:

Ode to my Ailing Friend, by LDB

I hear you're feeling poorly and I'm sorry, yes, 'tis
   true;
I'm certain you'll be quite recovered in a day or two.
So meanwhile, please don't text me every hour, or
   even less,
To tell me that your virus has now moved into
   your chest,
That your head's on fire, you're coughing gobs
   of sputum white and green,
You hate your life, your suff'ring is the most
   the world has seen.

Stiff upper lip! Go to it with a will, and bear in
   mind
You're not the only representative of humankind
To suffer so: and some have even lived to tell the
   tale
As well you may. Your antibodies know just what to
   do
If you'll only rest and let them, without getting in a
   stew.

You'll soon enjoy your health again, hearty, well
   and hale.

For now, only remember that I've had it up to here
With all your gripes and wailing, and that's why
   I'm steering clear.

YEARBOOKS

The year Sheila was born, I bought some cheap notebooks and stuck in photographs of the family engaged in everyday activities. The books acted like magnets, inviting the children to pore over them, remembering the places they'd gone, the things they'd done, and the people they'd met. As they repeatedly turned the pages, the weakness of the system became apparent: my prized yearbooks were falling apart. If they were to survive as treasured family heirlooms, which given the time and effort I'd put into them, they better had, an investment in acid-free, archival materials was required. No sorry pools of acid on my bookshelves!

The first picture each September features our home-school: the children and their teacher, yours truly. Next come individual back-to-school photos of each child posed in front of a piece of shrubbery; some years (inertia being a potent force) it took until November to accomplish even this simple task. I invested in a quality camera and, even though it was a bulky SLR, took it everywhere to record field trips, recitals, the new violin teacher, or outings with friends. At home, it captured quiet moments reading on the sofa or in a tent fashioned from sheets draped over dining-room chairs. It recorded science experiments in the bathtub; Jim, our faithful window cleaner; the children cooking dinner. I made a "Before and After" book: a twig coming into blossom, then covered with apples; a flower-bed newly planted, then rich with the plentiful bounty of late summer; Fiona's hands before and after she stopped biting her fingernails; an autumn leaf next to a leaf skeleton. I took photos of overnight guests. When twelve-year-old Diana first spent the night, I realized as her father drove up to fetch her that I had forgotten to capture her and Fiona on film. *Never mind, I'll get them next time.* There was no next time. Diana was killed in a car crash two weeks later. Never have I so regretted not taking a picture.

My yearbooks would win no prizes for artistically arranged pages or novel use of thematic stickers. Rather, the pages are filled with photographs cut into random shapes, labeled with comments both pithy and apposite. My primary goal was simply to get the photos into the book, with enough commentary to explain to future generations who that curious-looking creature with the decomposing pumpkin might be. As the girls grew older, they loved to plan the pages and help cut and glue. Whether digital or paper, their future yearbooks will be something to behold.

THE BEST WAYS TO LOVE YOUR TEENS IS TO LOVE THEIR FRIENDS

Remembering my own excruciatingly awkward and lonely teenage years, I wanted to let my children's friends know that I both noticed them, and cared. I was particularly drawn to those who wouldn't make eye contact, for this is often a hallmark of low self-esteem. In an effort to offer them acceptance and respect, I blasted them with questions about their private lives that had my children cringing with embarrassment. For the most part, my victims took it in stride. They knew I meant well and some even seemed to like it. Some even looked me in the eye when they said goodbye.

Even teens who seem to have it all together can be deeply touched by a thoughtful word. Some years ago, I wrote a letter to a girl who had been spending quite a bit of time at our house, listing ten reasons why I considered her an Honorary Bernhoft. I subsequently learned that she framed the letter and hung it in her dorm room. How easy it would have been not to have written that letter. How glad I am that I did.

Strong families are in perilously short supply these days and need all the help they can get. Reaching out to our children's friends has brought great joy and continues to make our family stronger. True, it didn't exactly make life easier when Sheila descended on us with a half-dozen bohemian youths from Idyllwild Arts Academy, but making those young people welcome for a weekend filled our house with vitality and happiness. All the reward I needed was their presence, and if one person said, "Sheila, your parents are awesome," it was enough.

MAKING OUR HOUSE TEEN-FRIENDLY

When we moved from London to Everett, we found a housing market so depressed that we were able to buy a large house on a bluff for the price of a one-bedroom apartment in San Francisco. We unloaded our pitiful supply of scruffy furniture and, listening to our voices echo off the walls of empty rooms, wondered how we were to fill this house—what sort of home did we want it to be?

Iain was just two and Andrew but a bump in my tummy; it seemed impossible that they would ever be out of diapers, let alone wanting to hang out with friends. But I put myself into subjunctive mode: *assuming that* popular wisdom is correct and the children will one day be teenagers, and *also assuming that* the teen years are inevitably out of control and downright awful (the climax to the bad news of parenthood I'd been warned about over Iain's cradle) didn't it make sense to keep these volatile creatures close to home to monitor the damage? And the best way to achieve that was to make them want to bring their friends here. So the answer to the question of what sort of home we wanted was "a place where children, particularly teenagers, feel welcome." This decision came as balm to my housekeeping woes: I've never yet seen a teenager run a white-gloved finger along a mantelpiece to detect telltale specks of dust, nor look askance at piles of books threatening to topple all over the living-room floor. And I had a sneaking suspicion that a teen-friendly house would also be inviting to adults—at least those who were more interested in relation-ships than appearances.

Having set my sights on a teen-worthy house, I spent the following years working to accomplish that goal. This was the motivation behind the annual Family Christmas Present that was unveiled around teatime every December 24. The most successful of these was unquestionably the pool table.

There had been some heavy hints from our eldest son that his life would be vastly improved by a pool table, but knowing how expensive they were, I demurred. Just to be sure, Robin and I went to the pool store to check; sure enough, they were prohibitively expensive. Phoning home, we explained to Iain that we couldn't afford such exorbitant prices—which was, strictly speaking, the truth. What we neglected to mention was that a secondhand table was well within our budget. The seller reluctantly agreed to deliver it on Christmas Eve while Robin and I conspired to distract Iain; but when we unveiled our masterpiece, we were met not with the cries of astonished joy we so confidently expected, but rather a savvy "I knew you'd get one" from our eldest son. So much for our duplicity at the pool store.

Teens generally come as a package deal, with parents and younger siblings who all need to be made to feel wel-come. I used to labor under the delusion that hospitality was something that happened after the house was clean. Books written by women with a quite extraordinary knack for managing any number of children while keeping their homes orderly, spotless, and inviting, threw into painful relief my own struggles to keep even one bathroom remotely clean. While they worried about scented guest soaps and immaculate guest towels, I sought the quickest way to deal with a bathroom festooned with toilet paper and toothpaste. My attempts to instill order on the kitchen took constant vigilance and almost all my time, so I gave it up as a bad job. It looked as though, if I were to realize my dreams of hospitality, visitors would have to make do with a house that was more than slightly scruffy, run by a well-intentioned but visibly frazzled woman to whom Martha Stewart was but a name from a distant galaxy.

I joined a women's Bible study that involved monthly luncheons in members' homes. Filled with dread at the prospect of putting my home on show, I was first to volunteer as hostess—at least that way I'd gain points for willingness. Obviously I was way out of my housekeeping depths, so I went for authenticity: "This is how I live, and I'm glad you're here." Far from being censorious, my guests seemed genuinely pleased by the welcome; and if there was any malice behind one woman's enthusiastic "I do admire you, opening your home when it looks like this," I chose to ignore it.

And so my hospitality style was established, and it has served me in good stead ever since. The recipe is simple: mix together congenial people from every generation, add food, music, maybe a group activity or game, and entertainment happens. Fears preceding any social event—*What if nobody comes? What if they turn up their nose at my cooking? What if they despise me for my messy house?*—always proved groundless.

They say that the mother is the heart of the family—*If Momma ain't happy, ain't nobody happy*—and I was eager to keep this particular momma healthy, both physically and mentally. A nutritious diet and twice-daily walks with the dog took care of the physical component, but how to keep the grey matter between the ears in tip-top shape? Research suggests that the brain keeps forming new connections as long as it is asked to perform new functions, to learn new things. Accordingly, on my forty-fifth birthday, I resolved to do at least one new thing every year. First came learning the cello, which continued for the next five years. (I chose the cello because the children's enthusiasm for their string instruments was flagging and I hoped to lead by example.) I practiced for an hour after they went to bed; for years, they drifted off to the strains of me struggling to master fifth position and vibrato. Eventually I returned to the piano, serenading them instead with Schubert Impromptus or Brahms Intermezzi. My "one new thing every year" included ice-skating, calligraphy, learning Italian, waterskiing, gymnastics, salsa dancing, drawing wildflowers, karate, and stand-up comedy.

Did I become an expert in everything I tried? In *anything*? Not by a long shot! The magic was in the process, not the product. My adventure in waterskiing is a perfect illustration.

Every summer we spent a week at a family camp on Keats Island near Vancouver, British Columbia. I watched legions of young people, including my own children, learn to ski; a few floundered helplessly behind the boat the first few times, but an inspiring number of them took off at the first attempt and by the end of the week were dropping a ski and looking like pros. Then there were those intimidating women closer to my age who had been skiing all their lives; I had to remind myself forcibly that behind the flawless tans and rippling muscles lurked a human being with the same personal shortcomings and sense of inadequacy as myself. I am easily intimidated by great physical beauty and athletic ability, and both were in abundant supply at those summer camps.

And yet I longed to ski. In my declining years, I wanted to be able to look back and say "At least I tried." So one year I did it. Remembering Evan's piano lessons, I set my sights low: every day, I would risk the scorn of the super-fit, don a pair of skis, get into the water (no matter how cold), clutch the rope tightly, and do my best to stand up. Yes, I had visions of flying across the water, casually brushing back my hair with one hand and waving to the admiring onlookers. Yes, I saw myself coasting back to the dock and into the waiting arms of my adoring children, to cries of "Gosh, Mum, you were terrific! We're so *proud* of you!"

Dream on, dream on. But I did achieve my goal: every day I plunged into the icy drink and tried my best. Fortunately, it was so cold that few others were foolhardy enough to brave the water, so at least there were no impatient lines of would-be skiers tapping their feet as I toppled over again, and again, and again. But something about my pathetic ineptitude brought the sympathetic out in droves; by the end of the week, half the camp was waiting to welcome me with cheers and applause as I made my wobbly way back to the dock. All the world loves an underdog, and an underdog in an undertow is better yet. I scratched one more thing off my lifetime "to-do" list. Afterwards, a teenager confided to me that my efforts had given her the confidence to get behind a boat herself for the first time. It was worth it just for that.

My mother raised me with the maxim "if a thing's worth doing, it's worth doing well." However true this may be in the routine chores of everyday life—making a bed, for instance—I found it distinctly stultifying in more creative arenas, where a better motto might be, "If a thing's worth doing, it's worth doing badly." Take drawing wildflowers, for instance. At family outings to a park, or during Andrew's Special Olympics soccer practices, there was often time to spare after Kidu's obligatory walk, so I started to take along a drawing notebook and pencil. The wildflower sketches that resulted will never grace the walls of any natural history museum, but the act of drawing them made me look more intently at the natural world, and to observe is to wonder. Moreover, my amateurish scratchings inspired more than one friend to remember, *I used to do stuff like that*, dig out sketchbook and pencils, and follow suit.

Waterskiing or wildflowers, both well worth doing badly.

GIRLS' GROUP

Fiona's teenage years were fast approaching. Thus far, she seemed a well-balanced, even likeable young lady, but just to be on the safe side, better be proactive, I thought. Suppose I gave her circle of friends a monthly venue where they could practice social skills, eat, spend an hour or so discussing their worldviews, and finish with some serious "chillaxing." I had a hunch that teenage girls have considerably more going on between the ears than just clothes and, like, you know, *stuff*, and wanted to put my hunch to the test. Accordingly, Girls' Group was born.

Over the years the format changed very little; occasionally the girls dressed up for a more formal dinner, but most of the time the evening was casual and went as follows:

> *4:30–5:00 Girls arrive bearing their assigned food: sal-
> ad, main dish, vegetables, drinks, or dessert. Noise
> level increases exponentially.*
> *5:30–6:30 Girls eat. Noise level flattens out just this
> side of deafness-inducing. They clean up the kitchen
> and pray the rosary before serving dessert.*
> *7:00–8:00 I read a chapter and we discuss it. The book
> could be anything that makes us think and question*

our beliefs. Why do we live the way we do? How do
we know what is right and what is wrong? Is there a
deeper truth than the Golden Rule? As Catholics,
we found conversion stories to be powerful food for
thought. This girl "had it all" but felt there was
something lacking in her life. What was she miss-
ing? Why did she feel she had "come home" when
she came into the Church?
   8:00–9:30 Free time before parental intervention to
   whisk the girls home.

Some girls were ready to carry on talking past the allot-
ted hour, but others grew restless; so, while the formal session
usually disbanded close to eight o'clock, discussion sometimes
continued in small groups. The girls mostly welcomed this
opportunity to discuss the more profound things in life, listening respectfully to each other. When one girl threatened to
dominate the discussion, I requested that every speaker wait till
at least two others had aired their views before speaking again.
This worked well, and I have used the technique since then in
groups of all ages.

Recognizing that the day would come when these girls
would be faced with an interview, either for a job or a place in
college, I had them practice putting themselves forward well,
with a firm handshake, direct eye contact, and clear speech.
Amid howls of protest, I declared our house a "like-free zone,"
telling them that they were free to sound like teenage morons
anywhere and everywhere else, but at my address they like
weren't, like, allowed to, like, say "like." Unless, of course, it
was in a simile—my love may still be "like" a red, red rose.

Feeling distinctly countercultural and more than a little com-
bative, I imposed a twenty-five-cent fine for each errant "like."
Money certainly mounted up in the "like jar," but I didn't
want to impose an undue repression of free speech, nor yet
burden our charity of choice with too massive a contribution,
so once it had done its duty of making the girls aware of this
linguistic peculiarity, the jar was retired. Its memory, however,
lingers on.

DANCES

At school, I spurned ballroom dancing as fit only for wimps
and losers. It was the era when "dancing" consisted of intro-
spective gyrations some distance from your partner for the fast
tunes, and horribly embarrassing, sweaty clutches during the
slow ones. Too vain to wear glasses, too poor to afford contacts,
I had to accept the grunted invitation, "Wanna dance?" literally sight unseen, and more often than not lived to regret it. Oh,
hideous memories! Thanks to my mother I knew how to dance
the Highland Fling, but that was not much help when the music was Pink Floyd.

What would it take to ensure that the children knew basic
steps of the waltz, foxtrot, tango, salsa, and swing? Our basement looked big enough to accommodate up to fifty teens,
some dancing, some socializing. I decided on a date and
time, invited the dancers to bring finger foods and soft drinks,
purchased a video of an arrestingly elegant Austrian woman

demonstrating basic ballroom steps, set aside an hour before the dance for those who wanted to get a head start on the waltz or tango, and sat back to observe the fun. I wondered how much supervision would be required to keep things running smoothly and soon got my answer: Hardly any. Dance steps seemed to be contagious: if a girl knew how to waltz, she taught someone who didn't; if a boy knew a nifty swing step, it was soon shared with the whole group. As the room temperature rose, sweetened sodas were quickly eschewed: the thirst-quenching drink of choice was water. Buckets and buckets of cool, refreshing water. Swing dancing is thirsty work!

We held two dances a year, one around New Year's and one in the summer to celebrate the end of the school year. The first half of the summer dance was held outside on the lawn, to the intense delight of the mosquitoes. We added square dancing to the mix once we found a priest friend who knew how to call the *do-si-do*. Folk dancing, like folk music, proved an outstanding way for young people to spend time together, having outrageous good fun.

My children picked up new dance steps effortlessly, their background in Irish dancing, with its feet-twittering rapidity, having evidently strengthened their foot-brain connections to an impressive extent. When one of our plays called for a polka, they were instant adepts. Once I stopped exerting a ballroom influence on our biannual dances, swing and freestyle took center stage, but I don't think anyone will ever regret having the foxtrot and waltz firmly under their arches, so to speak. I

was tickled pink at how much more fun our domestic dances were (not to mention cheaper and more convenient) than
seeking out, paying for, then driving back and forth to, conventional dance lessons.

THE TEEN YEARS ARE DONE—NOW WHAT?

Let's assume that life with teens has not been a picnic in the
park. Before you dust off your hands, watching your teen dive
into the murky waters of adulthood as the first digit on the
birthday cake finally transmogrifies into a "two," let me offer
a word of advice: not so fast! The twenties may be no better. Life for the twenty-something packs a whole new world
of stresses that are altogether different from those of college,
but no less—well, stressful. I asked Lorna and Sheila for their
input. They both agreed that stress in college is very different
from that in real life. In many ways, college is more acute, but
it's mostly short-term: finishing assignments, memorizing a
concerto movement, spending ten straight hours in the business school finishing a case study. And it's all clearly oriented
towards a goal: graduation. Stress in real life is more about the
long-term: what am I going to do with my life? I may be happy
with my job now, but will I be in the long run or do I want a
career? Then there's the question of where to live and what I
want out of life: what is my life's goal, and how do I get there?

Sheila offered an excellent metaphor: college stress is a
short-term hard boil, real life an existential simmer. Every

young adult must find out how to manage her own life, and may not be ready for a mature relationship with her parents until she has.

Of all the manifold benefits of homeschooling, none is dearer to me than the closeness the children now enjoy. When they get together during vacations, it truly is awesome to see the love and respect with which they treat one another. *(Love and respect? You mean, the motto worked?)* Whether standing by the bedside of their dying Granny, flying off to visit each other on long weekends, or chilling in the hot tub here at home, they are a force to be reckoned with.

Having such well-bonded, independent-minded children does have its drawbacks, however. When faced with some physical, emotional, or spiritual crisis, they are swift to consult the most reliably helpful source of advice they know: each other. The very idea that their parents' experiences some forty years ago at Harvard or Oxford might have any relevance whatever in the twenty-first century apparently never occurs to them.

Perhaps it comes of being a successful launching pad.

Epilogue

*W*hen Sheila and I were in Austria for her tenth birthday trip, I noticed a slight cramping in my left big toe. On this, our last day in Vienna, we had the entire day to spend walking while we waited for our night train to Venice. It was bitterly cold and the occasional snowflake dusted our clothes and hair. We had ridden on the Wiener Riesenrad, the enormous Ferris wheel that plays such a prominent part in the movie *The Third Man*, drunk coffee and cocoa at the coffee house where Brahms was once a frequent patron, watched the famous Lipizzaner stallions being trained, toured the castle, admired a massive collection of ancient musical instruments, and it was still only three o'clock. The only way for us to stay warm was to keep walking. My pace flagged, but I dismissed the insistent tugging of my big toe. "Tight shoes and cobbled streets," I told Sheila. We finally got on the train and I thought no more of it.

Back home, the cramping worsened. Walking ceased to be the pleasurable escape it had always been. My left hand became involved. While accompanying Lorna in a piano concerto competition, I wondered why the low G did not sound at the end of the Mozart slow movement. It seemed odd for such a fine instrument to have a defective key, then I realized: the problem was not with the piano. It was with me.

Robin had played out his political aspirations and was moving into the field of environmental medicine. He was booked to go to his first meeting of the environmental medical academy in Florida when I went to see a neurologist, who gave me the devastating diagnosis of Atypical Parkinson's. "How long do I have to live?" I asked. "Oh," he said with a sneer, "it won't affect how long you live, just the—ah—*quality* of your life." When I went home, I sat for a long time staring at the same view I'd looked at when Andrew was born. Again, everything was changed. Again, I wanted to rewind the day and put in a different tape. I could hear the children playing outside; the distance between us felt immeasurable. Only Kidu crawled up on the couch and pushed at my hand with his nose. He understood my desolation.

At the conference, Robin received good news. The main speaker was the national authority on Parkinson's and its environmental causes, notably mercury. I had a mouthful of amalgam in my tooth fillings, which translates into high blood levels of mercury. It spreads itself around the body and is particularly attracted to nerve cells, where it causes enormous damage. For the first time since receiving the diagnosis, I had hope.

We traveled to Texas to have my dental work redone by the finest dentist in the country. One week later, as we were returning to Washington, I experienced a complete remission of symptoms. But this did not last, and since then my condition has gone steadily downhill. We learned that our idyllic situation on the bluff overlooking the Puget Sound was downwind from Boeing, and that I had been breathing a steady diet of dilute airplane glue, which is a serious neurotoxin. Would we be forced to move again?

I have an illustrious history of challenging fate by making rash statements. Halfway through my second year at UCLA, I sat in my apartment above a millionaire's garage in Brentwood, and reviewed the sorry state of my love life. The swimming pool was overflowing its banks in the torrential rain, which perfectly matched my mood. Dramatically, I threw down my gauntlet in the face of fate as I declared, "I know one thing: I'll never marry an American." (Peal of thunder stage left.) Sure enough, two weeks later, who should come riding over the horizon on his white charger but Robin.

When we moved into our house in Everett, I said, "This is the only place I will ever live. They'll have to carry me out of this house in a long, narrow box." I had a nasty suspicion at the time that I was tempting Providence yet again, and now my intuition was proving correct. We were looking at another move.

We chose Ojai based on three criteria: other homeschooling families, a large patient base for Robin's new practice, and environmental cleanliness. The irony of moving within seventy miles of Los Angeles to escape foul air was not lost on us. However, the pollution of Los Angeles makes for a lot of sick people willing to drive a couple of hours into the mountains to get their systems cleaned out. Robin's environmental medical practice began to thrive while my personal medical condition did anything but.

The biggest change for me since moving here has been the end of our homeschool. The impossible happened—it simply ran out of children. Ill health has forced me to abandon my dream of playing a homeschooling Mary Poppins, appearing with trademark umbrella wherever illness or a new baby has temporarily taken the mother out of the picture. I have had to abandon my one class, ("Teaching History Through Story," for K–8 grade, which I plan to write up for publication) and now have zero piano pupils. The ebullient Enkidu has been replaced by two mostly sedate but gloriously neurotic rescue Great Danes; they fill my days with their stories and make few demands beyond hearing mine (they particularly like ones about them) and being scratched under the chin. Entropy Academy exists only within the (thankfully acid-free) pages of the yearbooks. As launching pads go, however, it has been pretty successful.

At this point, kindly allow me a brief digression. Each one of the children (apart from Andrew, who doesn't much care about Absolute Truth) would wholeheartedly endorse George Santayana's avowal that "history is always written wrong, and so always needs to be rewritten." He might have added, "This is never more true than when the writer is your mother." One major benefit of appointing myself family historian is that where uncertainty arises, what I say goes.

While I have tried not to let this giddy power to create history go to my head (looking to twentieth-century Russia and China for warning), I have also held true to the spirit of Robin's Irish grandfather. A great raconteur, he swore that a storyteller who did nothing to improve his tales was "no better than a journalist." Perish the thought!

When it came to their updates, however, I got the information directly from the horse's mouth, and can therefore attest to its accuracy.

Iain made a seamless transition from homeschooling to Gonzaga University, where he graduated atop his class with a double major in English and philosophy. He switched coasts shortly thereafter, and received his doctorate in American literature from Boston University. Iain now lives in Providence, Rhode Island, with his wife Jiyoon and their two sons, and teaches literature at the Rhode Island School of Design. Homeschooling prepared him well for his decade-and-counting in academia, he feels, particularly in how the ample one-on-one attention enhanced his skills of writing, revision, and reasoning.

Having no perceptible affinity with either heat or sunshine, Fiona moved back up to Seattle full time. There, she was happy to rejoin the choir at our ex-parish; she was even happier when she found it had a new member, a baritone named Greg. Suddenly her life's direction became crystal clear: marriage won the day. They now live in their first house just north of Seattle with Naomi who, at one year of age, fills Fiona's days with the miracle of discovery that is new motherhood's joy. When asked, Fiona says she "liked pretty much everything" about homeschooling, and gives it the best endorsement possible: she plans to "keep the magic happening" by homeschooling Naomi, and any siblings the family may be blessed with.

Lorna transferred from the University of Pennsylvania to Stanford in the fall of 2011, where she graduated with distinction, Phi Beta Kappa, in English while tripling up on research in neuroscience and the California criminal justice system. She then hightailed it over to Boston to work as a consultant and ponder with her nephew Julian the life cycle of squirrels—she swears he knows more than she does. Hearing the sororal siren call, she moved to Seattle last year, where she is living with Sheila and doing programs in computational finance and forensic accounting. She is pursuing these postgraduate certificates less for career advancement than for a reason right out of homeschooling: a love of independent learning driven by intellectual curiosity. Fiona told her recently, "I can't imagine you ever not being in some kind of school." Neither can Lorna.

Sheila homeschooled for ninth grade here in Ojai, attended public school for tenth, and spent eleventh and twelfth grades at Idyllwild Arts Academy, perched on a mountaintop six thousand feet above Los Angeles, where she practiced her beloved viola to the maximum extent permitted by law. The flexibility of homeschooling allowed her to devote time to music, uncovering her primary passion. Then, when the opportunity to go to Idyllwild and pursue this passion further arose, she was poised and ready to take full advantage. She went on to brave the frozen wasteland of Ohio at the Cleveland Institute of Music, where she flourished musically as well as academically, majoring in viola with a minor in finance. She now lives in Seattle, where she loves cooking with fresh ingredients from Pike Place Market, running on the waterfront, and dressing her customers in beautiful suits at Flagship Nordstrom Men's Fine Clothing Department.

Evan graduated *magna cum laude* from Villanova Preparatory School, and is now on the cusp of graduating from Gonzaga University with a major in business with a focus in economics and finance and a minor in philosophy. As well as this passion for learning, he has shown quite a talent for leadership. He manages a mentorship program for underprivileged children and also shepherds young freshman through their first week at Gonzaga. When he's not visiting his sisters in Seattle or working at the local coffee shop, Evan can be found shooting baskets and playing the guitar with a group of close friends.

He says that homeschooling taught him the importance of finishing his work, of doing things fully and completely. He found that if he got right down to his work and did it promptly, he had plenty of time to pursue other interests.

Andrew spends his days at the Ojai Enrichment Center with other developmentally disabled adults. He may struggle to write his name legibly, but roughly half the population of Ojai seems to know it anyway. Chillin' with Andrew is like being with a movie star—we walk into a café and the place lights up with "Hi, Andrew!" "Andrew, how're you doing?" and, if I'm lucky, "Is this your mom? Hello, Andrew's mom!" He increases my street cred no end. Although mostly nonverbal, he occasionally makes his strong opinions known. Recently, he advised a visitor that it is unwise to take in stray cats because they're liable to explode. He has an intensely serious facial expression that he adopts when spouting gibberish; it's usually our first sign that he's off in some parallel universe.

SO REALLY, WHAT WAS IT ALL ABOUT?

When the children were little, people would say to me, "Just wait 'til they start kindergarten, the next thing you know they're graduating high school." It's not like that in a home-school. When Iain left home to go to university, it was like ripping off the most enormous Band-Aid that had been firmly fixed for eighteen years: agonizingly painful! But at the same time, we had lived fully every moment of those eighteen years together and now he was ready to move on. Yes, it was excruciating—but it also felt so much the right thing to do, the next "Best Thing" for him, that I was happy and at peace.

Our educational choice for Sheila, on the other hand, took us completely by surprise: I never dreamed we would send a child away to boarding school. And yet, when the opportunity arose that April, we recognized that Idyllwild was the perfect setting for her. Another day, another Band-Aid. It was agonizing, but we knew Ojai could never give her the breadth of musical experience she would enjoy "up the mountain," which she needed if she was to become a professional violist. Sometimes love involves letting go sooner than planned.

After Sheila left, it was just Robin, Andrew, Evan, and me. I was almost completely out of touch with Evan's education. He drove himself to and from school, so no conversation there; in response to my questions he would grunt that his grades were "fine." Checking them online, I saw that he had grunted true, but somehow lacked the heart to point out that we must never take good grades for grunted. It felt odd, this asking after his grades, instead of discussing Bernoulli's principle and how it affected the trajectory of his latest paper airplane. It gave me a piercing appreciation for the marvelous, intense sharing that we had so much enjoyed homeschooling together.

So often, the best conversations occur when the two of you are doing something side by side—driving places, washing the dishes, making applesauce. That's really what homeschool is all about: making applesauce. Doing stuff together, talking all the way and finding, when the task is done, that your memory banks are full of gems to take out and reflect on at leisure. Gems that are the true education that remains when you've forgotten all the facts you were taught.

There are certain cathedrals in England that have an unusual feature. In the apse of the building, where the choir sits, the seat bottoms fold up to give the monks more room to stand. The rigors of the ecclesiastical hours being what they are, the bottoms of the seats were often fitted with a little ledge, or *misericord* (mercy seat), on which the monk could prop his weary behind while still appearing to stand. Under this ledge is a hidden space where can sometimes be found carvings of subjects surprisingly out of keeping with the rest of the cathedral—rustic scenes, common farm animals, serfs engaging in bucolic activities that may be downright inappropriate. I first discovered these marvels in Wells Cathedral when I was in my twenties, visiting with an elderly friend of my mother's who was a keen photographer and passionate local historian. I like to think that the first thing my children will do when they visit an English cathedral with their own children will be to turn up the choir seats and peer underneath, "just in case." With any luck, they'll find me there.

Acknowledgments

*T*he gestation period of a giraffe is fourteen months; of an elephant, two years. The very longest I could find is a frilled shark, at three and a half years. I was going to say that no living thing even comes close to the time it has taken me to write this book, but then I remembered the giant sequoia, and hastily withdrew that claim. No animal, I should say.

In the course of these many years, I have been aided and inspired by many, and I hesitate to start naming names for fear of forgetting the legions who offered advice, criticism, and kind words. Arielle Zibrak first helped tame the excesses of my unruly prose, and I recall fondly the fruitful hours at a favorite Ventura coffee shop.

Julia Fogassy graciously prepared the manuscript for its first run in 2011, when I spoke at the Seattle Catholic homeschool convention; I am most grateful for her know-how, efficiency, and compassion.

My English friend Howard sparked a lively controversy about the proper use of commas, and his transatlantic editing came up with a few howlers: when he first encountered America's quintessential campfire dessert, he wrote, "I haven't the foggiest notion what 's'mores' might mean. A foreshortened 'some mores' perhaps… but some more of what? The expression is simply too recondite to be used to any good effect."

Rose Fujinaka's help was invaluable, both as grammarian and techno-whiz extraordinaire. Ever gracious, ever good humored, she was a joy to work with; I miss her cheery e-company most e-dreadfully.

Entropy is all very well, but it's not much help when it comes to publishing a book, and still less marketing it. That takes someone who really knows what she is doing, and that someone for me is…Katy Bowman! I am deeply honored to be associated with her publishing company.

A huge "thank you" to all those parents who entrusted their children to the tender ministrations of Entropy Academy, and to the children themselves, who will always be dear to my heart.

Last, my husband, Robin, ever-encouraging, always supportive. Truly, I could have done none of this without you.

About The Author

After graduating from England's Royal College of Music and Oxford University, Alison Bernhoft swapped Oxford's eight hundred years of history for the modern-day chaos of Los Angeles and an MA at UCLA. Having ripped herself from family, friends, and homeland in an act she now describes as wanton self-vandalism (a do-it-yourself Attila the Hun, perhaps), her bold declaration, "I'm definitely only staying for one year" slithered gently into "Perhaps only two…"

That was thirty-five years ago.

Had she stayed in England, she would most likely have missed out on the single most formative educational experience of her life: homeschooling. Alison's particular passion lay in making complex intellectual ideas simple, and she utilized every ounce of creativity and problem-solving skills she possessed to teach her own six children, as well as others who found the Entropy mix of laughter and serious education irresistible.

After a brief foray into the intoxicating world of public speaking, Alison's desire to utilize her spiritual gift of exhortation to encourage other mothers to find joy and fulfillment teaching their own was curtailed by atypical Parkinson's. The only voice she now has in the homeschooling community sounds through the pages of *Entropy Academy*, and her blog, beyondentropy.blogspot.com.

She very much hopes that her readers will be inspired to read their favorite chapters of *Entropy Academy* out loud—preferably with an English accent!